D1263541

TOWARD A NEW VIEW
OF
AMERICA

TOWARD A
NEW VIEW OF AMERICA

ESSAYS IN HONOR OF

Arthur C. Cole

EDITED BY

Hans L. Trefousse

BROOKLYN COLLEGE AND THE GRADUATE CENTER, CUNY

Burt Franklin & Company, Inc.

Library of Congress Cataloging in Publication Data

Main entry under title:
Toward a new view of America.
"Publications of Arthur C. Cole": p.
CONTENTS: Cole, A. C. Southward ho!—East, R. A.
The strange pause in John Adams' diary.—Rayback, J. G.
The presidential ambitions of Aaron Burr, 1800-1801. [etc.]
1. United States—History—Addresses, essays,
lectures. 2. United States—Foreign relations—20th
century—Addresses, essays, lectures. 3. Cole, Arthur
Charles, 1886-   I. Trefousse, Hans Louis. II. Cole,
Arthur Charles, 1886-
E178.6.T69   973   76-49063
ISBN 0-89102-066-7

CONTENTS

PREFACE

Arthur C. Cole belongs to a generation of men who had a tremendous impact on American historiography. Many of them were giants in their day. But unlike his contemporaries, Cole is still modern. Their ideas have been successfully challenged; his contributions are as stimulating today as when they were first proposed. Their books are no longer widely read; his *Irrepressible Conflict* is still popular. They appear to belong to another age; Cole really seems to be a part of the present.

What is the reason for this difference? The answer is clear: In the 1920s and '30s, it was fashionable to take an antiabolitionist, if not proslavery, point of view. Ideological considerations were minimized; and barely concealed racist prejudices affected the conclusions of many historians. Arthur C. Cole, however, never forsook his egalitarian convictions. He never lost sight of the fundamental justice of the antislavery cause. It is no accident that in 1934 a distinguished reviewer of *The Irrepressible Conflict* found only one shortcoming. While characterizing the book as "a solid and notable contribution to the social history of the American people," he criticized its author for betraying an "attitude too closely akin to that of the anti-slavery propagandists of 1860."

Cole's ideas are now widely accepted, but in their day they were as unorthodox as they were scholarly.

Arthur C. Cole's fame does not rest on *The Irrepressible Conflict* alone. The first scholar to write a comprehensive history of the Whig Party in the South, in 1912 he was awarded the American Historical Society's Justin Winsor Prize for the book, which has since become a classic. While teaching at Urbana, in 1919 he published the *Era of the Civil War,* one of the volumes in the *Centennial History of Illinois.* It was followed by *The Irrepressible Conflict* in 1934 and by *A Hundred Years of Mount Holyoke College* in 1940. Among the articles he contributed to various journals, his famous exchange with J. G. deRoulhac Hamilton in 1931 and 1932 in the *American Historical Review* on "Lincoln's Election an Immediate Menace to Slavery in the States?" is perhaps the most notable. (He took the negative view.) Cole also served as managing editor of the *Mississippi Valley Historical Review* (now the *Journal of American History*), as president of the Mississippi Valley Historical Association in 1940-41, and he taught American history not only at the University of Illinois, but also at Ohio State, at Western Reserve, and finally at Brooklyn College, where he became Professor Emeritus in 1956. His academic career included visiting professorships at the Universities of Pennsylvania and Wisconsin, Columbia, the Brookings Institution, and, after retirement, the Whitney Professorship at C. W. Post College.

In addition to having been a meticulous and methodical scholar, Arthur C. Cole was also a dedicated advocate of academic freedom and other liberal causes. As a foe of American involvement in the First World War, he was investigated in 1917 by a committee of university trustees in the course of a loyalty probe in Illinois, only to be completely exonerated. Taking a prominent part in launching a teachers' union at the University of Illinois, he later became an active member of the American Association of University Professors and of the American Civil Liberties Union. He challenged the program of compulsory military training at Ohio State University and repeatedly took part in investigations of alleged violations of academic freedom. During the Second World War, serving on a special committee of the Air Force to study the feasibility of reducing Germany by strategic bombing alone, he concluded that the proposition was false. Always in the forefront of righteous causes, he was a true representative of the libertarian tradition in America.

Now, in tribute to Arthur C. Cole's memory, it is fitting that colleagues and former students should join together to present a volume of essays in his honor.

The opening selection of this collection was written by Professor Cole himself. When he delivered the Walter Lynwood Fleming Lectures in Southern History at Louisiana State University in 1944, his theme was "The Yankee in the South." In a series of addresses, he traced the influence on Dixie of Northern enterprise, religion, and culture, as well as the attitudes of Yankee immigrants toward the great sectional conflict. This is the first time that any of those essays, in this case the introductory lecture, "Southward Ho," has been published.

The other essays in this volume also represent challenges to widely accepted viewpoints in American history, and we believe them to be particularly appropriate as a way of honoring an unusual scholar.

H. L. T.

PUBLICATIONS OF ARTHUR C. COLE

Books

The Whig Party in the South. Washington: American Historical Association, 1913.

Editor, *Constitutional Debates of 1847.* Vol. XIV, *Collections of the Illinois State Historical Library.* Springfield: Illinois State Historical Library, 1919.

The Era of the Civil War, 1848-1870. Vol. III, *Centennial History of Illinois.* Springfield: Illinois Centennial Commission, 1919.

The Irrepressible Conflict, 1850-1865. Vol. VII, *A History of American Life.* New York: Macmillan, 1934.

A Hundred Years of Mount Holyoke College: The Evolution of an Educational Ideal. New Haven: Yale University Press, 1940.

Articles

"Nativism in the Lower Mississippi Valley," *Proceedings of the Mississippi Valley Historical Association for the Year 1912-1913,* 6, (1913): 258-275.

"Camels in the United States: An Experiment of the War Department," *History Teachers Magazine,* 4 (1913): 156-157.

"The South and the Right of Secession in the Early Fifties," *Mississippi Valley Historical Review,* 1 (1914): 376-399.

"Lincoln and the Presidential Election of 1864," *Transactions of the Illinois State Historical Society* (1917): 130-138.

"President Lincoln and the Illinois Radical Republicans," *Mississippi Valley Historical Review,* 4 (1918): 417-436.

"The Passing of the Frontier," *Mississippi Valley Historical Review*, 5 (1918): 288-312.

Lincoln's House Divided Speech: Did It Reflect a Doctrine of Class Struggle? An Address Delivered Before the Chicago Historical Society on March 15, 1923. Chicago: University of Chicago Press, 1923.

"Abraham Lincoln and the Traditions of American Civil Liberty," *Transactions of the Illinois State Historical Society* (1926): 102-111. Danville, Ill.: Illinois Printing Co. (1926).

"Abraham Lincoln and the South," Lincoln Centennial Association *Bulletin* (1928).

"Lincoln's Election an Immediate Menace to Slavery in the States?" *American Historical Review*, 36 (1931): 740-767.

"Our Sporting Grandfathers," *Atlantic Monthly*, 150 (1932): 88-96.

"The Puritan and Fair Terpsichore," *Mississippi Valley Historical Review*, 29 (1942): 3-34.

TOWARD A NEW VIEW
OF
AMERICA

THE YANKEE
IN THE ANTE-BELLUM SOUTH

Arthur C. Cole

FIRST LECTURE

SOUTHWARD HO!

Partly, perhaps, because of the lure of genealogical lore—whether as related to individuals or as concerned with social and national groups—some of the most fascinating pages of history are to be found in those dealing with the stories of human migrations, of man readjusting his habitat upon this terrestrial sphere in response to the urges of his soul or the pressures exerted upon him by divers forces. The movements from the cradle of the human race, the invasions of barbaric hordes sweeping upon the centers of well-defined civilizations, the exiles imposed by political, religious, and racial persecutions, and the attempts to satisfy a hunger for a better living or for a greater liberty to be found in new lands of opportunity are all well-known phases of man's course, generally ever westward, until an array of new national states created the institutions of the modern world, or at least of Western civilization. The story of the American nation begins with the story of the peopling of the mainland of North America by groups that came in varying proportions from nearly every country of western Europe, crossing the broad Atlantic to conquer the primeval forest and the natural resources and native peoples of the Western Hemisphere. Its greatest human theme is to be found in the ever westward movement of large elements of this population and of the generations that it produced, a stream swelled by fresh ac-

1

cretions from across the sea; this movement, step by step, carried a pioneer stock from the Atlantic seaboard to the foothills of the Appalachians, stormed the mountain barrier just beyond, spread out over the fertile reaches of the great valley of the Mississippi, mastered the inhospitable aridity of the Great Plains area, penetrated the breaks of the Great Divide, and flowed down the valleys that led to the Pacific shore. By this movement the human representatives of a western European civilization conquered a vast continent in a period of three centuries.

It was no wonder that the vicissitudes of this movement often revealed a sharp cleavage between those who with their indomitable energy were the active agents in this conquest, and those who remained behind to enjoy in ease—if not in luxury—the more settled life of well-established institutions generally founded upon the sweat and blood of earlier pioneer forces. When the representatives of eastern or older states added to their disregard and neglect of the pioneer forces not only a sense of superiority but even an inclination to exploit their pioneering brethren of the West, it was not strange that lack of sympathy and of understanding should engender mutual distrust and suspicion and oftentimes antagonism. Of such forces was born the sectionalism of East and West, a theme in American history which has not even yet been exhausted, a cleavage that was fundamentally more basic than any division between North and South.

It is almost an axiom to the student of the westward movement that the flow of population has generally proceeded along isothermal lines, along which the migrants at least sought to carry the habits, the preferences, and the multifarious institutions of their homelands. Thus Englishmen liked and sought out the temperate zone for their new home in the Western world, the Spanish preferred something more like the mild, and often semitropical clime of the Mediterranean, while the hardy Norsemen and Swedes founded a new Scandinavia in the more rigorous upper Great Lakes region and the uppermost parts of the Mississippi Valley, a land of ice and snow such as they knew at home. By the same token the restless residents of New England followed the westward urge to found a great Yankee belt—a new Connecticut and its Massachusetts counterparts—in the territory due west of those states. And in the same way Virginians, Carolinians, and Georgians proceeded along the parallels of latitude to corresponding areas in the Mississippi Valley carrying with them their institutions of all sorts.

This line of migration, which in itself made for much of the distinction between the institutions of Americans located on either side of the Mason and Dixon line and the Ohio River, was for a long time presumed merely to perpetuate differences fundamentally based upon the distinctive origins of the earlier settlers of the North Atlantic Seaboard on the one hand and on the South Atlantic Seaboard on the other. This was the old Cavalier-Roundhead theory of sectional differences between Northerners and Southerners. These allegedly contrasting origins and the enduring force of social heredity were presumed to have furnished an almost insurmountable barrier to the unity of the two sections that did come to define distinctive and antagonistic objectives, largely in the three decades that preceded the struggle that in these southern parts—for no really very good reason at all, as it seems to the speaker—you prefer to call the War between the States.

This theory, for some decades thoroughly discredited as to its basic validity for explaining group origins, seems to have survived in the minds of many to strengthen the assumption that this unfortunate conflict of four-score years ago may have been rooted in a force as unchangeable as human nature itself. In any event the average man is satisfied to accept the assumption that a population unity in the South that resulted from more or less insurmountable barriers was early defined as a necessary preliminary to the ill-fated effort to achieve a national unity within the limits of the southern states themselves.

The student of American population movements, however, is aware of the multiplicity of forces that early qualified the homogeneity of the southern people. Both non-English and non-English-speaking stocks made important contributions—actually or relatively—however much they failed to refresh themselves in

the period after 1830. Some of these accretions had worked
their way westward from the Atlantic Seaboard up the streams
and along the simplest lines of the westward movement. Others
had come down the Great Valley, the great nursery of the
American pioneer, and then had spread over the upland South
from which in time they again moved in a more literally wester-
ly direction.

But the currents which have been noted were part of the
stream properly known as the Westward Movement and in the
days of its active flow the trans-Appalachian region generally
was West, rather than North and South. In the process of this
movement its human constituents were, in the interpretation of
Frederick J. Turner, nationalized or Americanized rather than
sectionalized. In the early nineteenth century, however, one
finds increasing evidence of the cleavage that brought the conflict of the sixties and, as this happened, the situation becomes
one which poses the question of a northern population contribution to the evolving South and its significance in the way of a
distinctive contribution and of a problem of assimilation—or, as
in many cases, a rejection and withdrawal.

For the purposes of this study, then, the story of the Yankee
in the antebellum South is the story of the coming of a group of
outsiders from across the Mason and Dixon line and the Ohio
River, i.e., from what were in the antebellum period the non-
slaveholding states. Only to the extent that this group found a
special origin and inspiration from the New England area will
the term "Yankee" have anything of its narrow meaning. As
you perhaps greet me to day as a "Yankee"—hopefully without
the traditional prefix—the South had a hundred or more years
ago to be prepared to receive an accretion that came from all
parts of the section that it was increasingly coming to look
upon with suspicion—if not with fear.

The stream was not altogether new to the nineteenth century. It had been anticipated by various earlier arrivals—even
back in colonial days. When victims of religious persecutions in
early New England left to enjoy the more tolerant clime of the
southern colonies—not to pioneer but to settle in a more static

sense; when the young collegian, graduate or otherwise, went south to accept congenial employment as a tutor in the home of a southern planter—as did most conspicually, Philip Fithian in the "Nomini Hall" home of the "King" Carter family; when business opportunity, real or fancied, beckoned an ambitious Yankee peddler or trader to find prosperity in the Southland; when the call of duty summoned to new and distant fields the pious and energetic representatives of organized religion; and when other attractions secured a response from other groups, these immigrants to the land of Dixie were the vanguard of the stream that it shall be our problem to appraise.

There were many indications before the turn of the eighteenth century that if not a stream, at least a trickle of population was about to flow into the South out of Yankeedom. The way had been prepared by random colonization schemes, such as one, based on a royal grant (in 1774) of lands between the Yazoo and the Mississippi river; Major Phineas Lyman of Durham, Connecticut, its chief promoter, conducted a sturdy band of Connecticut farmers to the Natchez region where in later years—after his own death—they became prosperous planters with extensive estates, fine dwellings, and large slaveholdings. Though many did not survive the hardships of the pioneering stage, as in the case of members of the family of Captain Matthew Phelps who went out to join the colony, the story of his voyages by Anthony Haswell (as published in 1802) probably added to the interest in those distant parts.

Some Northerners were content to anticipate someone else's settlement, if not their own, and embraced opportunities for speculation in land. At least there is evidence that thousands of acres of Yazoo lands granted by the Georgia legislature in 1795 were sold to the New England Mississippi Land Company. Somewhat later a considerable group of Bostonians "were bled very freely," as one commentator put it, in a speculative bubble in town lots in Brunswick, Georgia, of which only a rapidly decaying hotel of some beauty was to remain in the forties. This is a theme which if adequately pursued might reveal extensive Yankee interests behind which lay at least the possibility of southward migration.

Evidence of an early interest in the South is meager and scattered. Yet it apparently became something of a tendency for young college graduates to make a trip to the South for relaxation and a chance to canvass the opportunities to seek their fortunes in those parts. Abiel Holmes, father of Oliver Wendell Holmes, visited the South after his graduation from Yale College in 1783 and upon ordination became pastor of the Congregational Church at Midway, Georgia, where he served for four years; his experiences left enduring impressions which he passed on to the next generation. In 1798 upon his graduation from Harvard College, William E. Channing, the later critic of slavery, accepted a position as tutor in a Richmond family, where he spent a year and a half and acquired a lifelong respect for Southerners and their convictions. Five years later a young friend of Webster, Freeborn Adams, spent some time in Virginia and the Carolinas canvassing the opportunities "for the distribution of medicine," the meantime making observations on the charms of the fair sex—"ribs," he called them and pronounced them "rather ugly," or at least "poorly polished." In turn twenty-five years later the young Ralph Waldo Emerson enjoyed a five-months' sojourn in Charleston and St. Augustine which helped, as he later explained, "to cast out the passion for Europe by the passion for America." While these are instances of Yankees who went South and returned again, the stories of the exodus of the more numerous group who remained and became a part of the citizenry of the South, are generally lost as mere details in a longer southern career.

In the meantime other Yankees were making a more substantial adjustment and contribution to life in the South. Take one example where we do have adequate data. In 1795 a twenty-year-old Massachusetts youth arrived at Charleston with a dollar and an eighth in his purse; needing a haircut he paid 37½ cents for the same and "gave the odd bit" to the barber as a tip. An advertisement inserted the following day in the *State Gazette* netted a situation in a few hours. Out of employment six months later, he entered into a partnership with a newly arrived

Bostonian to operate a local bookstore. The Charleston fire of 1796 and a yellow fever epidemic which carried off his partner did not prevent prosperity from crowning his efforts. His first profits were wiped out by an unfortunate speculation in trade with Havana, but he recouped with successful cotton shipments to Liverpool. For three years after 1800 his business "doubled, and trebled annually." In November 1803, he returned from a voyage to England with a large stock of books and a printed catalog listing 50,000 volumes. Then the reopening by South Carolina of the foreign slave trade brought a disastrous diversion of planters' purchases to the newly imported chattels and forced the bookseller to liquidate his business.

The story of the enterprising young Ebenezer S. Thomas is all the more important because of a long list of the contemporary commercial houses of Charleston—some two or three dozens— he could later recall only one that was being run by a native of South Carolina. The local aristocracy disdained sordid business affairs and left them primarily to Yankees and Europeans. Many of these merchants achieved a success that enabled them to enjoy a style of living equal to that of the wealthiest planters.

In January 1819, after various previous informal meetings, the sons of New England in Charleston foregathered in a local coffeehouse to organize more formally as the New England Society of Charleston. Its chief founder and first president was Nathaniel Russell, one of the local merchant princes who resided in an especially palatial mansion. Forty-seven members— merchants, preachers, educators, etc.—were promptly listed on its roll with a dozen others added in a few months. As the historian of the centennial of the organization has said, "The New Englanders fell into the very natural and patriotic habit of gathering around a cheerful fireplace in one of the old inns, or at the residence of one of the members on 'Forefathers' Day." Incorporated by the state legislature in December 1820, the society became one of the most significant organizations in the community. Its example was in due time followed by the organization of a similar society in New Orleans, of which unfortunately much less is known; it presented to the public distin-

guished speakers, among whom may be listed Sergeant S. Pren-
tiss, the Maine Yankee who won such an enviable political success in the state of Mississippi. The Charleston society combined
in its meetings educational and convivial features and in a century under a series of eight distinguished presidents presented
addresses by four hundred men of distinction. It often lent a
helpful hand to New England settlers in distress and showed a
generally fine civic spirit.

Equally suggestive both of the opportunity for Yankee ambition to find outlets in the South and of the eagerness of the
enterprising to embrace this opportunity was the career of
Bronson Alcott and some of his contemporaries as peddlers of
fancy goods and Yankee notions in southern parts. Sailing in
October 1818 from New Haven to Norfolk, from which he
planned to launch his career as a schoolmaster, he noted fifteen
peddlers and tin men as sailing companions, and was exposed,
as it developed, to the peddling fever that each year recruited
ten to fifteen enterprising youths from the little town of Wolcott, Connecticut. When his efforts to secure an opportunity to
teach brought no satisfactory results, he bought a peddling out-
fit from a Yankee dealer and was soon going on his rounds. A
net profit of a dollar a day seemed a tidy return to the average
peddler and Alcott had sufficient success to repeat his experience four more times. On his third trip he set out for Charleston
with a cousin and one hundred other Connecticut boys expect-
ing to be employed on a canal-building project at Columbia. But
the canal project failed and the two cousins walked the 600
miles to Norfolk, from which Alcott eventually peddled his way
back home. His fourth trip was made with a peddler's wagon in
the company of his brother and his cousin. After six months
they sold out to another Yankee dealer, whereupon young Alcott arranged to teach penmanship at Warrentown, North Carolina, which he found, according to this diary, "the lonesumist
[sic] place" and vowing "never . . . again," he walked the 500
miles to New York City. Nevertheless October found him and
his cousin again in his peddler's wagon on his last trip, which
again carried him well into North Carolina from which he re-

turned the next July. This story lacks only the accident of a decision to settle down in the South to make Alcott a permanent figure in the story of the Yankee in the antebellum South. Probably only the current prejudice, against the Connecticut peddler that prevailed in the North as well as in the South, stood in the way of such an outcome.

Teacher, preacher, peddler, and printer—lawyer, visitor, editor, adventurer, and tinker—and more filled the roll of these early Yankee migrants. Almost inevitably the contagion for southward migration was spread by those who formed its vanguard and who wrote home of their experiences. Not only the mails but in due time the printing press bore testimony to this opportunity. Two volumes from the pen of James K. Paulding offered the public in 1817 his anonymous *Letters from the South, Written during our Excursion in the Summer of 1816.* Two years later Estwick Evans, who left Hopkinton, New Hampshire, in February 1818 dressed in buffalo skins, published an account of *A Pedestrious Tour, of Four Thousand Miles, through the Western States and Territories, during the Winter and Spring of 1818,* which included a trip down the Ohio and the Mississippi to New Orleans. Five years later Henry Cogswell Knight, under the pseudonym of Arthur Singleton, offered his *Letters from the South and West.* Next appeared, in 1825, the account of the Massachusetts-born James Pearse, a more ambitious *Narrative ... a General Account of His Life; and more Particularly of his Five Years' Residence in the States of Mississippi and Louisiana.* In 1818 at the age of twenty-two he had sailed from New York City for New Orleans where he says he found little "to please a pious or a sober man." He next visited his brother in Natchez and engaged in farming and other pursuits in Mississippi, of which he wrote in some detail.

Such accounts were usually from the pens of those who did not remain to become Southerners, and Pearse's book was "designed for the use of men of ordinary life, who wish to emigrate from the northern and western states"—and frankly intended to discourage the popular trend in the younger generation to be lured by "many pompous stories from the South." His account of much unfavorable weather, of frequent illness in his family, and of "a system of thought and conduct, so entirely different" from what they had known was hardly calculated to lure others to follow in his footsteps.

More enticing presumably were the frequent editions of Zadoc Cramer's *The Navigator; Containing Directions for Navigating the Monongahela, Allegheny, Ohio, and Mississippi Rivers,* to which was appended in certain issues "An Account of Louisiana." In 1816, too, William Darby brought out *A Geographical Description of the State of Louisiana.* A native of Pennsylvania transplanted to Ohio, Darby migrated to Natchez, became a cotton planter, and married a widow of "quite handsome property"; later he made extensive explorations and surveys of Louisiana but returned to Pennsylvania, after Louisiana officials declined to publish his surveys. Ten years after his publication was brought out in Philadelphia, D. Hewitt of the same city included in the monthly issue (April 1826) of his *Universal Traveller* detailed information on routes to New Orleans, Charleston, and other objectives. Soon the field was adequately covered in the commercial guidebooks or directories that listed the attractions of the West and of the South for the aspiring emigrant. It was not long before the French commentator, Michael Chevalier could state (in his *Manners and Politics in the United States*), "There is not a family in the North that has not a son or a brother in the South," a comment that was reaffirmed by many a later writer.

But no movement can be appraised adequately without some gauge of its size or extent. Fortunately such a measure is made possible by the data in the census of 1850, assembled and dispensed under the supervision of the ablest director who had as yet held that office, the distinguished Southerner and Louisianan, James D. B. DeBow.

In his *Compendium* to the sixth census, DeBow supplies data on the population origins of the residents of southern states and cities. One is inevitably impressed with his declaration that there were 726,450 persons living in slaveholding states who were natives of nonslaveholding states, as against the 232,112

persons in nonslaveholding states who were natives of slave
states. This nearly three-fourths of a million Yankee residents of
the South outnumbered the foreign-born element there nearly
two to one. If it can be assumed that an equal number of their
offspring were born and probably raised under some influence
of an outside parental origin, the Yankee element cannot be
dismissed as a mere drop in the southern bucket.

But more important than the number of this Yankee stock in
general was its concentration in the larger centers of population
in the South. Certain towns and cities had almost become, in
the minds of contemporary observers, Yankee towns. In 1849
James H. Hammond of South Carolina, himself the son of a
Yankee educator from Massachusetts, wrote to John C. Calhoun
designating Augusta as "a Yankee town you know" and this
label was at least somewhat confirmed by other commentators
including a correspondent of Senator Calhoun who put Savannah in the same class. Savannah had a total population in 1850
or a little over fifteen thousand. Of these, 1,249—nearly half of
them from Massachusetts—were northern-born. With nearly
2,500 foreign-born, the city's native Georgia stock, including
Negroes, was less than five thousand. The Richmond *Whig* in
1850 conceded of its own community, "Many of the citizens of
Richmond are Northern men by birth." Charleston continued
to have a conspicuous Yankee element in its population up to
and even after the secession of the state.

Alabama had a total Yankee population of just under five
thousand, only a little over one percent of the white population
of the state, but one of its early historians conceded that "the
impress of the characteristics of these early settlers, and the
States and communities from which they came, was strongly
made in the sections where they resided." Mobile had somewhat
less than two thousand Yankees, not quite ten percent of the
urban white population. F. L. Olmstead found the Northerners
as well as the foreign-born prominent in the business and community life of the state capital, Montgomery.

Mississippi had nearly as many northern-born residents as
Alabama out of a population much smaller. The Yankee ele-

ment was conspicuous in towns like Natchez and Vicksburg where there were prominent "colonies" of Pennsylvanians, among other northern elements, who particularly welcomed newcomers from their own native state.

Louisiana led other communities not only in its total but in its Yankee population. Nearly 15,000 of the latter were conspicuous in a population not native to the state of a little over 125,000. New Orleans had a population of 116,375, nearly half of which was of foreign birth and less than one-tenth native to the free states. But the large floating population included, especially in winter, additional thousands of visitors from Yankeedom, seekers after health and pleasure as well as nonresident agents of northern commission and mercantile houses.

It would seem that no really southern community had a population of over ten percent of Northerners. But New Orleans, Memphis, Mobile, Savannah, and a few others approached that figure and found themselves the subject of special interest—and at times concern—for that fact.

The new state of Texas, more western than southern in many ways, had its fair quota of Yankee residents. After all the original promoter of American settlement in this area, while it was still a unit of the Mexican republic, was Moses Austin, a Connecticut Yankee, and many of the early pioneers hailed from northern parts. Whole boatloads of settlers embarked from northern parts in the early thirties to establish themselves on this new frontier. The officers in the new independent republic that broke off from Mexico were to an amazing degree Yankees from New England. Many of these Yankee Texans in due time took their pens in hand and wrote extensive accounts of their adventures in the Lone Star republic. Their wide circulation in print whetted many a later appetite for adventuresome pioneering in the Southwest.

The flow of population to Texas was largely interrupted by the Mexican War. In the fifties, however, it was again in evidence, in greater strength than ever. In the spring of 1851 the Quincy (Illinois) *Whig* noted that a number of the "most respectable and thrifty farmers" of that part of the state had sold their holdings and made preparations to emigrate to Texas. Two years later the same movement was manifest in other parts of the state, with many but not all planning to settle in the northern part of Texas. After the panic of 1857 there was another exodus of settlers and downstream steamers out of St. Louis were crowded with emigrants. "HO, FOR TEXAS!" announced the Belleville *Democrat,* September 3, 1859, as it proceeded to recount the preparations of fifteen or twenty families in the county—"excellent citizens they are too," it added—to start out for Texas in a single overland train.

Indeed, the panic of 1857 was said by a somewhat sullen southern writer (Hundley, 209) to have made many Northerners, "turn doleful visages toward the South." "Many of you, indeed," he stated, "leaving your families in the Free states, turned your steps Southward in search of employment. Never was there such an Exodus from the Northern to the Southern States before."

In the year of the next census, on the eve of a bloody civil war, the Baltimore *American* summarized this phenomemnon of Yankees in contemporary Dixie:

> It is computed that at least one million of the citizens of the South are natives of the Northern States, who have settled in the South and in many instances intermarried with southern families, and are among the most loyal and public spirited of the population. This is especially true of Georgia, South Carolina, and Louisiana. Charleston has a large population of the natives of northern states among her population, and the city of Savannah is, in its habits and aspects, more like a sober, business New England town than a Southern city. New Orleans and Augusta each have a large northern element, and there, as elsewhere, northern adopted citizens are among the most valuable and reliable men in the community. . . .

During the antebellum period there circulated a humorous

definition of nowhere as "a place where no Yankee has ever been and never will be." According to this definition the South could claim status by the very presence of its "Yankee" citizens. The lure of the South had brought them to its farms and cities. The stream that had flowed was infinitely more powerful than that of the eighties when a romantic preacher, the Reverent T. H. Harley, proclaimed *Southward Ho!* as the title for his notes on a "Tour to and through the State of Georgia," a trip far more prosaic and untouched by the lure or romance than many of the forces that brought the Yankees of the antebellum period.

An earlier preacher commentator had really sensed the power of these forces and their romantic meaning. According to the Reverend William Henry Milburn, whose own missions had occasioned some years of labor in the deep South, that section, together with the West, had drawn off a considerable percentage of the population of the older areas of the North.

> . . . A quarter, almost, of the whole population of New England has been drained out it into new settlements. Her sons and daughters are ever moving westward, insomuch that whole villages may be found left with a strange overproportion of elderly people in them. Over the mountains they go, teaching or trading, farming or preaching. The young maidens inter-marry with the southerners or westerners, and the young men take to themselves wives of the daughters of the land. And thus are fused together, the comparatively stiff and formal, though strong, practical, straightforward, acute and resolute, qualities of the New Englander, with the fiery impulsive generosity, the passionate fever, the indolence, the semi-tropical ease, of the far South. . . .

Southward Ho!, indeed, in one form or other, in terms of hard Yankee practicality if not of romantic word-mongering, may well have been the slogan of the thousands who made their way by land or sea to a sojourn in Dixie—Would it be a permanent home? they wondered. The question as to the impress of this northern element upon the social, economic, and political life of the South will be the problem of my later lectures.

THE STRANGE PAUSE IN
JOHN ADAMS'S DIARY

Robert A. East

One of the tantalizing omissions in our pre-Revolutionary history is the absence of entries in the famous diary of John Adams between February 1763 and January 1765. There is good evidence that Adams was having fun at the time by writing on both sides of the Massachusetts political situation, and that these contrary writings were being published in rival newspapers of the day; but the diary entries are missing.

The period was referred to by Charles Francis Adams as a two-year "interval," which he unsatisfactorily tried to fill with a passage from the autobiography, written many years later.[1] The most recent edition of the diary merely makes a brief mention of the gap, in a footnote, together with a draft of an essay on agriculture.[2] One wishes that the editor had emulated the author of *Tristram Shandy,* and inserted a few blank pages at critical points to warn unwary readers.[3] There has been a disposition among scholars to pass over this period in John Adams's life, with little attention to anything other than his marriage to Abigail Smith in October 1764. Unfortunately for us (if not for Adams) the gaps in his diary during the period of his courtship leave in relative obscurity the question of what else was going on at the time.

As Governor Hutchinson noted in his *History of Massachusetts-Bay,* this was a most crucial period. Hutchinson identified

17

the first free use of the terms *Whigg* and *Tory* as centering around 1763, likening such expressions in Boston to the sympathy then being heard in England for "Wilkes and liberty," and said that in Massachusetts the activities of the Otises, father and son, had already given great impetus to the growth of the party spirit.[4] Yet all we have pertaining to John Adams's interest in these events in 1763, according to the traditional accounts, is one or two equivocal entries in his diary regarding the outrageous behavior of James Otis, Jr., in February 1763, and several newspaper articles submitted to the *Boston Gazette* that summer, two on the philosophical subjects of "Private Revenge" and "Self-Deceit" (as Charles Francis Adams termed them). This lack of personal reflection seems scarcely in keeping with the character of John Adams.[5] He had been an inveterate diary scribbler from college days, at least.

This lack of interest is not only uncharacteristic of Adams but is surprising in view of certain other circumstances. This presumably was about the time when Adams's "most intimate friend" at the bar, Jonathan Sewall, came visiting weekends in Braintree where he was courting the vivacious Esther Quincy, whom he was to marry in January 1764. (Her sister, Dorothy, was to marry John Hancock years later. Hancock himself had originated in Braintree, where his father had been a minister.) According to John Adams's recollection, Sewall invariably saw him at the Quincys' on Sunday nights, and (according to John Quincy Adams, in his short biographical sketch of his father's early years) the young men probably continued to have at that time that animated discussion of philosophical topics which had occasioned a confidential correspondence between them.[6] Esther Quincy was, of course, a distant cousin of the Abigail Smith whom John Adams was to marry later that same year. John thought Esther rather saucy, even if she looked good to Sewall.[7]

Jonathan Sewall, the subsequent noted Loyalist, was the nephew and executor of the late Chief Justice of the province, Stephen Sewall, whose death in September 1760 had revealed that he was a much better student of the law than of business affairs. Jonathan had petitioned the General Court for financial assistance in settling his uncle's estate, a petition that had failed, due, he thought, to lack of support by the Otises. According to Adams in later years, this feeling had immediately been seized upon by the administration—i.e., Bernard and Hutchinson. They had fastened young Sewall to their interests by appointing him a Justice of the Peace for Middlesex in 1762. Securing such a commission was the royal road to success in the law, as John Adams himself knew, for it was one he was to recall that he had been urged to travel as early as 1761.[8]

The politics of Sewall would seem to be important for an understanding of the political leanings of his friend Adams. For one thing, Sewall's "enemy," James Otis, Jr., had allegedly threatened to throw the province into a "flame" because Hutchinson had become the new Chief Justice in 1760, thus thwarting the ambitions of James Otis, Sr. The latter had thought that a position on the bench of the Superior Court had been promised to him as soon as one would become available.

Hutchinson always accused James Otis, Jr., of subsequently doing precisely what he had then threatened—of opposing the administration on so many issues as to prepare the way for a holocaust. From so "small a spark" did the Revolution come, says Hutchinson in his *History*. It was a point of view with which John Adams was to take issue, more or less, in his old age; but he had heard a story as early as 1766 that the mob had destroyed Hutchinson's house, the previous year, in order to prevent his writing any more history![9]

This, then, was the exciting political situation of which young John Adams must have been fully aware, to judge from the last entries in his diary in February 1763, just prior to his silence of nearly two years. The facts are clear. His closest friend, who was or had been spending a lot of time in Braintree, and often in his company, had become bitterly anti-Otis and proadministration, despite his earlier "patriotic" (i.e., anti-British) attitude. (Adams's assignment of Sewall's change in attitude to a later date, as a result of his troubles with the Otises, is obviously incorrect.)[10] Although John Adams in old age was to

remember Otis, Jr., with the greatest awe and affection, even
he, as we have seen, was noting sympathetically the "rage" of
the Boston bar against Otis in February 1763 on the issue of
making political use of "pettifogging" (i.e., untrained) lawyers.
He even once voted to insult Otis by specifically excluding his
name from an invitation of the bar for the judges. Adams was
obviously becoming, temporarily at least, disillusioned about
the erratic course of that great man,[11] however neutral he may
have remained about taking "sides" in politics himself. In other
words, the Otis question in early 1763 very likely left Adams in
somewhat of a quandary.

At this very juncture, in February 1763, a great political
uproar broke out. John Adams made his famous, and apparently disapproving, diary entry that month—almost his last entry
for nearly two years—about the activities of a "Caucas Clubb"
that was meeting in the long garret of Tom Dawes, on Boston's
South Side, to smoke and drink and to determine what was to
be done at town meetings (and no doubt to counteract the influence of the "court" party). About the same time the activities
of the "Junto" at the "Caucas Clubb" were being broadcast to
the world in the *Boston Evening-Post* by a writer who signed
himself "J." The same writer had already communicated a long
indictment of James Otis, Jr., whom he called "Bluster" and a
"tool" of the "Junto," and who, he had insinuated, was on
the way to becoming a madman (which of course he eventually
did become).[12] According to the *Boston Evening-Post,* the "Junto" even drew up newspaper copy for publication in the sympathetic *Boston Gazette.* The language of "J." in describing the
"Caucas" is strangely like that of John Adams in his diary, with
regard to the personnel and the smoking and drinking habits of
the habitués of Tom Dawes's garret. It sounds almost as if
Adams and "J." had had a common source of information; or
that Adams had checked on "J." 's newspaper account, and
found it correct.

This writer, "J.," affected to be a young man living a long
distance from Boston, at least thirty hours of travel time by
horse, and perhaps at Springfield which is given as his address at

the bottom of one of his pieces;[13] but of course, this is the greatest nonsense. The author of the sensational attacks on Otis was obviously at great pains to conceal his identity, and no doubt used such a device precisely because he did not live at any great distance from Boston. Within a year or two (the date is not certain), Boston wit Samuel Waterhouse, in his *Proposals for Printing by Subscription the History of Adjutant Trowel and Bluster,* was to point out with great glee that the identity of the "candid writer" who had attacked Otis had been successfully kept from him.[14]

But to us, the secret apparently is solved. John Adams in later years refers to the author of the savage attacks on Otis ("Bluster") in 1763 as being the same person (i.e., Jonathan Sewall) with whom he was engaging in a newspaper duel in 1766-67, when Sewall was writing over the signature of "Philanthrop," in defense of Governor Bernard.

In manuscript, the Adams reference to the writer who signed himself as "long J." is on the back of a draft of an article (presumably written in 1763 but never published) in the *Adams Family Papers.*[15]

One of the satires on Otis in the *Evening-Post* the April 1763 is signed "J. Philanthrop," and is obviously a combination of signatures.[16] It indeed seems probable that "J." in 1763 and "Philanthrop" in 1766 were the same person. In any case, John Adams always thought, and said, that this was his old friend Sewall, whose writings he said he recognized from their "style." Sometime after the repeal of the Stamp Act, Adams stated that he had known from the very first of the attacks on Otis in 1763 just who this "Raskall" was.[17] That is, Adams claimed several years later that he had known from early in 1763 that his old friend Sewall (i.e., "Philanthrop") had been the politically upsetting "J."

Adams seems to have had a lifelong obsession about the wickedness of Jonathan Sewall—witness how long he wrongly regarded Sewall as the author of the "Massachusettensis" papers—to the effect that his old friend had been behind many of the Tory "shenanigans" in Massachusetts.

Unless Adams's bitter accusations of Sewall in later years were nothing but suspicions, it is difficult to reject the thesis that Sewall and "J." probably were identical in 1763; also, more importantly, that since Adams "knew" this at the time, that Adams very likely had already begun to have doubts about his friends's political integrity by 1763, if not earlier.

Assuming this to be true (and it really makes very little difference since Adams thought it was true), from a "Whig" point of view it may account for the critical treatment of "J." as a tool of a "faction" and the instrument of a "party," which Adams expresses as the writer "U." in the *Boston Gazette* on August 29, 1763. It may also account for his sarcastic references to "Mr. J." in that same paper on July 18 (although this particular "U." article was one that Charles Francis Adams did not see fit to include among the "earliest printed productions known" of his grandfather's works).[18]

These articles by "U." in 1763, moreover, put Adams in an "antiadministration" newspaper in his first public appearance in print. (There is no other way to describe the *Gazette* even at that early date, as anyone will conclude on reading the angry exchanges on the subject of "sides" that had developed between its printers and those of the *Evening-Post* in January and February of that year.) It also shows him to have been in a critical frame of mind about the violent political writing and acts of personal violence that leading citizens were indulging in as "Private Revenge." Adams's essay on "Self-Deceit" in August also reveals him to be in an especially critical attitude toward his "worthy and ingenious friend, Mr. J.," as already noted.[19]

It should be borne in mind that Adams and Sewall had earlier thought of each other as "David and Jonathan," and had addressed each other as "Brother." However, Sewall seems to have referred to other persons than Adams as "Brother," for he was a most facetious and witty man and no doubt given to familiar expressions.[20] Perhaps it was Adams rather than Sewall who had stressed the role of "Brother Jonathan," and accordingly was the more apt to be disillusioned by any transgression on his friend's part, as in the latter's having been made a Justice of the Peace in 1762.

All this would seem to be acceptable, if regrettable, historical interpretation, and something of a subsitute for the "interval" in the Adams records for 1763 and 1764, if one takes, as we have said, a "Whig" version of the origin of Adams's political philosophy, i.e., of his being identified with the writings of "U." in the *Gazette* in 1763.[21] It may also cast some light on Adams's undoubted ambitions as a young man.

Fortunately, the situation may be seen in a somewhat different light. The "Whig" version of Adams's early career may be only a part of the story. The question has been raised, and apparently must be answered in the affirmative (as it is in the recent edition of John Adams's diary), whether Adams over the signature of "Ploughjogger" was not also the author of a second series of articles in 1763, which took a much more sympathetic attitude toward "J." and presumably toward the anti-Otis politics which the latter espoused. These articles, significantly, were in the proadministration *Boston Evening-Post,* and not in the antiadministration *Gazette* at all.

There seemed to be something of a contest between these two newspaper contributors. At the *Post* said on August 29, *"Honest Ploughjogger's Letter in Answer to Mr. U. is come to Hand, but an Account of its length must be deferred till our next."*

This ambivalence may throw some light on the mixed nature of Adams's political feelings from the earliest times; here may be a key to that mixture of conservatism with "whiggery" which eventually was to make him (and his eldest son, John Quincy Adams) so many domestic enemies in post-Revolutionary years.[22]

Such are the implications raised by the likelihood of John Adams having been the author of the "Humphrey Ploughjogger" letters in 1763. There is clear proof that Adams later wrote under this signature in the *Boston Gazette* in 1765 and 1767 (including the draft of an article in his diary), and in one of these written in 1765, he actually makes reference to "a good many papers" which "Mr. U and I" had written a year or two before.[23] Adams also asserted in old age that among his earliest publications were two or three pieces written under this signa-

ture "in the year 1762 or 1763."[24] Such articles do appear in
the later year, as already noted, although not in the *Boston
Gazette* but in the *Evening-Post*. (It may be significant that the
latter was the paper for which Adams had also originally designed the first of the "U." articles.)

An especially amusing bit of internal evidence may be ad-
duced from the "Ploughjogger" article in the *Evening-Post,* on
September 5, 1763. Listing his differences with "Mr. U.," that
"wonderful, lofty, sublyme riter," "Ploughjogger" humorously
remarks, "Next comes one thing that I do like, that is the line
of latin. I love to see, now and then, some latin, in the books I
reed. I almost think I understand it sumtimes, especially when I
see it in Mr. Flavels works, it comes in so natural." Compare
this with the sardonic quotation by lawyer Prat of Boston,
noted with head-shaking by Adams in his diary, January 1759:
"There is not a Page of Flavels Works without several sentences
of Latin. Yet the common People admire him. They admire his
Latin as much as his English, and understand it as well."[25]

Unless one rejects all of the circumstantial evidence, as well
as Adams's own statement at a later date, his identification with
the early "Ploughjogger" must be conceded, i.e., the fact of his
having carried on a "dialogue with himself in the two leading
Boston papers" in 1763, as has been brilliantly said.[26] It is almost inconceivable that John Adams would have taken the signature of someone else who had already written in a rival newspapers, and used it for political purposes in 1765 and 1767.
Moreover, the concern of colonial printers for the integrity of
signatures among contributors should always be remembered.[27]

As the name "Ploughjogger" suggests, the writer professed a
countryman's interest in agriculture, especially in promoting the
cultivation of hemp (sinister word!) in New England. Hemp had
just been added to the enumerated list, and was a common
topic. Indeed, "U." had also professed this in his articles, even
acknowledging his indebtedness to "Ploughjogger" on that
score.[28] However, "Ploughjogger" from the beginning, in March
1763, had also shown a deep interest in politics, not only (like
"U.") because of his disapproval of the violent actions and poli-

tical writing by "grate men," but because he clearly disapproved of "party" politics (such as Hutchinson later testified were beginning to take place, and of which the use of a "Caucas" was surely an indication). "Ploughjogger" also took to defending "J." He even asked "U." in his final number, on September 5, what were *his* motives in all this controversy?

In other words, if Adams was "Ploughjogger" as well as "U." in 1763, he ended up by asking himself questions about his own motives and ambition, in addition to putting in a good word for the writer whom he later said he had already suspected (i.e., "knew") to be his intimate friend. No doubt all this was deeply philosophical, but it was deeply political as well.

It must be admitted that there are other logical contenders for the honor of having been "Ploughjogger" at that early date (as Charles Francis Adams may have believed, despite his grandfather's statement, possibly because he thought that the old gentleman had gotten mixed up in his dates). One such person would be Peter Oliver, Justice of the Superior Court of Massachusetts and a famous Loyalist. Peter Oliver was a witty gentleman with marked literary gifts and a deep interest in agriculture which he had shown by his correspondence with Jared Eliot, whose *Essays on Field Husbandry Especially in New-England* Oliver had paid to have published in Boston in 1760. "Ploughjogger" tells us in his article in the *Evening-Post* on June 20, 1763, that he has seen pass his house, that "nice, good natur'd fine Gentleman" who wrote the "leeves at the end" of Eliot's *Essays* (i.e., the appendix). Adams, himself, of course, was never more deeply interested in agriculture than at this period of life.

There is no doubt that Oliver wrote this appendix, nor that lawyer Adams several years later thought Judge Oliver to be the "best bred Gentleman" of all the judges in Massachusetts.[29] ("Ploughjogger" had added in his article on June 20 that "folks say I know him.") And since it would have been logical for Oliver to have ridden past Adams's house in Braintree on the Old Plymouth Road to Boston from his country seat in Middleborough, Plymouth County, it seems reasonable to assume that Adams might have seen him.

It might be argued that another "Ploughjogger" possibility would have to be Jonathan Sewall himself. When in philosophical disputation with his old friend Adams he might indeed have learned (and thus could have mocked in print) Adams's sentiments and expressions; but there is no reason to believe that Sewall knew the details of agricultural life as "Ploughjogger" expressed them. Moreover, the protest by "Ploughjogger" in his last contribution to the *Evening-Post* in 1763, against "black, ugly pictures" being drawn of leading province characters including "Bluster," would have been out of character for Sewall, considering his anti-Otis feelings. So *his* pretensions likewise may be dismissed.

Suspicion of being "Ploughjogger" might also point at young Samuel Quincy (orginally from Braintree and, like Sewall, a close friend of Adams and subsequently a Loyalist in the badly split Quincy family). He must have been acquainted with the sardonic opinions of the caustic Benjamin Prat of Boston (whom "Ploughjogger" quoted), since he had studied law with him for three years; but "Sam" Quincy (it was his sister, Hannah, to whom John Adams had once come perilously close to getting engaged), presumably was living in Boston in 1763, where he had settled down after marriage in 1761. Thus, it is unlikely that he had been the person who had seen Judge Oliver "ride by my house" in the country. Nor is there any reason to believe that Sam had any great knowledge of, or love for agriculture, like "Ploughjogger."

Of course, one can imagine Sam Quincy and Sewall together "putting-up-a game" on their old friend Adams, in the September 5, 1763, "Ploughjogger" communication in the *Evening-Post* (which is the communication most difficult to explain). Sewall, at least, dearly loved a hoax (as witness his pulling the leg of the *Gazette* the next spring in connection with the "great calomel scandal" at Castle William), and his anti-Otis feelings could have been pared down by Quincy; but such amusing speculation must be laid aside as reasoning *reductio ad absurdum*.

Similar speculation could be made about "Daddy" Quincy (the uncle of Sam and the father of Esther and Dorothy), because of *his* writings on hemp (in which everyone was interested, as we have said). Even one of the Boston wits might be suspected.

But John Adams, himself, is still the overwhelming favorite for the honor of having been "Ploughjogger."

By September of 1763, however, Adams may well have suffered twinges of self-reproach for his criticism of the "Long J.," whom he suspected to be his friend; or, what is more likely, to have attempted to make retribution in the *Evening-Post* for having been drawn into political controversy in the *Gazette*.[30] It may be significant that in "U." 's last article in the *Gazette*, on September 5, there is no mention of "J." at all. On the other hand, "Ploughjogger" in the *Evening-Post* tells that "noble, high flown riter" who signs himself "U.," that he is wrong on many counts.[31] He excuses "U." 's belligerency to a certain extent because "there is sumthing in man that delites in fighting," and relates a story from boyhood, of once having seen two rams fight until one dropped dead with a split skull. Though it had been a "dredful cruel fight," yet he admits that he had "lov'd to see it," which surely is an autobiographical confession from John Adams himself.

Nevertheless, "Ploughjogger" professes not to like what is going on, and to question "U." 's motives in the most sarcastic terms:

> Mr. U. seems to run quite out of his way, to pick a quarrel with Mr. J.—I cant devise what his reason was.—I guess several things.—Sumtimes I think he has studied oratary, and oratary, our ministur says, is the art of gaining attention. And he mite think there was no way of gaining attention so shure, as to make fokes think him a party-man. For he would get the attenshon of one haff the world thro love, and of tother thro hatred.—Sumtimes I think he made a pass at Mr. J. to let fokes know his reason for signing himself U.—But upon the whole, I beleeve it most likely Mr. U. has been a deputy for sum town, and been made a justice by the Governor and

then was dropt by his town.

A long drawn-out debate on the subject of vanity and human wishes very likely occupied Adams in 1763, possibly in person with Sewall, who presumably was frequently in his company that year. Perhaps it had been occasioned by their reading in Burke's *Philosophical Enquiry,* or in Adam Smith's *Theory of the Moral Sentiments* which had recently appeared and was to influence much of Adams's later writing.[32] The morality of receiving favors from the governor was also involved. In any case, the passage reveals a severe, if humorous, self-explanation by Adams regarding his own motives in denouncing the motives of his friend. He plainly is skeptical about the makeup of a "party-man," himself or anyone else.

The difficulties in the way of accepting the idea of Adams having made such cross-fire criticism of himself in 1763, and of his holding conflicting attitudes toward the political writing of his old friend "J.," are of course very great. On the other hand, as argued above, these may help to reveal Adams's conservative-radicalism at an early date, and throughout his later career.

Adams's determination to remain politically neutral in 1763, when "sides" and "party men" began to appear under the whip-lash of Otis's eloquence and "J." 's witty retorts, is evident in both roles. The result seems to have been his concentration on the legal foundations necessary for a good society. Of course, Abigail may have made up his mind for him, after 1764.

Lawyer Adams's basic concern eventually was to become what was to differentiate his philosophy from that of many "Tories": i.e., his belief in a government of "laws and not of men." For many of the Tories were surely seen as men of privilege. As early as 1762, James Otis had referred in his brilliant *Vindication of the Conduct of the House of Representatives* to that "set" of men in America (much more dangerous to America than any group in England, he declared) who were seeking to embellish their power and interests.[33] This sort of thing, according to his sister, Mercy Otis Warren, had led to marriage contracts being made in colonial times between young persons of immature age and close relationship, so as to perpetuate a monopoly of office-holding interests.[34] This "set" was no doubt identical with that "crew of Villains" which Adams accused of once having raised the great "clamour" against Governor Pownall, and which he believed, in old age, to have matured a "plan" against the liberties of America as early as Governor Shirley's day.[35]

Whether these persons were right in their suspicions or not, it seems likely that Hutchinson was right in his accusation that the terms *Whig* and *Tory* had begun to be used in America even before the Stamp Act crisis. Although Otis's *Vindication* did not use these words directly, his argument was based upon the importance of the "glorious revolution" for American as for English affairs, which surely was a Whig interpretation of American rights. It was closely akin to the constitutional reasoning of "patriots" like John Dickinson in the years prior to 1776, although not, be it noted, in the thinking of John Adams. (Acceptance of the glorious revolution in Adams's legalistic analysis of American rights would have been destructive of the right of revolt against Parliamentary authority in America.)[36]

In her history of the American Revolution published in 1805, Mercy Otis Warren, the sister of James Otis and the wife of a famous Revolutionary statesman (and an intellectual bluestocking in her own right), blackened, in the most patriotic terms, the memory of the unfortunate Thomas Hutchinson, late Governor of Massachusetts Bay; but she reserved her deepest scorn for those Americans who, in her opinion, had deviated from their professions of republicanism.[37] There can be little doubt that the formidable "Mercy" had in mind her old friend and neighbor, the former President of the United States, John Adams, who since the days of Shays's Rebellion had acquired the reputation in certain quarters of being a political reactionary; and who, together with his eldest son, John Quincy Adams, had thrown up the first barricades in America against French Revolutionary doctrines in the 1790s.

All this may well have been a conservative Adams echo from the distant past. So also may have been his scathing denunciation in later years of secret committees of correspondence as "dangerous machines" which had produced a revolution in France and all over Europe. "What an engine!" he then exclaimed. He denied their desirability except in the very last extremities, and denied that he had ever belonged to any such a committee in pre-Revolutionary America.[38]

Adams in the role of "Ploughjogger" makes a great deal of sense, not because the role reveals him as a man of divided mind as regards his close friend, but because it reveals him as a man already possessed of the strong conservative streak that was to come out in his later career. He was a great man not in spite of his having a divided mind, but because of it. Rules of psychology apparently do not apply equally to the great and the near-great.

Nor does a Whig view of history explain all the facts.

Unlike most Revolutionaries, young John Adams had a sense of humor, for some things at least. In the years before 1776 there was to be a sad need of such humor as "Ploughjogger" had supplied in 1763, during that strange pause in John Adams's diary; but this was generally to be forgotten, in that more-or-less humorless movement that we call the American Revolution. [39]

Notes

1. John Adams, *The Works of John Adams,* ed. C. F. Adams, 10 vols. (Boston, 1851-1866), 2: 145.

2. John Adams, *The Diary and Autobiography of John Adams,* ed. H. L. Butterfield, 4 vols. (Cambridge, Mass., 1961), 1: 252.

3. Adams, *Works,* 2:145.

4. Thomas Hutchinson, *History of the Colony and Province of Massachusetts-Bay,* Lawrence Shaw Mayo, ed., 3 vols. (Cambridge, Mass., 1936), 3: 69, 74, 75.

5. Gilbert Chinard, *Honest John Adams* (Boston, 1933), p. 45, says that Adams "apparently" was little concerned about the political situation in 1763-64, in view of the lack of diary entries.

6. Adams, *Works,* 1: 61; 4: 8. John Adams wrongly gave the date of Sewall's marriage as 1766, in addition to vaguely placing Sewall's "corruption" by the administration at a later date. See note 7.

7. Adams's characterization of Esther is in the *Diary and Autobiography*, 1: 67.

8. Adams, *Works*, 4: 7; *Diary and Autobiography*, 3: 287, 288. Adams's account of the anti-Otis origin of Sewall's politics is accepted by modern scholarship but at an earlier date: Clifford K. Shipton, *Sibley's Harvard Graduates*, vols. 4-12 (Cambridge, Mass., 1933-date), 12:308, 309. Sewall's appointment as a "special" Attorney General was not until 1767: ibid., p. 311. John Quincy Adams was, of course, wrong in placing Sewall's difficulties with the Otises at a later date: Adams, *Works*, 1:61, but in this he obviously followed his father's vague recollections.

9. Hutchinson, *History*, 3: 64; *Adams, Diary and Autobiography*, 1: 300. For John Adams's somewhat similar recollection, see his *Works*, 10: 183, 281, 298, 300. The curious parallel between Adams's analysis of the causes of the Revolution and that of some Tories has been remarked upon elsewhere, e.g., Peter Oliver, *Origin and Progress of the American Revolution*, eds. Adair and Schutz (San Marino, Cal., 1963), p. 28 and note.

10. See note 6.

11. Adams, *Diary and Autobiography*, 1: 235-237.

12. Ibid., 1: 238; *Boston Evening-Post*, February 14, March 14, 1763. For further descriptions see the articles in the latter for March 21, including material on the "Corkass By a late Member of that Society," and on the "Junto" by "W. D——s."

13. *Boston Evening-Post*, March 14, April 25, 1763.

14. Samuel Waterhouse, *Proposals for Printing by Subscription the History of Adjutant Trowel* (Boston, 1766).

15. Adams, *Works*, 4: 6, 7; Hutchinson, *History*, 3: 118 and note; *Adams Family Papers*, August 1763; Adams, *Diary and Autobiography*, 1: 330ff.

16. *Boston Evening-Post*, April 4, 1763.

17. In microfilm reel 343 of the *Adams Family Papers*, misfiled with drafts of articles by "U." under August 1763 there is an address to "J. Phylanthrop" in which Adams says that since the repeal of the Stamp Act he has been in hopes of a respite from the "crew of Villains" who, however, now think they are out of danger and "have hired their old trumpeter J. Philanthrop, to start forth." (Cf. "U." 's reference to "Mr. J." with his "noble and ignoble Trumpeters," in the *Boston Gazette*, July 18, 1763.) Of this "Rascall," Adams declares, "I knew you perfectly well. I knew your Name, Character . . . Patrons, Prompters, Views . . . every syllable you have scribbled from the first of your Productions, as contained [the] character of Bluster [i.e., Otis] to the last of them . . . and that unless you desist I . . . will expose the whole Faction . . . from the time they raised the villainous clamour against Govr Pownal. . . ." However, as late as February 15, 1764, Sewall was addressing Adams as "Brother John."

18. *Works*, 3: 427ff.

19. *Boston Gazette*, August 29, 1763.

20. *Works*, 4: 6; microfilm reel 343 of the *Adams Family Papers*, under February 15, 1764, for a letter from Sewall to "Brother John" which also refers to "Brother Thacher." The witty correspondence of Sewall, mostly at a later date when he was a Loyalist, is in the *Proceedings of the Massachusetts Historical Society*, 2d ser., 10 (1896): 407-427.

21. Or, with his later emphasis on Otis's speech against the *Writs of Assistance* in 1761: Adams, *Diary and Autobiography*, 2: 55; Adams, *Works*, 10: 183, 272, 280, et passim.

22. Cf. my *John Quincy Adams: The Critical Years, 1785-1794* (New York, 1962), chaps. 7, 9. The most recent study of J. Q. Adams is Marie B. Hecht, *John Quincy Adams: A Personal History of an Independent Man* (New York, 1972).

23. *Boston Gazette*, October 14, 1765.

24. Adams, *Diary and Autobiography*, 1: 250, 290, 330, and editor's notes; microfilm reel 327 of the *Adams Family Papers*.

25. Adams, *Diary and Autobiography*, 1: 73. The observation about Flavel had originally been made by the caustic, one-legged Benjamin Prat, a Boston lawyer of original mind, who had died in 1762. Some of Prat's ideas, including such slurs on the "common" people, or on free schools which made the "lowest of the People infinitely conceited," did not sit well with Adams (ibid., 1: 152, 153); but the important thing to bear in mind is that the whole character of "Ploughjogger" is a satire on rustic "larning," for which Prat's remarks were quite appropriate for paraphrasing, by Adams or anyone else. He was no "country bumpkin" who "warnt book larnt enuff," and his sympathy with the "common" people in resenting airs of patronage would not be inconsistent with his use of the "Ploughjogger" slur. If anyone doubts that Adams was incapable of making such fine "rustic" distinctions, note his scornful use of the word "Peasants" (an expression otherwise almost unknown to American history) as applied to the less cultured "strip" farmers around Boston a few years later (ibid., 2: 18).

26. Ibid., 1: 250, editor's note.

27. See Roger B. Berry, "John Adams: Two Further Contributions in the *Boston Gazette*, 1766-1768," in the *New England Quarterly* 31 (1958): 90-95, especially 93n.

28. *Boston Gazette*, July 18, 1763.

29. Shipton, *Sibley's Harvard Graduates*, 8: 740; Adams, *Diary and Autobiography*, 2: 51.

30. Adams's insatiable ambition to become a public writer thus got him into political hot water, despite all his nonpolitical protestations.

31. *Boston Evening-Post*, September 5, 1763.

32. "U." had characterized his last number, "On Private Revenge," in the *Gazette* on September 5, 1763, as his "history of *sentiments*." Thirty years later, Adams was to utilize a whole chapter of Smith's *Theory of the Moral Sentiments* for his "Discourses on Davila."

33. Charles Mullett, ed., "The Writings of James Otis," University of Missouri *Studies*, 4, no. 3: 70.

34. Mercy Warren, *The Rise, Progress and Termination of the American Revolution*, 3 vols. (Boston, 1805), 1: 116.

35. "To J. Phylanthrop," microfilm reel 343 of the *Adams Family Papers*, (misfiled under August 1763); also Adams, *Works*, 10:243.

36. See the arguments of the House of Representatives (for which John Adams seems to have been the principal penman) in its dispute with Hutchinson in 1773, in James Hosmer, *Life of Thomas Hutchinson* (Boston, 1896), pp. 380ff. and 415ff., especially pp. 425, 426; also the argument of "Novanglus" in 1774 in Adams, *Works*, 4: 114 et passim.

37. Warren, *Rise, Progress and Termination*, 1: 79, 125. Parts of this must have been written as early as the 1790s, to judge from some of her remarks.

38. Cf. chaps. 7, 9 of my *John Quincy Adams*; Adams, *Works*, 10: 196, 197.

39. It was once remarked by Samuel Eliot Morison that it would have been better for the unity of the British empire had none but humorists ever looked into the constitutional issues (*Sources and Documents Illustrating the American Revolution* [Oxford, 1923], xiii). Even if the Revolution was basically a problem of home rule and nationalism, the same reflection might be made upon other questions. As Clifford Shipton says in his life of John Lovell, the famous Latin schoolmaster of Boston (*Sibley's Harvard Graduates*, 8: 445), "Like so many of the wits, he failed to comprehend the seriousness of the impending struggle." See also Shipton's remarks about Otis and the "Tory wits" in ibid., 11: 271. Unfortunately for the latter, the "Whigs" were in deadly earnest. It is editorially noted in the recent edition of John Adams's *Diary and Autobiography* (I: 261n) that the mob that was destroying the house and gardens of Andrew Oliver on the night of August 14, 1765 drove off the sheriff and Lieutenant Governor Hutchinson with brickbats when they tried to "interfere with the fun." All one can say is, some fun! It was not exactly the kind of fun that the "Tory wits" had had in mind.

THE PRESIDENTIAL AMBITIONS
OF AARON BURR, 1800-1801

Joseph G. Rayback

This essay, an outgrowth of research into Aaron Burr's role in the politics of New York State,[1] is primarily concerned with the way historians have handled and are still handling the charge that Burr conspired to defraud Thomas Jefferson of the presidency in 1800-1801. Their handling has been and is confusing and disturbing. While they have developed, as might be expected, a generally accepted body of factual evidence, they have not sufficiently questioned its authenticity. Morever, the accepted body of evidence is not complete; additional evidence is available and has been available for a very long time. Most significant, however, is the way historians and biographers have handled or mishandled the evidence and frequently the lack of evidence in order to plead a cause. The result has been the development of a prevailing attitude on the subject that is actually a gross distortion.

Except for the major biographies of Burr[2] and for Noble E. Cunningham's first book on the Jeffersonian Republicans,[3] almost all accounts of the presidential election of 1800-1801 start with the contest for the election of thirteen members of the New York State Assembly from New York City in the spring of 1800. These thirteen Assemblymen were expected to hold the balance of power in the New York legislature which would name presidential electors in November. Among historians gen-

35

erally this contest has become the most important of the year because, as everyone knew, Jefferson could not win the presidency without New York State's electoral vote.

Actually, even a very casual study of the national election would reveal that the New York City election was no more critical than the contest in the badly divided Pennsylvania Assembly or in the closely divided South Carolina legislature. Jefferson had to secure a majority of the electors in both these states as well as in New York in order to be elected. Why, then, the sense of exclusive crisis in New York City? Perhaps because it was Jefferson who called it the most critical vote;[4] perhaps because it was the first election in the three doubtful states;[5] perhaps because it was a popular and not a legislative election; perhaps because it involved Burr. At any rate for 150 years it has remained locked into the historical literature as the only critical contest for electors of the 1800-1801 campaign.[6]

In all accounts of the New York City election Burr emerges as the hero. The statements of his quondam friend, Matthew L. Davis—"to Colonel Burr we are indebted for everything"—and of Albert Gallatin's father-in-law, James Nicholson—who explained the victory as evidence of the "intervention of the Supreme Power and our friend Burr as the agent"—are most frequently cited to characterize Burr's role.[7]

More earthly accounts emphasize Burr's development of an unbeatable Assembly ticket, of his organization of Tammany into a powerful voting phalanx,[8] and of his tireless activity: He "travels every night from one meeting of Republicans to another, haranguing and spiriting them to most zealous exertions." Some wonder how he "can stoop so low as to visit every low tavern that may happen to be crowded with his dear fellow citizens. But the prize of success . . . is well worth all this dirty work."[9]

That Burr with the help of other Republicans developed an unbeatable ticket, the candidate personally persuading some crotchety old men and diffident gentry to head the ticket, is undeniable. But the Tammany connection—reiterated ad infinitum since Gustav Myers's *History of Tammany* was published—

is sheer fancy. Perhaps it is malicious fancy. Even historians who should know better view Tammany as the symbol of eternal and universal corruption. Burr at the head of Tammany makes him forever a party to corruption.

The evidence is different. As Jerome Mushkat has so well explained, Burr was *not* a member of the Tammany society. In 1800 the society was *not* a political organization. If the few hundred members had political leanings or loyalties, they were not Burrite; they were more likely Clintonian, Livingstonian, or Federalist. Tammany society was politically inert; it did *not* participate in the election.[10]

What, then, did Burr organize? A careful reading of the New York City press reveals that the Republicans had been developing a system of ward committees to manage political activities for several years; the members of these committees made up the city's "general committee." It is not clear in what condition these committees were after the defeat of the party in 1799. But Burr did not organize them in 1800;[11] they were already in existence. As his military career revealed, Burr had great capacity to energize men and to direct them, particularly under pressure. What he probably did was to quicken and replenish these committees. And these committees sometimes used the Tammany Wigwam (open to anyone who could foot the bill) for some of their meetings; such was Burr's connection with Tammany.

That Burr was tireless in his efforts to get out the vote—the Republican formula for success—is undoubtedly true. That he was *solely* responsible for the results is obvious exaggeration; no man has that kind of capacity. There were about forty members of the general committee who also contributed. The great emphasis that Matthew L. Davis put upon Burr's contributions, large as they were, must be regarded as puffery. Davis wanted Burr to be Vice-President. Significantly, he addressed his remarks concerning Burr's achievements almost exclusively to Albert Gallatin, the leader of the Republican caucus which would determine Jefferson's running mate.[12]

A few days after the New York City election the Federalists

in Congress held their caucus and named John Adams and Charles Cotesworth Pinckney of South Carolina as their presidential ticket; Pinckney's nomination was evidence that the Federalists recognized that South Carolina would be a crucial state.

Republicans waited almost ten days, until May 12, before they acted. There were aspirants for a place on the ticket alongside Jefferson from New Hampshire, Pennsylvania, and South Carolina. But it appears that the New York City election focused attention—whose attention has never been made clear—on New York's Republican leaders: former Governor George Clinton, Chancellor Robert R. Livingston, and Burr. Gallatin, the one man close to Jefferson who was supposed to have a good understanding of New York politics, was "engaged"—on whose behalf has never been explained—to "procure correct information of the wishes of the New York Republicans" concerning Clinton and Burr. Gallatin, in turn, commissioned his father-in-law, Nicholson, a friend of both men, to seek out the answer.[13]

Nicholson soon informed Gallatin that George Clinton had declined: "His age, his infirmities, his habits and attachment to retired life, in his opinion exempts him from active life." Clinton, in turn, had recommended Burr "as the most suitable . . . and perhaps the only man." All Republicans had the same opinion; their "confidence in A.B. is universaal and unbounded." But Burr "appeared averse." He had two reasons: because he had been "ill-used by Virginia and North Carolina" in the previous election and did not believe that any "arrangement could be made which would be observed to the southward," and because he and his friends believed he could be elected to the more important office of Governor of New York; they were reluctant that he make the sacrifice. If, however, the "business of the last election" could be smoothed over, Burr could probably be induced to stand.[14] The congressional caucus promptly nominated him.

A number of questions and charges have arisen over this episode. Did Clinton actually decline or were these thoughts put into Nicholson's mind by Burr and his friends? Was Burr actually reluctant, or was he playing coy? When these questions developed, Nicholson attempted to explain. Yes, Clinton did decline—almost. He thought Burr, Livingston, and John Langdon of New Hampshire were better candidates. But he would run if it were necessary to ensure Jefferson's election; at the same time he wanted to be at liberty to resign. Nicholson drafted a letter on the subject and showed it to Burr, who became "agitated." Was it because it indicated he was New York's choice? Though he announced that he would have nothing to do with the subject, two friends who were present persuaded Burr to a reluctant consent. Nicholson, now personally persuaded that Clinton did not want to run, altered his letter to give Clinton an "unqualified declension" and Burr an "aversion." This account, declared no less a historian than Carl Becker, was evidence of Burr's "machinations."[15] But Nicholson's account reveals no machinations; he expressed his own conclusions concerning his own investigations. There is no evidence that anyone, let alone Burr, tried to influence him.

Was Burr reluctant? Not enough attention has been given to this question. There is little doubt that Burr mistrusted the Virginians. That mistrust was recorded in various sources in 1800 and was recognized by Virginians themselves.[16] The mistrust was well warranted. Virginia had given Burr only one electoral vote in 1796; states to the south had given him only six more.[17] Virginia Republicans, moreover, mistrusted Burr. Their reasons are obscure and unresearched. Usually the mistrust is remarked with some afterthought about Burr's morals, but no one has yet published an account written before the election of 1800 by a contemporary Virginian that explains the mistrust. Oliver Wolcott, Connecticut Federalist, has come the closest with a quotation from an unnamed Virginian in 1794: "I have watched the movements of Mr. Burr with attention, and have discovered traits of character which sooner or later will give us much trouble. He has an unequalled talent for attaching men to his views, and forming combinations of which he is always the centre. He is determined to play a first part; he acts strenuously with us in public, but it is remarkable that in all private consultations he more frequently agrees with us in principles than in the mode of giving them effect. . . . I shall not be surprised if Mr. Burr is found, in a few years, the leader of a popular party in the northern states; and if this event ever happens this party will subvert the influence of the southern states . . . and the cause of republicanism."[18] It is very tempting in the absence of any other evidence to conclude that Virginia's fear of the loss of its ascendency in the Union was at the root of its mistrust or fear of Burr, as Nathan Schachner has concluded.[19]

This mutual mistrust, together with the almost certainty that he would become Governor of New York in 1801, was enough to make Burr reluctant. He stated his reluctance on at least two other occasions: in his letter of December 29, 1800, to Samuel Smith when he declared that he had been made a candidate against his will and on January 26, 1804, in his last conversation with Jefferson.[20] These statements have been ignored, disbelieved, or scoffed at. Nevertheless, if they are read in a straightforward manner and in connection with Nicholson's conversations with Clinton and Burr on May 6/7, 1800, they are very credible. Burr entered the contest for the same reason that George Clinton would have—to promote Jefferson's fame and advancement.

Once in the contest he went to work, the only candidate who openly sought to influence voting. His contribution was a trip "eastward" to affect "a division of the New England vote," which most contemporary observers credited to Adams. Not too many people commented on this eastern trip. One was Alexander Hamilton who, sensing a Republican victory, reported that Burr was "intriguing" with all his might in New Jersey, Rhode Island, and Vermont."[21] It was the nefarious word "intrigue" used without expanation by the man whom John Adams called "the most restless, impatient, artful, indefatigable, and unprincipled intriguer" in the Union[22] that has captured attention. If Hamilton had used "campaigning" or "electioneering," his comments would have received less attention. Another who may have noticed the trip was Gideon Granger, who in

November 1800 "sent [George] Erving from Boston to inform
Virginia of the dangers resulting from [Burr's] intrigues."[23]

The election of 1800 was a race to the wire. Not until the last
electoral college—South Carolina's—cast its vote was it known
whether Federalists or Republicans had won. South Carolina's
vote, however, appeared to make the race a dead heat—Jefferson and Burr had tied.

Why did a tie vote occur? During the course of the campaign
Federalists had carefully arranged to avoid a tie. Among Republicans it was assumed that arrangements had been made. Burr
expected and informed Robert R. Livingston that Jefferson
would receive votes in Rhode Island that Burr would not receive.[24] Jefferson anticipated that he would receive votes in Kentucky, Tennessee, South Carolina, and Georgia that Burr would
not receive.[25] Significantly, if all these anticipations had
evolved—and this factor needs emphasis—Burr would have received seven votes fewer that Jefferson. He could and probably
would have lost the vice-presidency. But no one actually arranged anything. The tie vote occurred, as Jefferson himself recognized, because of bad management.[26]

The impression that historians have developed through decades, however, is that Burr was responsible. As late as 1953
Irving Brant, author of the admirable six-volume biography of
James Madison, declared: "From first to last, the work of Burr
and his agents supports the charge . . . that he deliberately produced the tie which threw the election into the House of Representatives."[27]

On what evidence does this charge rest? Actually on very
little. One bit of "evidence" involved the New York electoral
college, which Burr, as a member of the Assembly, had helped
elect on November 6, 1800. The twelve electors, accompanied
for some unknown reason by De Witt Clinton, met at Hudson,
New York. There, at a preelection dinner at the home of Edward Livingston, the general conversation revolved around rumors that one of the electors would not cast his vote for Jefferson but would give it to Burr. The man suspected was Anthony
Lispenard of New York City's Sixth Ward. According to the

"evidence" he had secured his election to the college "to accomplish personal and of course private views," and he would
not pledge himself to vote for both Jefferson and Burr. It was
through Lispenard that Burr would produce a tie. To prevent
any mischievous consequences, however, Clinton prevailed upon
Isaac Ledyard of Queens to propose an open ballot; and, when
he found his colleagues "unanimous and pertinaceous" in their
attitude, Lispenard "quailed" and agreed. Burr's "scheme" was
foiled and Jefferson was preserved.[28]

This "evidence" ignores the firsthand account of one of the
electors at Hudson, who told Martin Van Buren that some of
the electors were indeed apprehensive, concerning not only the
vote of Lispenard but also of another of Burr's old friends,
Peter Van Ness of Columbia County. According to his report,
however, all the electors held a private meeting at the home of
Ambrose Spencer and agreed unanimously that William Floyd,
one of the signers of the Declaration of Independence, would
propose an open ballot. All electors voted for Jefferson and
Burr. This would not have occurred, Woodworth declared, if
Burr had exerted a contrary influence over Lispenard, who
would have voted any way Burr pleased. But, Woodworth concluded, "Burr's conduct in the affair was unexceptionable."[29] In
short, the Burr "scheme" in New York is fiction.

Other "evidence" concerning Burr's production of a tie vote
involves an extremely complicated set of communications concerning Rhode Island's vote and the absolute necessity of securing a unanimous vote for both Jefferson and Burr in Virginia.
The key letter in this structure was written by David Gelston to
James Madison on October 8, 1800. It informed him that Burr
expected that votes would be withheld from him in two or
three states. He did not name the states. Gelston also expressed
alarm that even more votes—especially Tennessee's—would be
withheld. New York, Gelston assured Madison, would be "faithful and honest." "Can we, may we," he asked, "rely on the
integrity of the Southern States?" Gelston repeated the message
in a letter on November 21. Madison, who interpreted these
letters to mean that Burr was fearful that he might lose the
vice-presidency if the South acted as it had in 1796, determined

to keep Virginia honest. James Monroe and Jefferson became involved in the effort.[30]

Twenty-three years after these events Madison concluded that he had been duped. He had been assured falsely that the votes of one state—he did not know that it was the Federalist state of Rhode Island—would break the impending tie between Jefferson and Burr only in order to secure the full vote of Virginia for Burr, thereby assuring a tie.[31] Irving Brant has accepted Madison's conclusion completely; Burr was guilty of treachery.

The reasoning is specious. It ignores completely that Rhode Island was a somewhat doubtful state and Burr's actual belief—which he relayed confidentially to his uncle Pierpoint Edwards in late November—that Rhode Island would go Republican or at least give Jefferson one vote.[32] It ignores rumors, some of them current in New York City, that votes would be withheld from Burr in Vermont, Kentucky, Tennessee, and Georgia. It ignores the fact, fully known to Madison, that there were electors in Virginia only too eager to withhold votes from Burr.[33] The danger that Burr would run in third place or lower, as Madison concluded originally, was real. Gelson's letters revealed no duplicity; they expressed apprehension.

Still more nebulous "evidence" concerns South Carolina, from which came more than one prediction that the "compromise" of 1796 would be repeated: Electors would be named to vote for Republican Jefferson and Federalist Pinckney, which would make Burr a sure loser. Though Burr has been charged with influencing the vote, his involvement in the South Carolina election has never been developed.[34] Nathan Schachner, his best biographer, states that Burr had to campaign there to protect himself. But accounts from Jefferson's informant in South Carolina, Philip Frenau, mention no Burrite activity at the sessions of the legislature that chose electors. The only evidence of activity exists in a letter from Timothy Green, a New York lawyer, to Burr, declaring that he had been working against the "compromise."[35] What happened at the electoral college which voted Jefferson 8, Burr 8, when it was expected to vote Jefferson 8, Burr 7, Clinton 1, is unrecorded anywhere.

Examination of the evidence concerning New York, Rhode Island, Virginia, and South Carolina actually leads to only one conclusion: Burr made no effort to produce a tie, and he deceived no one into creating a tie. The examination, however, raises an interesting question. If, as his accusers charge, he could produce a tie merely by a little electioneering in New England, by a few letters from a friend to Madison, and some quiet activity on the part of another friend in South Carolina, why—with a little effort—didn't Burr produce an electoral college victory? It would have taken only one vote among 138.

Long before the tie vote was known, some Federalists recognized the possibility that the Federalist-dominated House of Representatives would make the final decision on the presidency. Among the earliest was Hamilton. There was a time when historians regarded his role in the election as decisive, claiming that it was he alone who persuaded a sufficient number of congressional Federalists to change their votes and allow Jefferson to become President. Fortunately, that myth has been rejected. It is now generally recognized that he had little, if any, influence on the final result; the only question that remains is how far his influence had declined.

Nevertheless, Hamilton cannot be ignored. He played a part in developing the historiography of the election, and his conduct needs a reappraisal. It was hardly ethical. There was his effort to persuade Governor John Jay, after the New York City election, to call a special session of the legislature to provide for election of presidential electors by district—thereby depriving the Republicans of votes—an action that can only be described as an effort to steal the election.[36] There was his last-hour publication of the *Letter . . . Concerning the Public Conduct and Character of John Adams, Esq.,* an effort to steal the election from Adams, one of his abiding hates. Among historians of the Hamiltonian persuasion it was fashionable once to regard this publication as a peccadillo compared with Burr's acquisition and republication of it in the Philadelphia *Aurora.* The letter, however, may have cost the Federalists the vote of South Carolina.[37]

Most important of his activities was Hamilton's campaign against Burr. It did not start, as it popularly assumed, with the election of 1800; rather it began after Burr was elected United States Senator in 1791 over Hamilton's father-in-law, Philip Schuyler. From that point on, though he maintained outwardly friendly relations and even engaged in legal causes with him, Hamilton sought to destroy Burr by destroying his reputation. Hamilton's pursuit was unrelenting, obsessive, almost paranoid. Even before it was certain that the election had ended in a tie—as rumors spread that Federalists would support Burr—he began a campaign to prevent Burr's election. He wrote letters, not many letters, perhaps twenty to less than ten men, leading Federalists in the House of Representatives and the Senate. All were intended to persuade Federalists that Jefferson was the better man because Burr's character was evil. Terms such as "unprincipled," "dangerous," "Catiline," "bankrupt," "crafty," "unscrupulous," "unmindful of the truth," "contemptible hypocrite," "cunning," "inferior" to describe Burr abounded in the letters. Hamilton also maintained that Burr's morals were so low his most partial friends would not defend him.[38] It was a thorough job of character assassination.

Hamilton's efforts, however, did not influence Federalist congressmen. Some had long discerned Hamilton's hatred and fear of Burr and dismissed his arguments. Before long every Federalist in the House of Representatives decided to vote for Burr. Their motives have been frequently examined. Essentially they were bent on mischief. Many hated Jefferson and his attitudes, Virginia planter attitudes, which would be harmful to their own primacy and to the commercial interests of the North. They were only too willing obstruct his succession, to nullify his victory, to grieve his supporters. They might even break up the Republican party. Among them were some who hoped that Burr would more likely accept Federalist attitudes. At the same time there were also some, even in Virginia—and this group has not been researched—who thought that Burr's character was "less exceptionable" than Jefferson's; that his principles in respect to foreign affairs and the navy were more acceptable; that he was a man of energy, vigor, courage, and generosity; that he was "better fitted" for the presidency.[39]

In all the analyses of the Federalists there are some curious omissions. Historians have developed their interpretations out of the letters of about a dozen men; there were another four dozen in the House who have gone unconsulted. Historians have made but little analysis of the Federalist press. How did it stand? Nathan Schachner declares that Federalist newspapers were almost unanimously for Burr, but he quotes only one. He says there were dissenting notes from papers under Hamilton's control.[40] What papers did Hamilton control? And what about the talented and articulate Federalist rank and file? Gallatin stated that Federalists in Maryland and Virginia did not support the movement for Burr, but the correspondence of Leven Powell, Federalist Representative from Virginia, indicates that they did. Would more widespread sampling provide different insights?

While Federalists were determining their course, two Republicans were also acting. From Washington on December 14, 1800, Jefferson, who assumed he had won the presidency, offered the position of Secretary of the Navy to Robert R. Livingston of New York.[41] On the next day—December 15 he sent his long and famous letter to Burr[42]—a letter sometimes described as curious or enigmatic. The letter is easy to understand. Jefferson told Burr that he had been elected President, that Burr would have three to four votes fewer, but—reassuringly—four to five votes above "Mr. A." There is a hint that Burr might not have won the vice-presidency; in that case Jefferson would have provided him with a post of greater service, though how any historian could accept these assurances in view of Jefferson's later statements is a puzzle.

Meanwhile in New York City there was talk of Federalist support of Burr in the event of a tie. Whether this talk influenced Burr is impossible to say. But on December 16, 1800, a month after the Sixth Congress had met in its second session, he sent General Samuel Smith, an old friend from the Revolutionary War and a Representative from Maryland, a short letter:[43]

It is highly improbable that I shall have an equal number of votes with Mr. Jefferson; but if such should be
the result, every man who knows me ought to know
that I would utterly disclaim all competition. Be assured
that the federal party can entertain no wish for such an
exchange. As to my friends they would dishonor my
views and insult my feelings by a suspicion that I would
submit to be instrumental in counteracting the wishes
and expectations of the people of the United States.
And I now constitute you my proxy to declare these
sentiments if the occasion shall require.[44]

On December 23, when it was nationwide knowledge that a
tie was probable, though the vote of Republican Tennessee was
not yet known, Burr replied to Jefferson in a letter given too
little attention. After apologizing for the failure of his arrangement in Rhode Island, he reassured Jefferson: "I do not appre-
hend any Embarrassment even in Case the Votes should come
out alike. . . . My Friends are . . . informed of my wishes and
can never think of diverting a single Vote from you. . . . They
will be found among your most zealous adherents." He expected Jefferson to have at least nine states. In addition he replied
to Jefferson's half-offer of a more active office: "I shall cheerfully abandon the office of V.P. if . . . I can be more useful in
any Active Service."[45]
Of this exchange, only Burr's letter to Smith secured public
circulation, probably first by word of mouth and then, because
the occasion required, by publication in the *National Intelligencer* on December 31.
Republican reaction to the December 16 letter was one of
relief. Two comments, both written on January 16, 1801, ex-
emplify the sentiment. One came from Caesar Rodney of Delaware: "I think Col. Burr deserves immortal honor for the noble
part he has acted on this occasion." Another came from Jefferson: "The Federalists were confident . . . they could debauch
Col. B. from his faith. . . . His conduct has been honorable and
decisive and greatly embarrasses them."[46]

But the Federalists refused to accept the obvious; they had a mission to accomplish and they pursued it. Among them the letter was ignored and the word was passed that Burr did not mean it, that he was willing to accept the presidency as a gift from the Federalists.[47] Significantly, none of the Federalists who recorded such reports revealed the source of their knowledge.

It is this Federalist refusal to accept Burr at his word that has been used against him. With one exception all the major historians of the Virginia persuasion who have examined the subject have come to the conclusion that Burr was lying, that he wanted the presidency, and that he was working for it desperately. These include Henry S. Randall, Jefferson's first biographer who influenced every account that followed; Irving Brant, Madison's biographer; John S. Pancake, author of the article "Aaron Burr—Would-Be Usurper"; and Dumas Malone, Jefferson's latest and greatest biographer, who has depended heavily on Brant and Pancake.[48] Only Noble E. Cunningham among the Virginians has disagreed.[49]

Irving Brant, whose examinations begin chronologically earlier than any of the others, questions Burr's knowledge on December 16, when he wrote his letter to Samuel Smith. He hypothesizes that Burr "knew"—from southern dispatches arriving in New York City on that day—that Jefferson had won the presidency.[50] Accordingly, Burr's disclaimer of competition for the office was a lie. The reasoning is baffling. Brant assumes Burr's knowledge, but he provides no evidence that he investigated the time of day Burr wrote his letter, the time he posted it, the time the mail was dispatched southward, the time of the arrival of the news of Jefferson's victory, and the time the news reached the streets to jump "from house to house" in the *evening* of December 16. Unless he comes up with the right answers to most of these time problems, his assumption is not reasonable.

But if his assumption is accepted and if Burr did "know" that Jefferson had won the presidency, why would Burr write a letter disclaiming all competition for the presidency? There was no more competition. If Brant's reconstruction of the situation is correct, Burr's letter was both unnecessary and ridiculous. Burr was very, very seldom ridiculous.

Brant's indicting attitude is really a preliminary to further analysis. He points out that on December 29, Burr, in Trenton, reminded Samuel Smith in Washington that he was coming to Philadelphia and offered to meet him there. He also informed Smith that he had been receiving letters about the election, indicating "jealously and distrust." These letters, he thought, were answered "by those which I have written you." But, Burr added, he had also received a letter from an old Republican, asking if "I would engage to resign" if elected President. The suggestion, Burr declared, was "unreasonable, unnecessary, and impertinent." He had made no reply. "If I had made any I would have told [him] that as at present advised, I would not." Then he gave vent to his anger. "I was made a candidate against my advice and will; God knows, never contemplating or wishing the result which has appeared." And now he was being insulted by those who had asked him to become a candidate.[51]

This letter, according to John S. Pancake, ably seconded by Brant and Malone, reveals that Burr was easily insulted, that he lied when he said he was not in competition with Jefferson, that he thought he had been technically nominated for President, and that he would not resign if elected.[52]

Their conclusion is impossible. All Burr was doing was expressing irritation at being questioned over a situation which he would have preferred to avoid by a man who helped put him into the situation. His suggestion that he would not resign can be as reasonably interpreted as the flouting of an impertinent man as it can be interpreted as design.

However, there are other aspects of the letter which need analysis. It reveals that Burr and Smith had been corresponding between December 16 and December 29 and that Burr probably had repeated his statement of December 16. It also contains the cryptic statement: "I presume . . . that before this time you are satisfied that no such event is or ever was to be apprehended by those who laugh at your absurd claims—Write me therefore of something else."[53] What does that mean? Was Smith already revealing the great perturbation that he supposedly revealed in January?

It was in January, according to some Jeffersonian historians, that Burr stopped writing "wheedling letters" and "shrouded himself in mystery at Albany."[54] He was, according to others, now following the advice of Robert Goodloe Harper, Maryland Federalist, who on December 24 had advised him "to keep the game perfectly in your own hand. . . . Do not answer this letter, or any other that may be written to you by a Federalist . . . nor write to any of that party."[55] It was also early in January, according to the same historians, that Burr sent his "most confidential agent," David A. Ogden, a well-known Federalist attorney of New York, "to tamper with" some Republicans.[56]

What was Burr actually doing? On January 4-6 he was in Philadelphia for his "secret" meeting with Samuel Smith. Several explanations have been given for this meeting. Irving Brant suggests that Smith went to Philadelphia because he was alarmed at Burr's "second unpublished letter" (apparently the letter of December 29).[57] John S. Pancake suggests that Smith was alarmed both by Burr's letter of December 24 (not quoted) which Smith received on December 29 (which appears to be the letter Burr *sent* on December 29) and because of the appearance of Ogden, Burr's alleged agent, in Washington (Smith says nothing about Ogden until January 11).[58] The confusion of dates in these accounts is a formidable barrier to understanding.

What happened at this "secret" meeting, about which the Philadelphia *Aurora* made an amusing report?[59] There are no firsthand accounts. One, several degrees removed, came from Gabriel Christie, a Representative from Maryland, who nearly two years later recalled what Smith told him after he returned from Philadelphia. In effect Smith understood that Burr had declared that the House had to make a choice for President— "that if they could not get Mr. Jefferson they could take him."

Smith, so Christie reported, returned from Philadelphia "much mortified" because he had expected that Burr would give him "full authority to say he would not serve if Elected President."[60] Another report came from a Colonel B. Hichborn of Massachusetts, who informed Jefferson on January 5, 1801, that he was lodged in the same house with Burr and Smith and was convinced that some Republicans were willing to join the Federalists in voting for Burr.[61] About three years later Hichborn stopped by the White House to add to his report. Burr, he vowed, had insisted that the nation had to have a President, that if necessary "our friends must join the federalists and give a president." Mr. Jefferson could be Vice-President. Jefferson recorded this information in his *Anas*.[62]

What happened after the meeting? It is not clear. Smith obviously returned to Washington to be confronted with the presence of David A. Ogden,[63] whom, according to John S. Pancake, he had already confronted.[64] Setting aside this problem, it is clear that Ogden did arrive in Washington. Claiming that he had traveled with Burr from Trenton to Philadelphia and that he was authorized to speak for him, he purportedly approached the New York and New Jersey Republican delegations with suggestions that Burr was willing to serve as President and that his election would be advantageous to them. Ogden's persuasive ability was poor. Not only did the Republican delegations turn him down, but one of the "half and half" Federalists from New Jersey joined them. These developments, supposedly, again alarmed Smith; he informed Burr of what was happening.[65]

Events now become less confused. Burr replied to Smith on January 16: "I have said nothing to a Mr. O[gden] —nor have I said anything to contravene my letter of the 16th ult, but to enter into details would take reams of paper and years of time."[66] On the same day he also wrote Gallatin suggesting that he consult Edward Livingston concerning "the proposed usurpation, and indeed all the other occurrences and projects of the day"; he "will tell you my sentiments."[67] Gallatin, however, had already concluded that Burr had "sincerely opposed the design [to make him President] and will go to any lengths to prevent it." [68]

Shortly after writing these letters, Burr removed to Albany, where he played a minor but active role as a member of the Assembly. He was there on January 27, voting for John A. Armstrong to fill a Senate vacancy; he was still there on February 19, after making a report on the preservation of Dutch records.[69] In between he arranged for his daughter's marriage, which occurred at Albany on February 2. During this time Judge Woodworth saw him "almost from day to day" and had repeated conversations with him: "The Col. throughout . . . reprobated the conduct of the Federalists in their effort to defeat the will of the people."[70]

To make a conspiracy against Jefferson out of these events is difficult; it is necessary to be selective. Burr's accusers have been selective and imaginative. They have judged his failure to reply to Harper and to write letters to Federalists as evidence that he had followed Harper's suggestions. They accuse him of entering a conspiracy of silence and allowing the Federalists to do what they would.[71]

They have concluded that the Burr-Smith meeting in Philadelphia produced further evidence of complicity. Yet the conclusion is obviously based on distortions, neglect of evidence, and neglect of circumstances. Although it appears clear that it was Burr who suggested the meeting,[72] no one has sought to determine the exact date of the suggestion or the purpose. Christie's account is used to suggest that Burr had no purpose, an impossibly strange conclusion, but it leaves the way open for another conclusion—that Smith was the principal in going to Philadelphia because he was alarmed by a letter from Burr and by Ogden's proselytizing in Washington. This conclusion requires use of (1) a letter (December 24), which no one quotes, of (2) another letter (December 29), which somehow managed to arrive in Washington on the same day it was sent from Trenton, and of (3) statements made by various persons long after the Philadelphia meeting. From all this Smith purportedly learned that Burr would not resign if elected.

What emerges most clearly from this welter is that Burr's accusers have been willing to accept without question second-, third-, and even forth-hand evidence of what happened. They have not even asked: Who was Colonel B. Hichborn? How did he get involved? Why did he wait so long to elaborate on his enigmatic and irrelevant message of January 6?

After Smith returned to Washington, he supposedly became alarmed again because of Ogden's activities. This purported situation raises a number of questions which have never been answered. If Smith was already "mortified" because he knew Burr wanted the presidency, why did he write Burr about Ogden's activities? Did Smith talk to anyone except Christie? If Ogden was unable to tempt the New York and New Jersey Republican delegations, among whom Burr had his closest friends, does not this mean that they knew Burr was not competing for the presidency? Does it not mean that there was no conspiracy?

Actually a study of the twelve readily available letters that Burr wrote between December 16 and January 16, and after as well, reveals strongly that he was totally consistent: He was not engaged in a conspiracy to win the presidency.[73] No one has produced any direct evidence that contradicts a straighforward reading of these letters. All that has been produced is implication, innuendo, interpretations.

Significantly, Burr's accusers have totally ignored the January 16 letter, except to criticize him for not using "reams of paper" to explain himself and to suggest that he continued to "hint to private" that he would accept.[74] To whom? How? To these questions some answers are usually offered from Jefferson's *Anas*. On February 12 Jefferson recorded that James A. Bayard, the Federalist senator from Delaware, had been approaching various Republicans in Burr's name. There is no evidence at all, however, of any contact between Burr and Bayard; from Bayard there is firm denial. On February 14 Jefferson recorded that John A. Armstrong had informed him that Gouverneur Morris, Federalist senator from New York, had asked: "How comes it that Burr, who is four hundred miles off, has agents at work with great activity, while Mr. Jefferson, who is on the spot does nothing?"[75] What agents? Surely not Ogden, Morris's good friend, who had long since gone. Whom were they working on?

Why, moreover, does Jefferson act so sanctimoniously? Didn't
he even have a floor leader for his agents—Gallatin? There were
fifty-three Republicans in the House; would a search through
their papers reveal the temptations, if any, to which they were
subjected?

There is an aspect of the evidence that needs further consideration: Burr's alleged statement at Philadelphia that the nation had to have a President and that he would accept an election. He might have made that statement. But it would have to
be considered in context. The tie vote might have wrecked the
republic. The new government was only twelve years old, un-
tested by any crisis, and it was now being tested over an issue
that had destroyed many an older government—the issue of
succession to power. It could have provoked civil war. Federalist behavior provoked both a trauma and a fear. There was
much talk that Federalists would prevent a decision, that they
would somehow enact legislation elevating the President pro
tempore of the Senate to the presidency. This "solution" became known as "usurpation." When this kind of talk died
down, all that was left was fear that no decision would be made
and that the republic would shatter. All sorts of proposals for
solution were made, but the one most everyone, Federalist and
Republican, preferred was a decisive election: The nation had to
have a President. Burr, at Albany, was well aware of the possible
usurpation; he talked of the use of troops to enforce the popular will.[76] Like most everyone else he felt the absolute need for a
President. How then could he refuse an election? But willingness to accept cannot and should not be equated with conspiracy to secure.

The balloting for President in the House of Representatives
began on February 11, 1801, and lasted through seventeen ballots until noon of the next day with the same results: Jefferson
8, Burr 6, divided 2. Three ballots on February 14 brought the
same result. Then the Federalists' united front crumbled. On
February 17 Federalist congressmen from Vermont, Delaware,
Maryland, and South Carolina ceased voting and the count became Jefferson 10, Burr 4, divided 2.

James A. Bayard, who held the key vote throughout the balloting and who had become the leader of the small bloc of six Federalist congressmen from Vermont, Delaware, and Maryland who decided collectively not to continue voting for Burr,[77] used bitter words in summarizing his disappointment. "Burr," he informed a constituent, "has acted a miserable, paltry part. The election was in his power, but he was determined to come in as a Democrat, and in that event would have been the most dangerous man in the community. We have been counteracted in the whole business by letters he has written to this place." To Hamilton he reported: "The means existed of electing Burr, but this required his cooperation. By deceiving one man (a great blockhead), and tempting two (not incorruptible), he might have secured a majority of the States."[78] Bayard, in short, conclusively confirms that Burr was not involved in any conspiracy. His testimony has been given scant notice.[79]

The controversy over Burr's role does not end with Jefferson's victory. Almost as news of the result spread through the nation, it was followed by a rumor that Jefferson had made a deal through Samuel Smith with Bayard concerning the Federal patronage in order to win Bayard's crucial influence.[80] The allegations have no place in this analysis; the whole relationship among the three men has been well researched and thoroughly explained by Morton Borden in his biography of Bayard.[81] It is important only because the rumor was strongly current in New York City as Jefferson became President and because Federal patronage in New York City soon became a contentious issue.

The contention began simply enough in April 1801, when Burr presented a memorial to Jefferson from the New York Republican delegation in Congress requesting the appointment of Edward Livingston as United States District Attorney, John Swartwout as United States Marshal, David Gelston as Collector of Customs, Theodorus Bailey as Naval Officer of the Port, and Matthew L. Davis as Supervisor of Customs. Except for Postmaster these were the most important federal appointments in New York City. It is generally assumed that all these men were Burrites. The assumption is incorrect: Livingston belonged to his own faction; Bailey was a chameleon who tended to and became a Clintonian; Swartwout was as yet a free agent who temporarily became a Burrite; only Gelston and Davis were firm Burrites.

Since he was already "reforming" the court system, Jefferson, without hesitation, named Livingston and Swartwout as District Attorney and Marshal. He also gave Gelston the Collectorship. Then he stopped. Why?

The assumption usually made is that Jefferson had finally become aware of Burr's clandestine effort to secure the presidency.[82] In view of the "fact" that Jefferson was "warned" in November by Gideon Granger of Burr's "intrigues" and of the "fact" that in February Jefferson had "learned" that Bayard was working in Burr's name and that Burr had other agents working in Washington, the assumption seems strangely unreasonable. But perhaps Jefferson had not been aware, or perhaps he had dismissed his awareness, which raises questions about the trustworthiness of his *Anas*. At any rate he purportedly became aware again.

His new information came from Samuel Osgood, a prominent New York Republican, who had written Madison on April 24, 1801, suggesting that Burr had tried to win the presidency for himself and charging that Livingston, Swartwout, Gelston, Bailey, and Davis were all in Burr's pocket: If "it had been in their power, we have reason to believe, that Mr. Jefferson would not have been President." Osgood suggested that Jefferson consult George Clinton, who was expected to become governor again, on appointments. Almost simultaneously, John A. Armstrong, Senator from New York, also suggested to Gallatin that Clinton ought to be consulted.[83]

Jefferson followed the suggestion; he asked Clinton's advice on both New York City and upstate appointments. Clinton's reply has disappeared. However, no more Burrites were appointed to federal offices in New York. This ostracism did not escape notice. As early as the end of May 1801, Federalists in New York City were speculating that Jefferson was no longer consulting Burr, that in fact Burr was out in the cold.[84]

This kind of blatant discrimination against a man whom Jefferson had acknowledged as a major factor in his election needs explanation, if not apology. Strangely, aside from the suggestion that Jefferson had become convinced that Burr had intrigued against him, historians of the Virginia persuasion have produced very little explanation of Jefferson's ingratitude, which became more than obvious with his letter to Burr of November 18, 1801, dismissing rather cavalierly Burr's request, made ten weeks earlier, for consideration of Matthew L. Davis's appointment.[85]

Their propensity is to cite a few lines from Jefferson's recording of his last conversation with Burr, on January 26, 1804, as explanation: "I had never seen Colonel Burr till he came as a member of the Senate. His conduct very soon inspired me with distrust. I habitually cautioned Mr. Madison against trusting him too much. . . . There has never been any intimacy between us, and but little association."[86]

The first and last sentences of this statement are obviously acceptable: All evidence speaks in corroboration. But if Burr's "conduct . . . soon inspired" Jefferson with distrust, why was he so eager to enlist Burr's aid in June 1797, five years after their first meeting, in developing a strategy for the next presidential campaign?[87] Is this a mark of distrust?[88] Why, further, did he entrust the legal problems of Dr. James Currie of Richmond to Burr in 1798-1799?[89] Is this a mark of distrust? And did Madison, whom Jefferson habitually cautioned, share that distrust? What then, did he think of his wife's act of May 13, 1794, entrusting little John Payne Todd, her son, to the guardianship of Aaron Burr?[90] If Jefferson is to be accepted at his word, as recorded in the *Anas*, it reveals him to be either a consummate dissembler or a hypocrite. It is most likely, of course, that Jefferson just plain lied; he had *not* formed his opinion "very soon" but at a later date, and that his comment reflected his reaction to later events, some of which he created himself.

If, therefore, it is not possible to accept Jefferson's recorded word, how can Burr's sudden isolation be explained? It may be that Samuel Osgood's charges about Burr's intrigues did perturb Jefferson, who began to believe some of the earlier rumors about Burr's behavior. It may be that Osgood, Armstrong, and George Clinton together reminded him that Burr led only one of the Republican factions of New York and that others had to be considered in the distribution of the patronage. These factors could have caused Jefferson to hesitate, to procrastinate—he was a master procrastinator—until Matthew L. Davis, seeking an answer to the petition on his behalf, penetrated into his seclusion at Monticello in the late summer of 1801 and angered him sufficiently by his crudities to refuse the appointment. Such is a rather kind explanation. Why, if the servant annoys, does one isolate the master? There must be a more adequate answer.

Perhaps the answer lies in the opinion of the Virginian recorded by Oliver Wolcott—in the Virginia Republicans' fear of Burr and his ability to develop a northern party. Whatever other conclusions may be drawn from the election of 1800-1801, it was more than obvious that Burr was a very powerful man, the one Republican outside Virginia with presidential potential, the one Republican capable of rivaling Jefferson. It has to be recognized that no President has ever willingly suffered a rival within his own party; it makes him too vulnerable. His instinct is to destroy.

That Jefferson and Republicans close to him worried about the problem of Burr is evident from the letters which Gallatin sent along with Matthew L. Davis on his way to Monticello on September 14, 1801. The letter confessedly rambles, but there are some clear points. Gallatin expressly asked if the Republicans eventually meant to support Burr as Jefferson's successor—a question that revealed the nature of Jeffersonian concern. To emphasize that concern, he also asked: "Do they mean not to support him at the next election for Vice President?" Why was this a serious question more than three years before the next election? Although Gallatin tried, he really did not answer the question satisfactorily. He stated that he had discovered a "total want of confidence" the previous winter "in a large majority of Republicans toward Burr," but he did not elaborate. At the same time he suggested that if Burr were supported for

Vice-President, the Republicans would either "run the risk of the Federal Party making [him] President" or of pledging themselves to support him for President at the next [1808] election. If Republicans supported only a presidential candidate and scattered their second vote, they would "pave the way for the Federal . . . candidate . . . to become President."[91] The prevailing thought in the message is a fear that Burr would succeed Jefferson. How could that event be prevented?

At this point Henry Adams's old charge comes to mind: Jefferson had determined to drive Burr from the party and now joined forces with De Witt Clinton, a rising power among the Clintonians in New York to accomplish his goal. It is a charge that Nathan Schachner also emphasizes.[92]

Part of the charge is readily corroborated. Jefferson was obviously willing to strike at Burr; his refusal to appoint Davis, as Gallatin emphasized, was "a declaration of war" against Burr.[93] As to the charge of alliance with De Witt Clinton, the evidence is not direct. Surviving correspondence between the Clintons, George and De Witt, and Jefferson in this period is scanty and unexceptionable; correspondence among Clintonian leaders in New York is also scanty and equally unexceptionable. Nevertheless there are clues. In his letter of September 14, 1801, Gallatin revealed that the support of another New York faction—besides Burr's—was being considered: "I dislike much the idea of supporting a section of Republicans in New York, and mistrusting the great majority, [merely] because the section is supposed to be hostile to Burr, [who] is the leader of the majority."[94] His dislike, however, was based on his feeling that the leaders of the section hostile to Burr—"the Livingstons generally and some broken remnants of the Clintonian party who hate Burr"—were so selfish and uninfluential that they would make an alliance with Burr to gain control of the state.

Gallatin's analysis of the political situation in New York was faulty. It ignored upstate New York. It was based primarily on his knowledge of the commercial-financial interests of New York City and exaggerated the influence of the Livingstonians; moreover, it suggested that the Livingstonians were anti-Burrite when they were first and foremost and always just simply pro-

Livingston. Nevertheless, he revealed the trend of thinking within Jefferson's administration—the desirability of supporting some anti-Burr force in New York.

Actually there was only one anti-Burr force in New York— the Clintonians, or, more accurately, the neo-Clintonians. The original Clintonians, led by George Clinton, had been the party of New York's upstate yeomanry. During the 1790s the party acquired a small city wing led by George's nephew De Witt. In the fateful spring of 1800, when Burr was leading Republicans in New York City to victory, Clintonian Republicans upstate also ran a strong campaign. When the legislature met in January 1801, the Assembly named a new Council of Appointments,[95] one of the most important ever elected in the history of New York under its first constitution. The new council was led by two younger Clintonians—De Witt Clinton of New York City and Ambrose Spencer, onetime Federalist from Columbia County and now a Republican from Albany. Borrowing a precedent set by Federalists during George Clinton's sixth term, the new council insisted on its right to nominate candidates to office equally with the Governor; it thereby assumed leadership of the Clintonian forces. De Witt Clinton and Spencer were in full control when George Clinton was inaugurated as Governor on July 1, 1801. George Clinton had become only a front.

In August 1801 they began to fashion what became notorious as the New York version of a spoils system and to fasten a neo-Clintonian domination upon the Republican party. It was an extraordinarily shrewd performance. First, it took care of the Livingstonians. As a faction they represented a wide-flung feudal family with many poor relatives and a very narrow but firm popular base among their manorial tenantry. Since they were impossible to dislodge, they often threatened to hold a balance of power. But they could readily be made quiet and cooperative with appointments. Jefferson had named their titular chief, Robert L. Livingston, as Minister to France and his much younger brother Edward as United States District Attorney in New York City. In 1801 Edward appeared as the one future leader of significance in the family. The council named him Mayor of New York City.[96] Within the same session it appointed Smith Thompson and Morgan Lewis, Livingston inlaws, and Brockholst Livingston to the State Supreme Court, and Thomas Tillotson, another relative, Secretary of New York State. That took very good care of the Livingstons and the Livingstonians.

The overwhelming proportion of the rest of the important appointments it reserved for the Clintonians: sheriffs, mayors, county attorneys, surrogates, judges, commissioners, clerks, registrars. These officials, along with the justices of the peace, were the backbone of the party. The climax of this great sweep of Federalists from office and their replacements by Clintonians was the selection of Spencer to be Attorney General and the election, by the legislature, of De Witt Clinton to the United States Senate.

Significantly, not a single important post was given to a Burrite in New York City or anywhere else.[97] Jabez B. Hammond suggests that this political ostracism had occurred because "Burr had rendered himself obnoxious to the animadversions and suspicions of the republican party by his conduct in relation to the pending presidential election."[98]

Interesting, but hardly possible. In August 1801 no charges had been made publicly against Burr. The only direct charge recorded against him had come from Samuel Osgood, who was a relative by marriage to De Witt Clinton, on April 24, 1801. It seems significant that a Clintonian should "inform" Jefferson of Burr's derelictions, that John A. Armstrong, a Livingston in-law, should advise Jefferson to consult George Clinton on appointments, and that Jefferson should immediately withdraw his favor from Burr.

None of this evidence reveals, as Henry Adams and Nathan Schachner would have it, a conspiracy between Jefferson and De Witt Clinton. It does reveal, however, a clear juxtaposition of mutual interests. Jefferson had to prevent Burr from becoming President. De Witt Clinton, whose power base at the time was in New York City, had to nullify, if not destroy, Burr in order to advance his own ambition—the presidency. It is out of such mutual interests that shaky but effective political alliances are formed.

By the time Burr arrived at Washington to preside over the Senate in December 1801 he was already persona non grata with Jefferson and under heavy siege in New York. And there were still no public charges against him. These were forecast, however, in three letters which James Cheetham sent to Jefferson in December 1801 and January 1802. Cheetham, at this time a devout Clintonian, was, in association with one of De Witt Clinton's relatives, David Denniston, publisher of the New York *American Citizen* and its country cousin, the *Republican Watch-Tower.* He was already known as De Witt Clinton's spokesman, in time editors of New York City papers came to call him the "jackal."

It was in early December 1801 that Cheetham, carrying a note from De Witt Clinton[99] and claiming falsely to have been the friend and confidant of Burr, beguiled Jefferson in detail with an account of Burr's efforts to steal the presidency. It included the story of Anthony Lispenard's intended duplicity as a New York elector and of De Witt Clinton's heroic check of Lispenard's intentions, of Burr's intrigues on his own behalf in Rhode Island and through Timothy Green in South Carolina, and of Burr's current dislike of the administration.[100] If Jefferson had ever before heard these specifications, he never recorded them, nor did any of his close friends. In the historical record they stand new and unclean.

About three weeks later Cheetham added to his information, reporting that Burr and other Republicans "whose plans I had unfolded to you" were conspiring to suppress John Wood's *History of the Administration of Mr. John Adams from 1797 to 1801.* The *History* was purportedly unfavorable to Adams and the Federalists. Burr, Cheetham alleged, was seeking to suppress it in order to secure the publication of a book more favorable to Adams. In a longer letter of January 30, 1802, Cheetham elaborated on the suppression, implying that the act was the beginning of a coalition between Burr and the Federalists, a regularization of the collusion in which they had engaged during the presidential contest.[101]

The Cheetham conversation and letters to Jefferson, which are given almost no attention by historians, except as corroborations of their own conclusions, are actually of vital importance. It is these letters which gave Jefferson his first substantial "information" of Burr's alleged conspiracy against him and of Burr's future plans. He had no such information before he received these letters—and despite Jefferson's inferences, he never claimed to have such information. It is, accordingly, very difficult not to conclude that it was these letters from a Clintonian that gave Jefferson the material he needed to comfort his conscience about ridding himself and his Virginia-dominated party of a rival. That he almost exclusively concentrated federal patronage in New York on Clintonians after he received the Cheetham letters was a most natural process. To signal the future he named Theodorus Bailey, a Clintonian, as New York City Postmaster and Samuel Osgood, another Clintonian, as Supervisor of Customs, the post for which Davis had applied. It was in this way that the Clinton-Jefferson alliance was formed. It was an alliance sought by the Clintonians; but Jefferson embraced it.

Putting Burr in the Clinton-Jefferson deep freeze did not destroy him. More was needed. It was found. During the first session of the Seventh Congress in which he presided over the Senate with scrupulous—too scrupulous—fairness, Cheetham attacked his tie-breaking vote, sending back to committee the ultrapartisan and probably unconstitutional bill to repeal the Judiciary Act of 1801 as evidence of his Federalist connections. The charge was quickly repeated by Duane in the *Aurora* and by other editors in Virginia and the South. Cheetham also gave publicity to a toast Burr offered at a strange—unexplained—dinner of Federalists on Washington's birthday: "to a union of all honest men."[102] This toast was somehow supposed to be Federalist in inclination, an assumption that raises questions about the morality of Republicans: Weren't they honest men?

Then on May 26, 1802, Cheetham published a complex and elaborate account of Burr's "suppression" of John Wood's *His-*

tory of . . . John Adams. It contained one truth: Burr foolishly
had sought to purchase all the printed copies of the book—
because he thought it would injure the Republican party. He
never completed the contract, however, because some printed
copies were released. Cheetham, ignoring Burr's failure, built
the impression that Burr was working on behalf of the Federalists, a traitor to Republicanism.[103]

On July 16, 1802, Cheetham struck again with a pamphlet, *A
View of the Political Conduct of Aaron Burr.* Here Cheetham
reached the zenith of his editorial abilities with a catalog of
"the most cruel and unblushing slanders."[104] In it he laid a long
charge intended to reveal that Burr always had been a secret
Federalist, never a true Republican, and that his career had been
one of duplicity and double dealing—without a single bit of ex-
plicit evidence. Burr, he declared, had never joined the "Republican phalanx" before 1800. The reports of his "herculean efforts" during the election were "false notions." Burr, moreover,
had been little known. If New York had been consulted he
would not have been nominated for the vice-presidency.[105] He
had always wanted the presidency because he needed the money. Then Cheetham laid out briefly the evidences of Burr's alleged conspiracy to steal the presidency:

1. He had engaged in secret correspondence with Federalists
from the day of his nomination at a cost equal to a year's
salary.

2. He had employed Abraham Bishop of New Haven, Connecticut, as agent to influence the Federalist Pennsylvania Senate to accept Republican electors. If this goal could be reached
there was an almost certain chance that Federalist Connecticut
and New Jersey would vote Republican.

3. He had employed Jonathan Dayton, United States senator
from New Jersey, to influence the New Jersey legislature.

4. He had tried to seduce Samuel S. Smith, president of New
Jersey College and a Federalist elector, to cast his vote for Burr.

5. He had used frequent "expresses" to communicate with
his uncle Pierpont Edwards in Connecticut instead of using the
mails.

6. He had given "attention" to his brother-in-law Tapping Reeve, a Federalist elector from Connecticut.

7. He had made a trip to Rhode Island from which he had brought false news that Jefferson (but not Burr) would receive votes; this news was then carried southward and used to convince the South that it must stand firm for Jefferson *and* Burr.

8. He had employed Timothy Green as his agent in South Carolina; Green had communicated with him through John Swartwout.[106]

9. He had written a letter to Samuel Smith of Maryland only after he had ascertained that the vote was tied.[107] The letter was not written for publication, only for oral communication, and was intended to "lull" the apprehensions of Republicans. If Burr had been honest he would have declared that he would resign if elected.

10. He had negotiated with a Federalist agent.

11. He had courted—wined and dined—Hamilton.

12. He had followed an "impeccable" course of "conduct" at Albany in order to disguise his designs.

13. He had used William P. Van Ness to subvert Edward Livingston of the New York delegation with the false information that Republicans in Albany favored Burr's election.[108]

In a second pamphlet, *Nine Letters on the Subject of Aaron Burr's Defection,* published early in 1803, Cheetham, after reviewing all his earlier charges, added his account of the alleged effort to give New York's electoral vote to Burr and greatly elaborated—in seventy pages—his account of the negotiations between Burr and the Federalists. He now named David A. Ogden as the negotiator, with Edward Livingston as intermediary.

Such was Cheetham's whole "case" against Aaron Burr. It has never been improved upon.

Abraham Bishop of New Haven, Jonathan Dayton of New Jersey, Samuel S. Smith of Princeton, Timothy Green and John Swartwout, David A. Ogden and Edward Livingston all publicly gave Cheetham the lie: they denied each and every one of Cheetham's charges.[109] Burr, however, remained mute.

Like many another politician, he was faced with a problem: He could reply to the charges, thus giving them greater currency and circulation, or he could keep quiet and allow the charges to fasten or to diminish in the public mind. He recognized the source of the attack. In his letters to his son-in-law Joseph Alston in the summer and fall of 1802 he named De Witt Clinton as the instigator; he knew Cheetham and Denniston as Clinton sycophants. He also suggested that their move against him was "a conspiracy [which] was formed last winter at Washington." But he refused to act against the charges: "It is not worth while to write anything by way of comment or explanation. . . . The malice and motives are obvious [and] will tend to discredit the whole. The charges which are of any moment will be shown to be fabrications. . . . These things will do no harm to me personally."[110]

Cheetham, nevertheless, continued to publish articles and pamphlets during the next year, and the Republican press led by Duane of the *Aurora* republished his charges. Few made any attempt to print denials or to defend Burr: They were given no material with which to defend him, until finally at the end of 1803 William P. Van Ness, under the pen name of "Aristides," published his pamphlet, *Examination of the Various Charges Exhibited against Aaron Burr*. A brilliant and caustic writer, he answered point by point the charges that Cheetham had leveled and then unveiled the fact that it was the Clintonians who were behind the effort to destroy Burr by defaming him. "Aristides" received much attention, but he was not republished by the Republican press,[111] and he did not convince those who had concluded that Burr was a scoundrel. Jefferson, who had no trouble swallowing Cheetham, described Aritides's account as a "falsehood" and "libelous."[112]

Despairing of correcting public opinion, his friends finally persuaded Burr in 1802 to institute a suit for libel against Cheetham. When Burr failed to press the case, his friends, still desirous of exposing the falsity of Cheetham's charges, instituted a "wager-suit" under the name James Gillespie v. Abraham Smith. Believing that Bayard and Samuel Smith held the secrets to any negotiations concerning the past election, they approached the two men for depositions. On April 3, 1806, both complied, and both completely exonerated Burr—as far as their knowledge extended—of any effort to win the presidential election in the House. Unfortunately, it was not until 1830, after the publication of the *Anas,* that these depositions were published.[113]

There are aspects of these postelection developments to negotiations concerning the past election, they approached the two men for depositions. On April 3, 1806, both compiled, and both completely exonerated Burr—as far as their knowledge extended—of any effort to win the presidential election in the House. Unfortunately, it was not until 1830, after the publication of the *Anas,* that these depositions were published.

There are aspects of these post election developments to which historians need to give attention and thought. Can more evidence be provided of the alliance between Jefferson and the Clintonians? Why has there been such little recognition of De Witt Clinton's campaign against Burr, particularly since Burr's followers, the "Little Band," were still angry about it as late as 1817? Why is there such little recognition that it was Clinton's editorial spokesman, Cheetham, who actually administered the fatal blows to Burr's political career? It was Cheetham's articles in the *American Citizen* and *Republican Watch-Tower* and his pamphlets that made public the rumbles about Burr's "intrigues." There was nothing specific and very little that even might be called ambiguous in the press of any party on the subject before Cheetham began his exposés. It was these exposes—and these exposés alone—republished throughout the nation, that befouled Burr's name and gave him a public reputation as a scoundrel who had sought to steal the presidency.

It seems rather obvious from even a casual inquiry that any truth that Cheetham included in his pamphlets is either accidental or incidental to his goal—Burr's destruction. Yet historians have never examined these charges carefully. Their tendency, based on earlier conclusions such as those of Henry S. Randall,[114] is to accept them as corroborations, when actually they are the original charges. Nor have historians given careful attention to the depositions and letters produced to refute the charges. Although they have the clear ring of truth, they are generally dismissed. In short, historians have allowed Burr to remain the victim of the Big Lie.[115]

Notes

1. Study of this problem developed in turn out of my research on Martin Van Buren. Anyone who works on Van Buren must inevitably give considerable attention to Aaron Burr. There are several reasons, not all of which I shall mention here. Historians connect their names in various ways: Most frequently they state that Burr taught Van Buren the art of political intrigue. How or why Burr taught Van Buren this art is a question few attempt to answer; when anyone does he usually points to the time when Burr lived at Richmond Hill in Manhattan at the same time that Van Buren was studying law in the Wall Street office of William P. Van Ness. Some biographers imply that Burr continued his tutelage after he returned from exile.

As it turns out, the period in which Burr was supposedly instructing Van Buren (October 1802-June 1803) was also the period when Burr became the target of the charges that Burr had conspired to defraud Jefferson of the presidency. Van Buren became involved in some sharp exchanges concerning these charges. Van Buren's awareness, however, was only a beginning. There are other connections. Van Buren became an active participant in politics during the New York gubernatorial campaign of 1804, when the political parties of New York were in the process of realigning into forms which were to remain relatively constant for fifteen years. Since Burr was supposed to have played a major role in the development of earlier alignments and his disappearance from the New York scene had a profound effect on later alignments, in which Van Buren became a major factor, I found it essential to study Burr's whole political role. The election of 1800-1801 is a major problem in developing any analysis of Burr's role. The inadequacy of past writings on the subject prompted this essay.

2. I include in this category Matthew L. Davis, *Memoirs of Aaron Burr* (New York, 1858); James Parton, *Life and Times of Aaron Burr* (New York, 1858); Nathan Schachner, *Aaron Burr: a Biography* (New York, 1937); and Samuel H. Wandell and Meade Minnegrode, *Aaron Burr* (New York, 1925). Holmes Alexander, *Aaron Burr: The Proud Pretender* (New York, 1937); Samuel E. Burr, Jr., *Colonel Aaron Burr: The American*

Phoenix (New York, 1961); Samuel L. Knapp, *Life of Aaron Burr* (New York, 1835); Charles B. Todd, *True Aaron Burr: a Biographical Sketch* (New York, 1902) follow the more general practice.

3. Noble E. Cunningham, Jr., *The Jeffersonian Republicans: The Formation of the Party Organization, 1789-1801* (Chapel Hill, N.C., 1957).

4. Jefferson to Madison, March 4, 1800, in Thomas Jefferson, *Writings of Thomas Jefferson*, ed. Paul L. Ford (New York, 1896), 7: 433.

5. In the spring of 1800 there was fairly general agreement that the five New England states together with New Jersey and Delaware, with 47 votes, were Federalist; that Virginia, Georgia, Kentucky, and Tennessee with 32 votes were Republican; that Maryland and North Carolina with 23 votes would divide about equally. New York (12 votes), Pennsylvania (15), and South Carolina (8) with 35 votes were doubtful and the real battlegrounds. If the computations were correct, the Federalists would receive 58 to 59 votes, or 11 to 12 votes short of victory, and the Republicans would receive 43 to 44 votes, or 27 to 28 votes short of victory. Obviously the Republicans had the greater distance to travel. If they could not carry New York, the first of the doubtful states to act, their chances were almost nil. See Jefferson to Madison, ibid.

6. The major exception to this condition as to others of my generalizations is Cunningham, *Jeffersonian Republicans*. See p. 176.

7. Matthew L. Davis to Albert Gallatin, May 1, 1800; James Nicholson to Gallatin, May 6, 1800, in Henry Adams, *Life of Albert Gallatin* (New York, 1879), pp. 238, 241.

8. Schachner, *Burr*, pp. 167-177, and Cunningham, *Jeffersonian Republicans*, pp. 176-183, are excellent examples.

9. Albany *Centinel*, May 6, 1800. Since the *Centinel* was a Federalist paper, these remarks are supposed to be pejorative; at the same time they illustrate Burr's activities.

10. Jerome Mushkat, *Tammany: The Evolution of a Political Machine, 1789-1865* (Syracuse, N.Y., 1970), pp. 26-29.

11. See ibid., p. 26; Cunningham, *Jeffersonian Republicans*, p. 181, n. 28.

12. Davis to Gallatin, March 29, April 15, May 1, 5, 1800, in Adams, *Life of Gallatin*, pp. 232-240.

13. Gallatin to Mrs. Gallatin, May 6, 1800, ibid., pp. 241-242.

14. Nicholson to Gallatin, May 7, 1800, ibid., pp. 242-243. Nicholson warned that Burr "must not be played the fool with."

15. Nicholson's explanation of December 26, 1803, and Carl Becker's critique are most readily found in *American Historical Review* 8 (April 1903): 511-513.

16. See, for example, Mrs. Gallatin to Gallatin, May 7, 1800, in Adams, *Life of Gallatin*, p. 243; Oliver Wolcott to Ogden Edwards, in George Gibbs, *Memoirs of the Administrations of Washington and John Adams*

edited from the Papers of Oliver Wolcott (New York, 1846), 2: 488; George Jackson to Madison, February 5, 1801, Madison Papers, Library of Congress, Washington, D.C.; Douglas Adair, ed., "James Madison's Autobiography," *William and Mary Quarterly,* 3d ser., 2 (1945): 206; Dumas Malone, *Jefferson and His Time* (Boston, 1962), 3: 322-324.

17. From the South Burr also received 3 from Maryland, 4 from Kentucky, and 3 from Tennessee.

18. Gibbs, *Memoirs* 1: 379-380.

19. Schachner, *Burr,* pp. 209-224.

20. See p. 49 n. 51 and p. 57 n. 86 ff. The latter, *Anas* entry, is given in full in Jefferson, *Writings,* ed. Ford, 1: 301-303. Burr also made his reluctance known to John Taylor of Caroline, October 23, 1800, Washburn Collection 4, Massachusetts Historical Society.

21. Hamilton to James A. Bayard, August 6, 1800, in John C. Hamilton, *Works of Alexander Hamilton* (New York, 1851), 6: 454-455.

22. John Adams to James Lloyd, February 17, 1815, in Charles Francis Adams, *Works of John Adams, Second President of the United States* (Boston, 1856), 10: 124.

23. Gideon Granger to Jefferson, March 9, 1814; Jefferson to Madison, March 10, 1814, in Jefferson, *Writings,* ed. Ford, 9: 454-458, 459-460; Irving Brant, *James Madison* (Indianapolis, 1953), 4: 24.

24. Burr to Livingston, September 24, 1800, Robert R. Livingston Papers, New York Historical Society, New York. See also Burr to Pierpont Edwards, November 26, 29, December 1, 1800, Aaron Burr Papers, New York Public Library. Burr received the promise of James Fenner of Rhode Island, a prospective Federalist elector, to give one of his votes to Jefferson. See citations to Aaron Burr Papers, Massachusetts Historical Society, in Cunningham, *Jeffersonian Republicans,* pp. 198-199.

25. Jefferson to Livingston, December 14, 1800; Jefferson to Burr, December 15, 1800; Jefferson to John Breckenridge, December 18, 1800; Jefferson to Madison, December 19, 1800, in Jefferson, *Writings,* ed. Ford, 7: 463-464, 466-467, 469, 470.

26. Jefferson to Burr, December 15, 1800, ibid., p. 467.

27. Brant, *Madison,* 4: 34.

28. Henry S. Randall, *Life of Thomas Jefferson* (New York, 1858), 2: 574-575; James Cheetham to Thomas Jefferson, June 1, 1801, *Proceedings of the Massachusetts Historical Society,* 3d ser. 1 (April 1907): 42-43; Brant, *Madison,* 4: 26; Malone, *Jefferson,* 3: 497-498.

29. Memorandum of Conversation with Judge Woodworth, February 9, 1858, Van Buren Papers, Library of Congress, Washington, D.C.

30. Brant, *Madison,* 4: 23-25.

31. Ibid., p. 26.

32. See p. 41 n. 24 ante.

33. See "James Madison's Autobiography," ed. Adair, p. 5 n. 39 ante.

34. The best account of the South Carolina contest is in Cunningham, *Jeffersonian Republicans*, pp. 231-235. See, however, John H. Wolfe, *Jeffersonian Democracy in South Carolina* (Chapel Hill, N.C., 1940), p. 158 n. 52.

35. Schachner offers no evidence for this statement (*Burr*, p. 185). Timothy Green to Burr, quoted in Burr to William Eustis, December 9, 1800, Burr Papers, Massachusetts Historical Society. Cunningham, in *Jeffersonian Republicans*, p. 235, notes this letter.

36. Hamilton to Jay, May 7, 1800, John Jay, *Correspondence and Public Papers of John Jay*, ed. Henry P. Johnston (New York, 1893), 4: 270-271.

37. Robert Troup to Rufus King, December 31, 1800, Charles R. King, *Life and Correspondence of Rufus King* (New York, 1900), 3: 359.

38. Among the recipients were James A. Bayard, George Cabot, John Marshall, Gouverneur Morris, Harrison Gray Otis, Theodore Sedgewick, and Oliver Wolcott. Henry S. Randall regarded these letters as giant black blotches on Burr's reputation and reproduced well and concisely all the significant passages besmirching Burr (*Jefferson*, 2: 582-589). Otherwise these letters and replies may be found most readily in Hamilton, *Works*, 6: 419-514. It is highly probable that Hamilton's campaign, in which he never once tied one of his terms to a specific incident, ultimately gave an additional foundation to Burr's later reputation. The pejorative terms used in the text appeared first in Hamilton's letters; they appeared next in the letters of Hamilton's correspondents—and spread to others. While I have hardly examined the whole correspondence of Hamilton's correspondents, I have the clear impression that these terms soon became vague and generalized descriptions. As generalizations, however, they served to influence many who did not want to examine the truth of them or who were only too willing to let Burr's name be defamed.

39. See Leven Powell to Burr Powell, December 23, 1800, January 12, 19, 1801, *John P. Branch Historical Papers of Randolph-Macon College* (June 1901), 1: 56-57; (June 1903), 3: 242-245. See also Gouverneur Morris, *Diary and Letters of Gouverneur Morris*, ed. Anne C. Morris (New York, 1888), 2: 401-403.

40. Schachner, *Burr*, p. 201.

41. Jefferson to Livingston, December 14, 1800, in Jefferson, *Writings*, ed. Ford, 7: 463-465.

42. Jefferson to Burr, December 15, 1800, ibid., pp. 466-467.

43. I have been unable to determine why Burr chose Smith for this communication, aside from their friendship dating back to the Revolution.

44. Washington *National Intelligencer*, December 31, 1800. The letter also appeared in the Washington *Federalist*, December 31, 1800, and is reproduced in Davis, *Memoirs*, 2: p. 75.

45. Burr to Jefferson, December 23, 1800, Jefferson Papers, Library of

Congress, Washington, D.C.

46. Caesar Rodney to James Nicholson, January 3, 1801, Nicholson Papers, Library of Congress, Washington, D.C.; Jefferson to Martha Jefferson Randolph, January 4, 1801, Jefferson, *Writings*, ed. Ford, 7: 478.

47. See, for example, Bayard to Hamilton, January 7, 1801, Hamilton, *Works*, 6: 505.

48. Randall, *Life of Jefferson*, 2: 585, 604-605; Brant, *Madison*, 4: 29-30, 34; John S. Pancake, "Aaron Burr: Would-Be Usurper," *William and Mary Quarterly*, 3d ser., 8 (April 1951): 205-209, 210; Malone, *Jefferson*, 3: 496-498. Other Jeffersonian historians who take similar positions include Claude G. Bowers, *Jefferson in Power* (Boston, 1936); Edward Channing, *The Jeffersonian System* (New York, 1907); John T. Morse, Jr., *Thomas Jefferson* (Boston, 1883); Albert J. Nock, *Jefferson* (New York, 1926). Gilbert Chinard, *Thomas Jefferson, Apostle of Americanism* (Boston, 1939) is more sympathetic to Burr.

49. The exception is Cunningham, *Jeffersonian Republicans*. Merrill D. Peterson, whom I regard as the most perceptive of Jefferson scholars, wisely refrains from making a judgment on the question of Burr's veracity, but he is strongly inclined to suggest that Matthew L. Davis's defense of Burr was an attempt to traduce Jefferson. (Merrill D. Peterson, *Thomas Jefferson and the New Nation* [New York, 1970], pp. 625-651, and *Jeffersonian Image in the American Mind* [New York, 1962], pp. 144-149.)

50. Brant, *Madison*, 4: 29-30. See p. 65 n. 107 post.

51. Ibid., pp. 30-31.

52. Pancake, "Aaron Burr," pp. 205-206; ibid., p. 30; Malone, *Jefferson*, 3: 497.

53. See Pancake, "Aaron Burr," pp. 205-206, especially n. 2 wherein Professor Pancake explains that the letter that he used was not an original manuscript but a copy; though he does not say so, his explanation suggests that the transference from the original to copy may have created the confusion in dates which I note on p. 50 nn. 57, 58, post.

54. Randall, *Life of Jefferson*, 2: 604.

55. The letter from Harper to Burr was originally published in the *Baltimore American* and was reprinted by the Philadelphia *Aurora* on July 12, 1808. It was again reprinted in *Niles' Weekly Register*, January 4, 1823, when Harper declared he had no idea whether Burr had received the letter. Most often, however, the letter is quoted from J. F. McLaughlin, *Matthew Lyon, the Hampden of Congress* (New York, 1900), pp. 385-386.

56. Pancake, "Aaron Burr," p. 206.

57. Brant, *Madison*, 4: 30-31.

58. Pancake, "Aaron Burr," 206-207.

59. Philadelphia *Aurora*, January 6, 1801.

60. Gabriel Christie to Samuel Smith, December 19, 1802, Samuel Smith Papers, Library of Congress, Washington, D.C.

61. B. Hichborn to Jefferson, January 5, 1801, Jefferson Papers, Library of Congress.

62. *Anas*, January 2, 1804, in Jefferson, *Writings*, ed. Ford, 1: 301.

63. Smith to Burr, January 11, 1801, Smith Papers, Library of Congress. Brant, *Madison*, 4: 30, reports this confrontation after the Philadelphia meeting.

64. Pancake, "Aaron Burr," pp. 206-207.

65. Smith to Burr, January 11, 1801, Smith Papers, Library of Congress. In this letter Smith assured Burr that neither Jefferson nor any other Republican believed Ogden was Burr's agent. It was his opinion that Ogden was making an effort to "disunite us." Such sentiments do not seem to speak any "alarm."

66. Burr to Smith, January 16, 1801, Smith Papers, Library of Congress.

67. Burr to Gallatin, January 16, 1801, Adams, *Life of Gallatin*, p. 245.

68. Gallatin to Mrs. Gallatin, January 15, 1801, ibid., p. 253.

69. A casual examination of the *Journal of the Assembly of the State of New York*, 24th Session—a rather dull session—will readily provide an outline of Burr's activities.

70. Memorandum, February 9, 1858, Van Buren Papers, Library of Congress.

71. Pancake, "Aaron Burr," p. 207; Brant, *Madison*, 4: 30; Schachner, *Burr*, p. 199.

72. Burr to Smith, December 29, 1800; Pancake, "Aaron Burr," p. 205.

73. The following letters have been cited in this essay: Burr to Smith, December 16; Burr to Jefferson, December 23; Burr to Smith, December 29; Burr to Smith, January 16; Burr to Gallatin, January 16. There are other letters which reveal the same consistency: Burr to John Taylor, December 18, 1800, Massachusetts Historical Society; Burr to Joseph Alston, January 15, 1801, Davis, *Memoirs*, 2: 144 ("The equality of Jefferson and Burr excites great speculation and much anxiety. I believe that all will be well, and that Jefferson will be our president"); Burr to Jefferson, February 12, 1801, Jefferson Papers, Library of Congress, in answer to Jefferson's somewhat panicky letter concerning a forged communication to Breckenridge allegedly asserting Jefferson's dislike for Burr. Thomas Jefferson, *Writings of Thomas Jefferson*, ed. Andrew A. Lipscomb and Albert E. Bergh (Washington, 1904), 10: 193-194; Burr to Gallatin, February 12, 25, 1801, Adams, *Life of Gallatin*, pp. 246-247; Burr to Davis on eve of House vote, Schachner, *Burr*, p. 199 (footnoted incorrectly). See also Edward Livingston to Burr, July 27, 1802 in Cheetham, *Letter to a Friend on the Conduct of the Adherents to Aaron Burr* (New York, 1803), p. 50. It is more than probable that a diligent search through the Burr correspondence in a dozen major eastern libraries and historical societies would produce many more of a confirming nature.

74. Pancake, "Aaron Burr," p. 209.

75. *Anas,* February 12, 14, 1801, Jefferson, *Writings,* ed. Ford, 1: 291.

76. Albert Gallatin wrote an excellent account of these apprehensions nearly fifty years later in a letter to Henry A. Muhlenberg, May 8, 1848, Adams, *Life of Gallatin,* pp. 248-251; Burr's attitude is mentioned in Burr to Gallatin, February 12, 1801, Adams, *Life of Gallatin,* p. 246; for another account of Burr's attitude see Memorandum, February 9, 1858, Van Buren Papers, Library of Congress. Another from Philadelphia is Alexander J. Dallas to Gallatin, February 15, 1801, Gallatin Papers, New York Historical Society, New York.

77. No one has satisfactorily explained how this bloc made up of James A. Bayard, Lewis R. Morris of Vermont, and John C. Thomas, William Craik, John Dennis, and George Baer of Maryland developed. The best account of the "break" in the Federalist lineup is in Martin Borden, *The Federalism of James A. Bayard* (New York, 1955), pp. 88-90. Robert G. Harper in a letter to his constituents, February 24, 1801, has provided an excellent contemporary observation. Elizabeth Donnan, *Papers of James A. Bayard, 1796-1815, Annual Report of the American Historical Association, 1913,* 2: 132-137.

78. Bayard to Richard Bassett, February 16, 1801, ibid., pp. 126-127; Bayard to Hamilton, March 8, 1801, Hamilton, *Works,* 6: 522-524. See also William Cooper to Thomas Morris, February 13, 1801, Davis, *Memoirs,* 2: 113: "Had Burr done anything for himself, he would long ere this have been president."

79. Brant, *Madison,* 4: 33, regards Bayard's statement to Hamilton as "absurd."

80. See Malone, *Jefferson,* 4: 12-13; Pancake, "Aaron Burr," 212-213. Burr in Philadelphia noted "the Federalists boast aloud that they have compromised with Jefferson, particularly as to the retaining [of] certain persons in office." (To Gallatin, February 25, 1801, Adams, *Life of Gallatin,* p. 247.)

81. Bordon, *Bayard,* pp. 86-93.

82. Malone, *Jefferson,* 4: 88; Noble E. Cunningham, Jr., *Jeffersonian Republicans in Power: Party Operations, 1801-1809* (Chapel Hill, N.C., 1963), p. 39. Channing, *Jeffersonian System,* p. 17, goes so far as to declare that "Burr's actions in the election of 1800 had filled Jefferson with disgust and loathing." One of the puzzling discrepancies in Jefferson's attitude and conduct develops out of his letter to Thomas McKean, Governor of Pennsylvania, March 9, 1801, in Jefferson, *Writings,* ed. Ford, 8: 12, in which he declares that he would have "cheerfully submitted" to Burr's election to the presidency. If he was truthful, why was he so vindictive?

83. Samuel Osgood to Madison, April 24, 1801, Madison Papers, Library of Congress, Washington, D.C.; John A. Armstrong to Gallatin, May

7, 1801, Gallatin Papers, New York Historical Society, New York.

84. Robert Troup to Rufus King, May 27, 1801, King, *Correspondence*, 3: 458-461.

85. Jefferson to Burr, November 18, 1801, in Jefferson, *Writings*, ed. Ford, 8: 102.

86. *Anas*, January 2, 1804, in Jefferson, *Writings*, ed. Ford, 1: 301.

87. Jefferson to Burr, June 17, 1797, ibid., 7: 145-147.

88. Malone (*Jefferson*, 3: 322) declares, "There is no way of knowing just what Jefferson thought of Burr at this time. The best guess is that he regarded him as a necessary evil. We must not assume that Burr's reputation was as unsavory as it afterwards became. . . . In any case Jefferson recognized that the cooperation of the most promising Republican politician beyond Pennsylvania was a virtual necessity." The statement is a perfect example of Jeffersonian attitudes that discolor the developments of the time.

89. Jefferson to Burr, May 20, 26, June 16, November 12, 1798, February 11, 1799, in Jefferson, *Writings*, ed. Ford, 7: 254-259, 347-349. Gabriel Chinard (*Jefferson*, p. 354) notes that the letter of February 11 was "affectionate and familiar."

90. Brant, *Madison*, 3: 501.

91. Gallatin to Jefferson, September 14, 1801, Henry Adams, *Writings of Albert Gallatin* (New York, 1879), 1: 50-53.

92. Henry Adams, *History of the United States of America during the Administrations of Jefferson and Madison* (New York, 1889), 1: 230-231; Schachner, *Burr*, p. 675.

93. Gallatin to Jefferson, September 14, 1801, Adams, *Writings of Albert Gallatin*, 1: 53.

94. Ibid., 52.

95. The Council of Appointment consisted of the Governor and one senator named by assemblymen from each of the four senatorial districts, elected for one year without possibility of reelection. The council made all military and civil, state and county appointments—about twelve thousand. In 1792 when George Clinton was Governor, the Federalists began to claim, contrary to fifteen years' tradition, that senator had the same right of nomination as the Governor. In 1801 when Federalist John Jay was still Governor, the Republicans made the same claim. The controversy that developed brought about a constitutional convention, over which Burr presided, and a constitutional amendment which confirmed the right of senators to make nominations equally with the Governor. It is under this amended constitution that New York's spoils system developed.

96. New York State had no law prohibiting its officers from holding a federal office. It was not uncommon for a politician to hold both a state and a federal office from which he drew two salaries or collected fees. The federal constitution, however, prohibited senators and representatives

from holding other offices.

97. Howard L. McBain, *DeWitt Clinton and the Origin of the Spoils System in New York* (New York, 1907), pp. 126-137, declares that not all Burrites were proscribed. Cunningham, *Republicans in Power*, pp. 42-43, accepts McBain's research. I have not been able to find a single Burrite appointed to an important office between 1801 and 1804 in the Civil List.

98. Jabez D. Hammond, *History of Political Parties in the State of New York* (Albany, 1842), 1: 172.

99. This letter has never come to light. That Cheetham carried a letter from De Witt Clinton would suggest at least a closeness of interest.

100. This information was communicated orally to Jefferson. When Cheetham could not see Madison, who was ill, he wrote out the same information for him. The letter, endorsed by Jefferson with the date December 10, 1801, is in *Proceedings of the Massachusetts Historical Society*, 3d ser., 1 (April 1907): 46-51.

101. Cheetham to Jefferson, December 29, 1801, January 30, 1802, ibid., pp. 51-57.

102. These events are variously covered in Malone, *Jefferson*, 4: 122-123; Schachner, *Burr*, pp. 222-225.

103. James Cheetham, *A Narrative of the Suppression by Col. Burr of the History of the Administration of John Adams* (New York, 1802); Davis, *Memoirs*, 2: 89-99; Schachner, *Burr*, pp. 224-227. It should be noted that the publisher of Wood's book was a man named Barlas. He was a private tutor to some of Alexander Hamilton's children.

104. *Poughkeepsie Journal*, March 27, 1804.

105. This "background" uses the first 42 pages of a 120-page pamphlet.

106. These eight charges cover pp. 43-50.

107. It should be noted that Cheetham "issued a handbill indicating Republican victory and a tie vote in South Carolina" as of December 2 on December 16, 1800. He did not publish the news until the next day, December 17 (*A View of... Burr*, p. 56). The need for a handbill would indicate that the "news" arrived after normal publishing time. Would Burr have seen this handbill before he sent his letter of December 16 to Smith? Cf. Brant, *Madison*, 4: 16 n. 50.

108. Charges 9-13 cover pp. 51-68; the remainder involves postelection "events" intended to reveal that Burr was hostile to Jefferson.

109. The denials were made in various ways. The most ready source is Davis, *Memoirs*, 2: 89-100.

110. Burr to Joseph Alston, July 3, 9, August 2, November 5, 1802, ibid., pps. 205, 208-209, 215.

111. In answer to Cheetham's allegation that Burr was hostile to Jefferson, Aristides pointed out with considerable evidence (borne out by later events) that George Clinton was the man in New York who was hostile to Jefferson. In my researches through the newspapers of the period I have

not found any Republican papers that gave Aristides anywhere near the space and consideration they gave Cheetham. It was the Federalist press that gave Aristides publicity—even small country weeklies gave it attention.

112. Jefferson to George Clinton, December 31, 1803, Jefferson, *Writings*, ed. Lipscomb and Bergh, 10: 439-441.

113. The most readily available source for the deposition is Davis, *Memoirs*, 2: 119-137.

114. It is interesting to note that Jabez B. Hammond, a Clintonian, who examined Cheetham's charges soon after they appeared, refused to accept all of them, but he accepted the charge that Burr conspired to steal the presidency. (*History of Political Parties*, 1: 134-144). Henry S. Randall swallowed the charges hook, line and sinker (*Life of Jefferson*, 2: 572-579).

115. If I undertook to correct or revise the current attitude toward Burr I would start at the beginning: with Cheetham and with the reports in the newspapers, with Burr's correspondence and that of his associates. These are almost unexploited.

"RATHER BE A NIGGER
THAN A POOR WHITE MAN":
SLAVE PERCEPTIONS OF SOUTHERN
YEOMEN AND POOR WHITES

Eugene D. Genovese

"When I was a boy," recalled Waters McIntosh, who had been a slave in Sumter, South Carolina, "we used to sing, 'Rather be a nigger than a poor white man.' Even in slavery we used to sing that. It was the poor white man who was freed by the War, not the Negroes.'"[1] Mr. McIntosh's remarks reveal two related but discrete slave attitudes: that the poor whites of the South ranked below black slaves in social standing or, more precisely, in "respectability"; and that slavery hurt the nonslaverholders almost as much as it hurt the slaves.[2] A measure of contradiction existed between the two attitudes, for if the former signified contempt, the latter implied sympathy and understanding.

The notion that the slaves felt unbridled contempt for lower-class whites comes primarily from the narratives of runaway slaves, at least if the self-serving pronouncements of the slave-holders are laid aside. Frederick Douglass opened his famous *Life and Times* with an account of Talbot County, Maryland, which he said housed a "white population of the lowest order, indolent and drunk to a proverb."[3] Henry Bibb, who noted that some poor whites wanted slavery abolished "in self defence," nonetheless dismissed most as "poor and loafering whites . . . about on a par in point of morals with the slaves." Specifically, he denounced them as "generally ignorant, imtemperate, licentious, and profane."[4] H. C. Bruce, whose ferocious hostility

79

toward white laborers made him a stalward supporter of big
business and conservative politics after the war, could think of
nothing worse to say of his old master than that he associated
socially with poor whites and used them to spy on his slaves.[5]

The slaves had much to complain about. Many districts
boasted a "nigger-breaker"—a harsh taskmaster to whom planters assigned difficult slaves for special attention. "Nigger-breakers," usually, although not always, poor farmers on-the-make,
temporarily acquired slave labor at low cost in return for per-
forming the pleasant duty of breaking the slaves' spirit.[6] A much
larger number of slaves focused their hatred on the lower-class
whites who rode patrol and enforced slave curfews, often with
excessive force and sadistic pleasure. Manda Walker, an ex-slave
from South Carolina, told an interviewer many years later:

> Why de good white folks put up wid them white trash
> patarollers I never can see or understand. You never see
> classy white buckra men a patarollin'. It was always
> some low-down white men, dat never owned a nigger in
> deir life, doin' de patarollin' and strippin' de clothes off
> men, lak pappy, right befo' de wives and chillun and
> beatin' de blood out of him. No, sir, good white men
> never dirty deir hands and souls in sich work of de devil
> as dat.[7]

Worse, the slaves knew that some poor whites earned their
living by tracking runaways with fierce dogs. The capital value
of the slaves did not guarantee that they would not be torn
apart by the dogs or shot by the pursuers, for many masters
willingly accepted the occasional loss of an incorrigible *pour
encourager les autres*.[8] And when poor whites were not torment-
ing the slaves in these and other ways, they might be annoying
them by peeping at or spying on them or by taunting and
insulting them or by blaming them for thefts and other mischief
committed by whites.[9]

Many slaves, however, had little or no contact with lower-
class whites apart from an overseer, and not always then. Slave

relations with overseers inquire separate and extensive treatment. Of immediate relevance, the slaves often used the overseers as a reference point for all lower-class whites. A cruel or unreasonable overseer reinforced the slaves' judgment of lower-class whites as their worst enemies. The slaves' most common method of condemning an unpopular overseer was to dismiss him as "poor white trash."[10] The slaves could hardly respect an overseer, or those for whom he stood in their eyes, when they saw him bow and scrape before his rich employer and then play the tyrant with the field hands.[11] The planters did not encourage slave contact with lower-class whites. In some districts the rich planters succeeded in buying out their poorer neighbors or in keeping them away from the slaves. An ex-slave from Virginia explained, "Marse Hunt wanted de culured slave chilluns to be raised in propah mannah."[12] Throughout the South the slaves of many of the larger planters lived in a society of blacks and well-to-do whites and were encouraged to view even respectable laboring whites with disdain.[13]

The slaves' attitude toward being owned by rich or poor masters was nevertheless much more complex than has generally been appreciated. Certainly, all the attributed elements of childlike devotion, false pride, and "identification with the oppressor" made their appearance. But the slaves' attitude also reflected a recognition of the better qualities of the great planters and represented acceptance of an aristocratic standard of behavior for themselves. They did not view every rich man as admirable and every poor man as "no-'count." If anything, they would have preferred that admirable white men be rich, and they attributed the failings of rich men to alleged lower-class origins. Their favorite expression was "de quality," which they associated with aristocratic bearing, courtesy, and courtly condescension, rather than with wealth per se. But in the end, they tried to estimate character rather than wealth—by aristocratic standards.

In this context the remarks made to Gus Feaster of South Carolina by his mother reflected a healthier attitude than critics have generally granted: "How is I gwine to ever teach you anything, when you act jest like a nigger from some pore white trash's pore land?" And after cleaning up her untidy son: "Now you is looking like you belongs to Marse Tom 'gin."[14] More to the point, the words of Charlie Moses, ex-slave from Mississippi, did not necessarily divide rich from poor when he referred to the "harsh treatment us colored folks was given by poor quality folks."[15]

However admirable features the slaves' attitudes revealed—a large subject in itself—it did lead straight to a dangerous class viewpoint. Ella Kelly, who had been a slave in South Carolina, exposed the outcome as well as anyone:

> Yes de overseer was de poor buckra, he was what you calls dis poor white trash. You know, boss, dese days dere is three kind of people. Lowest down is a layer of white folks, then in de middle is a layer of colored folks, and on top is de cream, a layer of good white folks. 'Spect itt'll be dat way till Judgment day.[16]

The slaves noticed their masters' sense of superiority toward marginal farmers as well as toward poor whites and, by associating themselves with "de quality white folks," strengthened their own sense of self-esteem. Here, a slave noted that only rich white people were welcome visitors at the Big House. There, a slave noted that Massa and Mistis lavished hospitality on other quality whites but had no time for those of lesser station. Another expressed no surprise that his master, who was Big Buckra, never associated with white trash.[17] And Rosa Starke, who had been owned by a big planter in South Carolina, reported that poor whites had to use the kitchen door when they went up to the Big House. Her mistress "had a grand manner; no patience with poor white folks."[18] So far did the slaves yield to their masters' class attitudes that some criticized Abraham Lincoln for his origins. With all the expressions of respect, gratitude, even adulation for "Massa Linkum," some felt impelled to mention, apologetically, his having been a poor man and not of "de quality."[19]

Yet, these accounts, like Ella Kelly's ambiguous remarks

about three classes in society, demonstrated resistance to racism
and total self-denigration. Racial slavery, by its very nature,
taught the slaves to despise their color and to worship white-
ness. The slaves, however, by accepting the class pretensions of
their masters, in effect announced that they rated themselves
much closer to "de quality"—to aristocratic standards—than
they rated the overwhelming majority of the white population.[20]

The slaves saw their masters' noblesse oblige toward the small
farmers as well as toward the poor whites and recognized in it
an extension of the plantation paternalism of which they them-
sleves were both beneficiaries and victims.[21] Thus, poor whites
and slaves both seemed to rely on rich whites for protection and
succor in times of stress. Did a farmer fall ill during the harvest
season? A neighborly planter would send a few slaves to save
the crop. Was the farmer's wife ill? A plantation mistress and
reliable black nurse would arrive to attend her. Did the farmer's
children need to learn to read and write or to be looked after
during their mother's illness? A planter's family would see that
they got what they needed. Did the local farmers occasionally
yearn for fresh beef or have difficulty raising enough vege-
tables? The planters—some anyway—would periodically throw a
big barbecue for the neighborhood and invite the less fortunate
to help themselves in the vegetable garden. Did a new man in
the area need help in raising a house and providing his farm with
seed and equipment? What were neighborly rich planters for—or
more precisely, what were the slaves of neighborly rich planters
for? Were there desperately poor people who depended on charity? Who bestowed charity more graciously than Ole Massa?[22]
The slaves, then, saw some masters ruthlessly drive the poor
whites out of the area and other masters extend every kindness;
in either case, the masters loomed ever larger as the dominant
figures on the countryside.

Even in straightforward economic relations the planters generally lent a helping hand to their yeomen neighbors, or at least
appeared to. The planters had the gins and marketing facilities
to process and ship their neighbors' small cotton crops; and
they had the gristmills and other equipment to meet their neighbors' needs. The yeomen paid for these services but not at

unfair prices, and the slaves, who did the actual work, saw the element of dependence of poorer on richer whites.[23]

The slaves could not fail to notice when "most of the local artisans and laborers turned to Charles Pettigrew, and he came, after the fashion of a feudal lord, to feel responsible for their employment."[24] Nor could the slaves have failed to notice when the planters condescendingly invited the local farmers and poor whites to join a fox hunt while commenting among themselves on the wretched condition of their guests. Or when the planters threw a barbecue for their disadvantaged neighbors. Or when a planter offered to pay to send a bright poor white child to school in the North.[25]

John S. Wise of Virginia and Eliza Frances Andrews of Georgia, among other slaveholders, might insist that the relationship between upper- and lower-class whites exuded equality—in some respects it in fact did—but their own accounts betray striking caste divisions. Miss Andrews assures us, in a retrospective note written in 1908, "While the structure of our social fabric was aristocratic, in the actual relations of the white population with one another it was extremely democratic." Yet, her journal entry for May 2, 1865, reveals that Confederate troops, whom her family was graciously feeding in the yard, became incensed because they were not being invited into the house.[26]

The presence of white sharecroppers and tenant famers on the plantations reinforced the slaves' sense of having a master who dominated an interracial community. Sharecropping and tenancy, usually associated with postbellum developments, had firm antebellum roots. The slaves saw an undetermined number of whites pass into dependence within a patron-client relationship.[27]

Planters of the second generation and certainly those of the third usually maintained strict caste lines with the whites beneath them. Small farmers and even laborers might receive courtesy and respect but could not, for example, expect an invitation to the Big House. Some of the more aristocratic planters, especially those with political ambitions, would go so far as to entertain poor neighbors in their parlors or, in rare cases, at table. But the planters had the greatest difficulty in hiding their conviction of superior breeding and status.[28] The slaves made their own judgment of the lower-class white response; however much the accuracy of that judgment might be challenged, its influence on the slaves themselves cannot be underestimated. Frank Adamson, an ex-slave from South Carolina, commented on his master, "Them poor white folks looked up to him lak God Almighty; they sho' did. They would have stuck their hands in de fire if he had asked them to do it.[29]

From the slaves' vantage point, the neighboring farmers and poor whites relied on the planters for protection and rode patrol and tormented slaves. But those whites who depended upon or feared a particular planter usually could be counted on to leave the slaves alone. Thus, that master protected the slaves from the worst racist excesses. As Lord Bountiful to the neighborhood, he increased his prestige among the slaves and made himself the more awesome. As sometime protector of the slaves, he deepened their sense of his being an indispensable shield against lower-class violence.[30] Among many ramifications of this dependence on a master, the slaves effected the classic attitude of "If the Tsar only knew." More often than not, they blamed the overseers for daily sufferings, not the slaveholders who hired and fired. And the slaves blamed the poor whites for the atrocities of patrollers who were, after all, protecting the slaveholders' property.

Yet, despite the overwhelming pressures toward racial antagonism—pressures that would take an even heavier toll during and after Reconstruction—impressive bonds of sympathy developed between slaves and some lower-class whites. If nothing else, the slaves displayed an astonishing compassion for the hard lot of the white laborers and marginal farmers. An ex-slave from Texas insisted that the poor whites of his district treated the slaves better than the rich did. Ex-slaves from Maryland said that poor whites behaved as decently as rich and that some got into trouble for expressions of hostility toward slavery.[31] In Mississippi two sons of a poor white, working as hired laborers on a big plantation, almost got lynched as "Negro sympathizers" because they became too solicitous of the slaves alongside of whom they were picking cotton.[32] The slaveholders remained nervous about the possibility of comradeship between poor whites and slaves. And well they might have, for here and there poor whites extended or alleged to have extended support to runaway or even insurgent slaves. The numbers were small, and probably exaggerated at that. But men of property, especially of such "troublesome property" as slaves, could not be too careful.[33]

Less dramatically, a poor white man might serve as a doctor and his wife as a midwife to slaves who appreciated the effort. A German grocer might win the respect of slaves for his kindness and generosity.[34] Lewis Clark, a successful runaway, told of Flora, a slave who took fifty lashes for raiding her master's storehouse in order to feed a sick and destitute white woman. Despite the slaves' own meager resources, they sometimes extended help to hungry or sick poor whites.[35]

Ex-slaves firmly insisted that at least some poor whites they had known were good, honest, respectable people. "He poor man," an ex-slave said of his overseer, "but him come from good folks, not poor white trash."[36] Another ex-slave said of an overseer, " 'Cose he wasn't no quality, lak ole Marster an' ole Mistis, but he was a good kin' man an' he didn't hab no trouble on de whole plantation."[37] An ex-slave from North Carolina added, "We thought well of the poor white neighbors," and others recalled particular poor whites as respectable family people.[38]

Planters in Louisiana complained to Olmsted about the effect of the poor Cajuns on the slaves:

> The slaves seeing them living in apparent comfort, without much property and without steady labor, could not help thinking that it was not necessary for men to work so hard as they themselves were obliged to; that if they were free they would not need to work.[39]

The Cajuns illicitly hired slaves, without their masters' knowledge, approval, or profit, to do odd jobs in return for liquor and money. Still, an articulate slave impressed Olmsted with his own version—a warm defense of the Cajuns as good, hardworking people.[40] The music of the blacks and Cajuns in southern Louisiana suggests close cultural relations, for if the blacks often sang Cajun songs, the songs themselves seem to have demonstrated a marked Afro-American influence.[41]

Throughout the South slaves came into close contact with white laborers who did skilled and unskilled work on the plantations. Carpenters and blacksmiths might arrive for particular jobs, and unskilled whites often supplemented the slaves during the cotton-picking season. Little is known about the relationship of the slaves to these white laborers, but that little hints at much more harmony than conflict. Those slaves apprenticed to skilled whites to learn a trade reported no worse than the usual range of behavior from kind to ill usage and at least appreciated the instruction.[42] The field hands who worked alongside hired white cotton-pickers significantly referred to their having "helped us." Several ex-slaves remarked pointedly that the overseers worked the whites too hard and too long. Others noted that the white laborers participated in the plantation social life on friendly and relaxed terms with the slaves.[43]

The principal negative comments came not from the slaves but from the slaveholders, who loudly denounced undue familiarity, and especially miscegenation. White laborers allegedly fathered the Mulatto babies who occasionally appeared on the plantations. White laborers, however, did not have the power to force black women except in the general sense that any man might attack any woman. The masters and their sons and overseers did have the power. Sexual relations between white laborers and slave women at least were voluntary acts, not the virtual rape that brought some slave women to submit to masters and overseers. In any case, whatever the extent of plantation miscegenation, white laborers accounted only for a small part.[44]

To the constant discomfort of the slaveholders, their slaves met local farmers and especially poor whites in illicit economic transactions. Despite periodic repressions, the police never succeeded in stamping out the flourishing trade in liquor and stolen goods. Slaves earned a little money from voluntary Sunday work for their masters and from selling the products of their gardens, hunting trips, pig and chicken-raising, and occasional handicrafts. When the slaves traded for liquor, their masters became concerned. When the slaves traded for weapons or forged passes, their masters became even more concerned.[45]

The slaves entered into more direct economic relations with yeomen farmers and artisans by illicitly hiring themselves out to do odd jobs on Sundays, nights, or during leisure hours. The planters railed that this practice undermined slave discipline and wore down their labor force, besides cheating masters of the compensation; but they never succeeded in eliminating it.[46] Many planters sensibly decided to profit from the inevitable by renting slaves to their neighbors. In that way they could protect the health of their property and maintain a sharp eye on those slaves who shirked work during regular hours to be ready for compensated overtime. When rented out by their masters, the slaves lost the payment and risked falling into the hands of someone who would abuse them.[47] In any case, some plantation slaves periodically lived or worked among neighboring white farmers or artisans.

The slaveholders' wrath fell particularly on the many peddlers and grog-shop keepers who infested the rural as well as the urban south. By reputation mostly Jews, Germans, and other foreigners, these petty bourgeois served as scapegoats for those who had to account for slave "demoralization." Yet, in a well-policed society populated with intolerant, violent whites quick to assume the role of vigilantes, not many foreigners could have behaved as alleged and survived. Peddlers and shopkeepers provided valuable services for the slaveholders themselves, especially the smaller ones, and most probably dealt carefully with the slaves. The slaves conducted the greater part of their illicit dealings with local white farmers, laborers, and ne'er-do-wells.

The rural slaves did not, however, often get drunk except during the Christmas holiday season, and their masters' anger arose from different sources.[48] First, the masters charged whites engaged in illicit trade with encouraging the slaves to steal. The slaves regularly raided their masters' hogpens, corncribs, or storehouses for the wherewithal to sell or barter. Second, some of the slaves and poor whites conducted their business amidst gambling and drinking parties at which racial etiquette gave way to a camaraderie the slaveowners considered subversive.

Some of those same poor whites undoubtedly rode patrol, worked as slave-catchers, and enjoyed a well-earned reputation as racist savages. The complexities of human nature being what they are, however, even some white thugs had their favorites among slaves of similar temperament, and they sometimes went to great lengths to protect and befriend them. D. R. Hundley, among other slaveholders, charged that those slaves who traded with dissolute poor whites often qualified not only as trouble-makers for their masters but as bullies to their fellow slaves.[49] But in more attractive instances poor whites formed healthier attachments with the slaves with whom they traded and helped them run away. At bottom, the slaveholders' concern with the illicit trade focused on its potential as a fount of social subor-dination. But their fear demonstrated the existence of some measure of mutual sympathy and friendship across racial lines.

The war brought some slaves and poor whites together in mutual support. If many planters left their poorer neighbors to shift for themselves, many others assumed responsibility, as best they could, for the wives and children of those who had gone to fight. In such cases the burden of caring for the whites fell on the slaves. George Briggs of South Carolina recalled, "When dese poor white men went to de war, dey left deir little chillun and deir wives to de hands of de darkies dat was kind and rich wives of our marsters to care fer. Us took de best care of dem poor white dat us could under de circumstances dat prevailed."[50]

The privations of war turned many lower-class whites against the Confederacy and sometimes led them into sympathetic rela-tions with the slaves. In the Sea Islands, for example, the slaves, according to their own accounts, might have believed their mas-ters' claims that the occupying Yankees intended to sell them to Cuba, were it not that local poor whites told them that the Yankees had come as liberators.[51]

The slaves demonstrated extraordinary compassion for the difficult position of the poor whites during the war. The slaves noted the complaint of the poor that they were being sent to risk their lives to defend the property of the rich. And the slaves also noted the instances of deserters from the Confederate army being hunted down and shot "like a dog." As an ex-slave recalled, "Dey used to say dey had to go and fight a rich man's war but dey couldn't help demselves no better'n us slaves could."[52]

Since the slaves had good reason to fear and hate the non-slaveholding farmers and poor whites, their expressions of understanding appear the more impressive. The evidence could be misleading, since the principal reports come from ex-slaves interviewed many decades later. But those intervening decades had, if anything, worsened relations between blacks and poor whites and could hardly have promoted affection. Sam T. Stewart of North Carolina remarked, "We didn't think much of the poor white man. He was driven to it, by the rich slaveowner. The rich slaveowner wouldn' let his Negroes 'sociate with poor white folks."[53] The many ex-slaves who recalled the lot of the small farmers and poor whites as hard and even as bad as their own knew what they were talking about. A substantial portion of the rural nonslaveholders suffered a standard of living not far above that of the slaves.[54] The slaves saw enough abject poverty, disease, and demoralization among the poor whites to feel sympathy and, at the same time, to see their own condition under Ole Massa's protection as perhaps not the worst of evils.

Lucretia Heyward of South Carolina spoke of having been sold, with her mother, to Edward Blunt, an overseer: "He been poor white trash, but he wuk ha'd and save he money and buy slave." Blunt, a rough man, did not treat his slaves kindly; yet, they responded with surprising objectivity. "Does I hate Mr. Blunt?" Lucretia Heyward continued. "No I ain't hate him. He poor white trash but he daid now. He hab himself to look out for, enty?"[55]

Tom W. Woods of Oklahoma spoke in more general terms:

If de nigger hadn't been set free dis country wouldn't ever be what it is now! Poor white folks wouldn't never

had a chance. . . . Dese white folks wasn't much better
off dan we was. Dey had to work hard and dey had to
worry 'bout food, clothing, and shelter, and we didn't.
Us darkies was taught dat poor white folks didn't
amount to much. Course we knowed dey was white and
we was black and dey was to be respected for dat, but
dat was about all.[56]

Reconstruction revealed that these attitudes had general currency among the blacks. Despite racial animosities and painful
daily confrontations, the ex-slaves and free Negroes who went
to the state legislatures repeatedly insisted that they wanted to
lift up the poor white man, whom they considered to have been
exploited and oppressed under slavery. The work of the black
legislators in education and economic development benefited
the laboring classes of both races. The blacks enjoyed the reversal of roles and their own emergence as paternalistic patrons of
white men, but the sincerity and effectiveness of their measures
cannot be questioned. The defeat of the blacks during Reconstruction in more ways than one signaled the defeat of those
very lower-class whites who muscled the conservatives to power.[57]

The full story of black relationships with yeomen and poor
whites must await much more work on Southern folk culture.
For too long most historians blithely assumed that southern
blacks merely copied the religion, music, and dialect of the
whites around them. W. E. B. Du Bois and Melville J. Hersko-
vits, among others, challenged this assumption decades ago, but
only recently have their claims for a distinct Afro-American
culture won wide acceptance.[58] Nevertheless, neither whites nor
blacks could develop a fully autonomous culture in a world in
which they lived and worked together so closely. The insistence
upon an Afro-American national-popular culture within a larger
American culture—"a nation-within-a-nation"—cannot be made
to rest on the absurd notion that whites and blacks somehow
avoided considerable cultural interpenetration.[59] However scholars sort out the elements for analytical purposes, the growing
concern with Afro-American culture in slavery must lead to a

fuller investigation of southern folk culture as a whole and, with it, of the influences of blacks and whites on each other.

Despite the inadequacies of the present record, which a new generation of social historians is likely to fill out, there already is enough evidence to force a new look at the antebellum relationship of blacks to lower-class whites. Undoubtedly, the slaveholders' regime succeeded in driving a deep wedge between them. But the hints of mutual sympathy and compassion in a world in which so much conspired to sow distrust and hatred suggest that the Reconstruction era was not fated to end as it did. A wiser and firmer social policy directed toward building interracial unity would have encountered enormous obstacles, but it would have had more on which to build than historians have yet investigated.

Notes

1. George P. Rawick, ed., *The American Slave: A Composite Autobiography*, 19 vols. (Westport, Conn., 1972), *Arkansas Narratives* vol. 10, pt. 5: 20. Subsequent citations to these volumes of interviews with ex-slaves will be abbreviated. Thus, this reference would appear as: Rawick, *Arkansas Narratives*, 10 (5): 20. In some cases the volumes are not divided in parts, so that the figure in parenthesis will not appear.

2. There was a vast difference between yeomen farmers—nonslaveholders or even very small slaveholders who owned enough land to support themselves—and "poor whites," who might be poor day-laborers or submarginal farmers who did odd jobs for the planters or dissolute, declassé elements whose numbers are not to be underestimated. In this paper, however, I must blur the difference because the slaves, whose testimony is being quoted, themselves often blurred it. It is not always possible to know what kind of people the slaves are referring to when they speak of "poor white trash," for they sometimes are referring to declassé elements and sometimes are referring to the moral quality of laborers or farmers considered respectable by whites.

3. Frederick Douglass, *Life and Times of Frederick Douglass* (New York, 1962), p. 27.

4. Henry Bibb, *Narrative of the Life of Henry Bibb, An American Slave* (New York, 1969), p. 24.

5. H. C. Bruce, *The New Man: Twenty-Nine Years a Slave; Twenty-Nine Years a Free Man* (New York, 1969), p. 28.

6. Douglass, *Life and Times*, chap. 15; Solomon Northup, *Twelve Years a Slave* (New York, 1970), p. 183, and generally chaps. 12-13. Not all "nigger-breakers" were poor men. See, for example, Benjamin Drew, *A North-Side View of Slavery: The Refugee or the Narratives of Fugitive Slaves in Canada* (New York, 1968), p. 200. (Hereafter cited as Drew, *Refugee*.)

7. Rawick, *South Carolina Narratives*, 3 (4): 171; also, *Oklahoma Narratives*, 7: 243; Bruce, *New Man*, p. 96.

8. Robert S. Henry, *Police Control of the Slave in South Carolina* (Emory, Va., 1914); Northup, *Twelve Years a Slave*, pp. 136-137, 158; Drew, *Refugee*, p. 157.

9. See for example, Rawick, *Oklahoma Narratives*, 5 (1): 77, 136.

10. Rawick, *Alabama Narratives*, 6:212, 340; *Oklahoma Narratives*, 7: 146; *Mississippi Narratives*, 7: 93; *North Carolina Narratives*, 14 (1): 180.

11. See, for example, Rawick, *South Carolina Narratives*, 2 (1): 235.

12. Rawick, *Ohio Narratives*, 16: 88.

13. See, for example, Rawick, *Alabama Narratives*, 6: 43, 164, 256-257; *Indiana Narratives*, 6: 165; *Mississippi Narratives*, 7: 78.

14. Rawick, *South Carolina Narratives*, 2 (2), 70.

15. Rawick, *Mississippi Narratives*, 7: 113.

16. Rawick, *South Carolina Narratives*, 3 (3): 82.

17. Ibid., 2 (1): 161; 3 (4): 165, 204.

18. Ibid., 3 (4): 147.

19. Ibid., 2 (1): 36; *Mississippi Narratives*, 7: 149.

20. See, for example, the lament of a poor white shopkeeper about the haughty attitude of some of the slaves: Gustavus A. Ingraham to Susan Fisher, December 27, 1840, in the Fisher Papers, Southern Historical Collection, University of North Carolina, Chapel Hill, N.C.

21. On the paternalistic aspect of the planters' relationship to small farmers and poor whites see Eugene D. Genovese, "Yeomen Farmers in a Slaveholders' Democracy," *Agricultural History* 12 (April 1975): 331-342, and *Roll, Jordan, Roll: The World the Slaves Made* (New York, 1974), pp. 91-93.

22. Susan Dabney Smedes, *Memorials of a Southern Planter* (Baltimore, 1887), pp. 30-31, 78; George C. Osborn, "Plantation Life in Central Mississippi as Revealed in the Clay Sharkey Papers," *Journal of Mississippi History*, 3 (October 1941): 281-285; Rawick, *South Carolina Narratives*, 2 (1): 105; 3 (4): 2, 39, 119, 148; *Texas Narratives*, 4 (4): 215; *Oklahoma Narratives*, 7 (1): 6; *North Carolina Narratives*, 15 (2): 345.

23. Raymond E. White, "Cotton Ginning in Texas to 1861," *Southwestern Historical Quarterly*, 61 (October 1957): 262, 268; Weymouth T. Jordan, *Hugh Davis and His Alabama Plantation* (University, Ala., 1948), p. 134; Frederick Law Olmsted, *A Journey in the Back Country, 1853-1854* (New York, 1970), p. 201; F. L. Riley, ed., "Diary of a Missis-

sippi Planter," *Publications of the Mississippi Historical Society*, 10 (1909): 427 et passim. For reports by ex-slaves see Rawick, *South Carolina Narratives*, 2 (2): 103; 3 (3): 129, 245; *Texas Narratives*, 4 (1): 62, 112, 217; *Indiana Narratives*, 5: 128, 137.

24. Bennett H. Wall, "The Founding of Pettigrew Plantations," *North Carolina Historical Review*, 27 (October 1950): 408. See also the remarks of Olmsted on the patronizing attitude of the Virginia planters: *A Journey in the Seaboard Slave States* (New York, 1968), pp. 200-201.

25. For examples, see D. Maitland Armstrong, *Day Before Yesterday: Reminiscences of a Varied Life*, ed. Margaret Armstrong (New York, 1920), pp. 77-78; Virginia Clay-Clopton, *A Belle of the Fifties* (New York, 1904), p. 247; Elizabeth Allston Pringle, *Chronicle of Chicora Wood* (New York, 1922), pp. 17-20.

26. Eliza Frances Andrews, *War-Time Journal of a Georgia Girl, 1864-1865* (New York, 1908), pp. 178, 200; also, John S. Wise, *The End of an Era* (Boston, 1901), p. 141.

27. Roger W. Shugg, *Origins of Class Struggle in Louisiana* (Baton Rouge, La., 1939); James C. Bonner, "Profile of a Late Ante-Bellum Community, *American Historical Review*, 49 (July 1944): 669; Rawick, *North Carolina Narratives*, 14 (1): 332.

28. Sarah Kathrine Stone Holmes, *Brokenburn, The Journal of Kate Stone*, ed. John Q. Anderson, (Baton Rouge, La., 1955), p. 5; Mary Boykin Chesnut, *A Diary from Dixie* (Boston, 1949), pp. 25, 137; John Hamilton Cornish Diary, February 22, 1842, in the Southern Historical Collection of the University of North Carolina, Chapel Hill, N.C.; Henry Graves memoir, n.d. but clearly written during the early period of the war, ms. in the Iverson Graves Collection in The Southern Historical Collection, University of North Carolina, Chapel Hill, N.C.

29. Rawick, *South Carolina Narratives*, 2 (1): 14.

30. For some indications of slave reliance on rich whites to protect them against poor, see, Drew, *Refugee*, p. 332; Rawick, *South Carolina Narratives*, 3 (4): 179; *Texas Narratives*, 4 (1): 10-11; *Oklahoma Narratives*, 7: 129; *Arkansas Narratives*, 9 (3): 285; 10 (5): 138.

31. Rawick, *Texas Narratives*, 5 (4): 101; *Maryland Narratives*, 16: 45, 67.

32. Osborn, "Plantation Life in Central Mississippi," *Journal of Mississippi History*, 3 (October 1941): 278.

33. Herbert Aptheker, *American Negro Slave Revolts* (New York, 1944), pp. 233-234; James Hugo Johnston, "The Participation of White Men in Virginia Negro Insurrections," *Journal of Negro History*, 16 (January 1931): 158-167, and *Race Relations in Virginia and Miscegenation in the South* (Amherst, Mass., 1971), pp. 101-104.

34. Rawick, *Oklahoma Narratives*, 7: 252; Thomas Wentworth Higginson, *Army Life in a Black Regiment* (Boston, 1962), p. 110.

35. Lewis Clarke, *Narrative of the Life and Sufferings of Lewis Clarke . . .* (Boston, 1845), p. 25. See also Rawick, ed., *God Struck Me Dead*, vol. 19, *American Slave*, p. 121.

36. Rawick, *South Carolina Narratives*, 2 (1): 206.

37. Rawick, *Alabama Narratives*, 5: 85.

38. Rawick, *North Carolina Narratives*, 15 (2): 345; *South Carolina Narratives*, 2 (1): 228.

39. Olmsted, *Journey in the Seaboard*, p. 674.

40. Ibid., p. 682.

41. Harold Courlander, *Negro Folk Music, U.S.A.* (New York, 1963), p. 164.

42. Contrast the favorable experience of James W. C. Pennington, "The Fugitive Blacksmith," in Arna Bontemps, ed., *Great Slave Narratives* (Boston, 1969), p. 209, with the unfavorable experience of Solomon Northup, *Twelve Years a Slave*, p. 103. See John Brown, *Slave Life in Georgia: A Narrative of the Life, Sufferings, and Escape of John Brown, a Fugitive Slave*, ed. F. N. Boney (Savannah, Ga., 1972), pp. 50ff. See also, Rawick, *South Carolina Narratives*, 2 (2): 77, 92.

43. See, for example, Rawick, *South Carolina Narratives*, 3 (3): 51; *Alabama Narratives*, 6: 106, 279; *North Carolina Narratives*, 15 (2): 345.

44. For a fuller discussion see Genovese, *Roll, Jordan, Roll*, pp. 419-423. Occasionally, a poor white woman serviced the slaves as a prostitute. See, for example, Rawick, *Arkansas Narratives*, 9 (4): 56.

45. Henson, *Father Henson's Story of His Own Life* (New York, 1962), p. 108; G. W. Featherstonhaugh, *Excursion Through the Slave States* (New York, 1968), pp. 158-159; Olmsted, *Journey in the Seaboard*, p. 592; Rawick, *South Carolina Narratives*, 2 (1): 147; *Texas Narratives*, 5 (4): 43. On various features of the illicit trade, including the attempts at suppression, see Genovese, *Roll, Jordan, Roll*, pp. 22-23, 641-643 and the references therein cited.

46. See Moore Rawis to Lewis Thompson, October 28, 1860, in the Thompson Papers, in Southern Historical Collection of the University of North Carolina, Chapel Hill, N.C.; Helen T. Catterall, ed., *Judicial Cases Concerning American Slavery and the Negro*, 5 vols. (Washington, D.C., 1926-1937), 5: 257, 260.

47. See, for example, Rawick, *South Carolina Narratives*, 2 (2): 77, 92.

48. On the extent of drunkenness among the slaves see Genovese, *Roll, Jordan, Roll*, pp. 641-646.

49. Daniel R. Hundley, *Social Relations in Our Southern States* (New York, 1860), pp. 229-230. Also, John Spencer Bassett, ed., *The Plantation Overseer as Revealed in His Letters* (Northampton, Mass. 1925), p. 52; James H. Hammond in J. D. B. De Bow, ed., *The Industrial Resources of the Southern and Western States* (New Orleans, La., 1852-1853), 3: 35; John Perkins in *De Bow's Review*, 15 (September 1853): 277; David Gavin

Diary, February 11, 1859, in the Southern Historical Collection of the University of North Carolina, Chapel Hill, N.C.

50. Rawick, *South Carolina Narratives*, 2 (1): 87.

51. Willie Lee Rose, *Rehearsal for Reconstruction* (New York, 1964), p. 105.

52. Rawick, *Missouri Narratives*, 11: 302; also, *South Carolina Narratives*, 3 (3): 234-235.

53. Rawick, *North Carolina Narratives*, 15 (2): 319.

54. Avery O. Craven, "Poor Whites and Negroes in the Ante Bellum South," *Journal of Negro History*, 15 (January 1930): 14-25; Genovese, *Roll, Jordan, Roll*, pp. 63, 532-533.

55. Rawick, *South Carolina Narratives*, 2 (2): 279, 281.

56. Rawick, *Oklahoma Narratives*, 7 (1): 354.

57. See especially W. E. B. Du Bois, *Black Reconstruction in America, 1860-1880* (New York, 1962), p. 543 et passim.

58. W. E. B. Du Bois, *Souls of Black Folk* (New York, 1961), among his many seminal writings. Also, Eileen Southern, *The Music of Black Americans: A History* (New York, 1971), pp. 94-99, 103; Charles W. Joyner, *Folk Song in South Carolina* (Charleston, S.C., 1971), p. 75; J. L. Dillard, *Black English: Its History and Usage in the United States* (New York, 1972).

59. I have briefly examined a few of these questions in *Roll, Jordan, Roll*: on religion, pp. 217-218, 239-243, and in general bk. 2, pt. 1; on the work ethic, pp. 295-296; on language, pp. 431-441; and on cuisine, pp. 540-561.

THE NATCHEZ NABOBS:
KINSHIP AND FRIENDSHIP
IN AN ECONOMIC ELITE

Morton Rothstein

In comparison with other cities its size, Natchez and its environs has received unusual attention from historians. The interest is understandable, for an unusually high proportion of America's wealthiest families lived there during the two generations before the Civil War.[1] Contemporary critics of this elite group referred to them on occasion as "aristocrats," "cotton snobs," or "nabobs," yet no one denied, then or since, that these landed magnates gave the town much of its unique character. Their legacy of romantic legends and magnificent houses fascinates those who cherish the myths of the "Old South," and their scattered records arrest the attention of scholars interested in the plantation economy. From the time that U. B. Phillips began his work on slavery to the more recent studies of Stampp, Gates, and others, historians have drawn examples of plantation life from individual histories among the "nabobs." In varying degrees, writers have been aware of the complex pattern of family relationships between large slaveholders of the area, but few examined them in detail.[2] The family ties and common interests of several leading Natchez planters reveal much about the social and economic development of an important southern locality and have implications for the region as a whole.

Among the Natchez area families were virtual dynasties, headed by outstanding entrepreneurs who often worked together as a cohesive group. They engaged in many business activities besides plantation management, particularly in commerce and banking. In contrast to the stereotype of the Southern planter as a somewhat naive agragian in chronic debt to his factor, the leading Natchez nabobs were men with impressive abilities to accumulate profits through their various enterprises.

We can trace some of the more meaningful family connections among a group of leading Natchez capitalists through the career of their outstanding member, Stephen Duncan. In 1860 he conservatively estimated his wealth at well over three million dollars and may have been the richest planter in the South.[3] Duncan, born into a prominent Carlisle, Pennsylvania family in 1787, came to Natchez in 1808, shortly after receiving a medical degree from the University of Pennsylvania. He allegedly arrived with only one hundred dollars to his name, but with important family connections. Duncan's mother was a Postlethwaite, another leading Carlisle family, and two close relatives, Samuel and Henry Postlethwaite, had been in Natchez since the turn of the century. Samuel, married to one of "Sir" William Dunbar's daughters, ranked as one of the town's more successful merchant planters.[4] In addition, Stephen Duncan's uncle, the renowned Philadelphian Judge Thomas Duncan, had married a Callendar, a family that held title to a two-thousand-acre tract downriver from Natchez as part of an estate administered by Judge Duncan.[5] With these connections, Stephen Duncan had no difficulty establishing a good medical practice while learning about land purchases and plantation management through helping with family business affairs. Within a few years he married Margaret Ellis, daughter of one of the earliest settlers in the area and heiress to considerable land. Through her, Duncan became related to the Farrar, Butler, Conner, and Routh clans, all of them extensive planters.[6] After acquiring tracts on the nearby Homochitto River, Duncan confined his doctoring to an occasional patient among his many new cousins, and his many new slaves, while energetically building his plantations into profitable enterprises.

In 1815, with the difficult years of land-clearing and adverse wartime markets behind him, Duncan's wife died. Five years later he married Catherine Bingaman, sister of the flamboyant Adam L. Bingaman and closely related to the noted Surget family. About the same time, another of Bingaman's sisters married James C. Wilkins, who was then, with his partner John Linton, the leading merchant in the Natchez area. Wilkins and Linton were also plantation owners, but spent much of their energies during the early 1820s marketing crops and importing merchandise for many of the families mentioned thus far.[8]

By the 1820s, Stephen Duncan had attained a solid position as a leading planter and banker and several of his Pennsylvania kinsmen followed him to the region. His sister's husband, Dr. James Gustine, had spent some time in Natchez during the previous decade, but returned to Carlisle to help his ailing father. In the late 1820s Gustine was back in Natchez to stay, bringing his wife and daughters, and acquired a nearby plantation to supplement his income from medicine. Dr. Lemuel Gustine, James's brother, made the same trek from Carlisle shortly afterward, and with Duncan's help also found a way to combine medicine with large-scale cotton farming.[9] Meanwhile, two of Duncan's numerous Carlisle cousins, lawyers instead of doctors, came in search of opportunity. Duncan Walker and Robert J. Walker became ardent Jacksonians rather than steadfast Whigs like Stephen Duncan and most of his circle, and remained outside the cohesive nabob group, but they did depend on their prosperous relative for financial help and political introductions in launching their Mississippi careers.[10] Duncan also encouraged another Postlethwaite, cousin to the first settlers, to join him in Natchez and set him up in business.

Stephen Duncan contributed more than a stream of relatives to the development of Natchez. He also aided several local entrepreneurs and worked on local projects. For example, he was Andrew Brown's silent partner in the town's leading lumber business, invested in several steamboat partnerships, and led in the promotion of a railroad link between Natchez and Jackson.[11]

Through his various family connections and business interests, Duncan formed strong personal friendships and economic ties with three other Natchez nabobs, attachments that lasted until his death in 1867. William Newton Mercer, William J. Minor, and Levin R. Marshall were, like Duncan, conservative Whigs in their politics, heavily involved in banking and commerce, and owners of plantations in neighboring states as well as in Mississippi.

Mercer was closer to Duncan than were the others; he was nearly the same age, had a Pennsylvania medical degree, and had a similar temperament that combined religiosity with shrewd managerial skill and a broad range of intellectual interests. In the early 1820s he abandoned a career as an army surgeon to marry Anna Farrar, a cousin of Duncan's first wife, and took over the management of the famous Laurel Hill plantation. After converting it, along with other holdings of the Ellis-Farrar-Butler families, into a highly profitable operation, he began channeling his returns into a variety of investments in southern and northern lands, mercantile and industrial enterprises, and banking. After his wife's death in the early 1840s, Mercer turned back much of his Natchez area property to the Farrar family and divided his time between Natchez and New Orleans, where he bought real estate, built a home, and served as one of the more active directors of the Bank of Louisiana.[12]

William J. Minor, son of the famous Don Estabon Minor of the Gayoso regime, entered the Duncan family orbit in two ways. His brother, Stephen Minor, Jr., married Charlotte Walker, younger sister of the famous Jacksonian politician. William went to school in Philadelphia in the mid-1820s and there met Rebecca Gustine, Duncan's niece, whose father had not yet made his final move to Natchez. In 1829 she married Minor and became mistress of Concord, the Minors' Natchez estate. William Minor, some twenty years youunger than Duncan, emulated his kinsman's example by purchasing new plantations during the 1830s, particularly in the Louisiana sugar areas, and by engaging in occasional mercantile and banking activities. Like Adam Bingaman, he had another diversion that tied up some of his surplus capital. Minor, Bingaman and Duncan Kenner, a distinguished cousin, maintained extensive stables of thoroughbred horses and vied for honors in some of the more publicized races of the age.[13]

Levin R. Marshall, a Virginian related to the famous Chief Justice, came to Woodville, Mississippi, in 1817 at the same age as the century and within a few years was cashier of the town's bank, a branch of the Natchez-based Bank of Mississippi. In 1826 he married Maria Chotard, one of William Minor's cousins and daughter of another prominent Natchez planter. In 1831, Marshall moved to Natchez as the cashier of the newly established branch of the Second Bank of the United States. His wife died three years later, and in a few years Marshall married Sarah Elliott Ross, widow of Isaac Ross, Jr., whose father had made the most publicized attempt at manumission in Mississippi's antebellum history. As one of the executors of the elder Ross's estate, Stephen Duncan had been deeply involved in the family's struggle. Each of Marshall's wives, therefore, provided a link with Duncan, and their intersecting business affairs strengthened those bonds. Marshall used his strategic position as a banker to help him acquire several plantations in Mississippi, Louisiana, and Arkansas, and he was absorbed in trade as a partner of a leading New Orleans merchant house.[14]

Thus far, the exploration of relationships between Duncan, Mercer, Minor, and Marshall attests to little more than the inadequacy of previous discussions about family ties in the elite group at one ante-bellum town. This is hardly novel for any southern area, or northern one for that matter. The social and economic significance of family was equally striking in Charleston, South Carolina, Montgomery, Alabama, and in other strongholds of the large-scale planters.[15] Economic historians have also long been aware of the extended family relationships, lasting over generations, that were so fundamental in the cohesion of the commercial-industrial elite in Philadelphia, the German-Jewish commercial banking fraternity of New York, the Quaker businessmen of eighteenth-century England, the Creek shipping magnates of the Mediterranean, and the illustrious Fuggers, to name a few of the more obvious examples.[16]

Nevertheless, the Natchez group differed from most of these other business elites in several respects. They built their enterprises on an agricultural base that was relatively remote from the business centers of the international economy. At the same time that their economic strength grew, they lost political influence in their state and locality. They eschewed specialization, and their loyalties were sharply divided between the Natchez area and the increasingly broader economic and social interests that they developed or maintained in other parts of the South and in the North. In a sense, their behavior resembles the landowning elites of the underdeveloped nations more than the "ingroups" of the North Atlantic economy.[17]

To some degree, they all led and supported much of the social development in the Natchez area. Each of the four men served as directors and supporters of Jefferson College, the area's only institution of higher learning.[18] Each of them served as vestrymen and major financial supporters for the Natchez Episcopal church, and contributed to other local churches as well.[19] Duncan supported at least one ill-fated newspaper, the Natchez *Ariel*,[20] was a leader in the Mississippi Colonization Society, helped protect the rights of free Negroes at Natchez, and contributed to relief work after epidemics and floods.[21] Minor was interested in the Mississippi Agricultural Society, served as captain of a militia company, and engaged in other civic activities.[22] Marshall's best known support of local culture was his role in bringing Jenny Lind to Natchez.[23]

Yet with all their strong attachments to the land, their homes, and their broad circle of family and friends in the area, they do not seem to have had a deep interest or commitment to the town or its vicinity. This was particularly evident after the Jacksonian tide swept through Mississippi, sharply diminishing their political leverage. Increasingly during the last two decades before the Civil War, they seem to have been alienated from Natchez society; Mercer spent less and less time there and more in New Orleans, White Sulphur Springs, and in the North. Minor moved his residence to Louisiana for a time and after he returned to the family home at Natchez, still spent less time there than on his plantations to the west of the Mississippi. In the 1850s, both Duncan and Marshall purchased homes in New York, where they spent as much of their waning years looking after business investments as they did in Natchez. Conservative Whigs and Unionists, all four were bitterly opposed to secession, and when it came, Duncan and Mercer were prepared to sell out all their southern holdings and leave after a half century in the region.[24]

Since each of the four men owned several plantations in two or more states, they had to cope with all the hazards of absentee ownership, including the appointment and supervision of overseers and managers, the coordination of planting, harvesting, and supply purchases, the occasional shift of livestock and work forces from one unit to another. Moreover, their large operations made them perhaps more vulnerable to the usual succession of disasters faced by any planter in the new Southwest—the heavy loss of slaves in the periodic onslaughts of cholera and yellow fever, the dangers of floods or drought, the devastation of plant diseases.[25] Each of the four paid meticulous attention to the details of plantation management in a continuous search for greater efficiency. They were painfully aware that a productive year with good prices might be followed by several bad crops and unfavorable markets.[26] There is little evidence of significant economies of scale to offset these inherent risks, but as members of an economic elite they did enjoy other advantages that were not available to their smaller neighbors. They had more direct contact with the distant markets for which they produced, and they had greater access to capital, credit, and favorable exchange rates.[27]

As early as 1816 Stephen Duncan purchased shares in the Bank of the State of Mississippi, which enjoyed a twenty-year monopoly as a state-chartered institution. In 1820 he became a director of the Bank, was joined in that role by Mercer in the late twenties, and also served as president of the institution, Mercer serving as chairman of the board of directors. In the early 1830s Duncan presided over the Bank's dissolution, forced by the advent of new banks under the Jacksonians.[28] During the following hectic period in state banking, Mercer and Duncan were associated with the Planter's Bank, Marshall and Lemuel Gustine, Duncan's brother-in-law, were leading lights in the Commercial Bank of Natchez, and Minor headed the Agricultural Bank of Mississippi. Through these banks, Natchez planters hoped to finance and market their crops without incurring the usual heavy cost of exchanging foreign credits for funds that could be used in New York or New Orleans.[29] In 1837 Minor, Frank Surget, and other members of the Agricultural Bank's board of directors pooled their cotton crop, some twenty thousand bales, and consigned it to W. & J. Brown & Co. in Liverpool on the Bank's account, with the proviso that Browns' New York branch would "make no charge for negotiating for us."[30] However, only Marshall's bank survived the debacle of 1837, and for the rest of the antebellum period the Natchez group had to rely on other devices.

Smaller planters may have had difficulty in obtaining loans during the 1840s and 50s, but members of the elite group could depend on each other for much of their working capital and long-term loans. Mercer and Duncan, as established patriarchs with wide investments and access to liquid capital through their banking connections at New Orleans and New York, frequently loaned sums ranging from five to fifty thousand dollars to friends and relatives within their charmed circle. From time to time they gave help to Marshall in his local banking business. Duncan provided William Minor with a succession of loans that enabled the latter to make basic adjustments in his planting operations without sacrificing a single thoroughbred. Minor, like all others who borrowed from this source, paid a strictly computed eight percent annual interest.[31] A major exception to the rule was Henry Clay, who received loans from Duncan and Mercer, his long-standing admirers, during periods of personal embarrassment and discovered in his late years that both interest and principal were canceled.[32]

The depression that followed the 1837 crash brought another change which worked to the disadvantage of the smaller producer in the Natchez area, the weakening of direct contact with

European buyers. From at least 1811 to the early 1840s, agents and partners in leading English firms visited Natchez regularly.[33] In the 1830s, ocean vessels took on cotton at the town's docks for direct shipment abroad. After that decade there is little evidence of either type of direct contact available to the average planter. On the other hand, Mercer, Minor, and Duncan maintained close relations with such outstanding Anglo-American firms as Washington Jackson & Company, Alexander Brown & Sons, George Green & Son, and George Peabody. At various times, they served as agents for these merchants, sending credit reports on neighboring "reliable" planters and collecting outstanding accounts.[34] Marshall, of course, had his own contacts through Reynolds, Byrne & Co., his partners in New Orleans.

Neither the ability to pool their liquid assets nor the retention of direct relations with Europe helped meet two additional business needs: a reliable eastern connection that could handle exchange transactions, and satisfactory agents in New York to handle sales on the domestic market of surplus cotton and all the sugar from the four men's plantations.

Once again, it was family connections that helped solve these problems. Four brothers named Leverich, from Newton, Long Island, embarked on mercantile careers in New York during the 1820s under the sponsorship of a friend and neighbor, George Rapalje, then at the zenith of his influence as a prosperous merchant shipper. Some years before another Rapalje from New York, presumably a relative, had married an aunt of Anna Farrar, Mercer's wife.[35] It was an ill-fated match and there is no evidence that the connection meant anything, but soon after James Leverich, the oldest brother, founded his firm in New Orleans, he was regularly visiting the Natchez area and doing business with John Routh and other leading planters.[36] For the next decade, James and Edward Leverich entrenched themselves firmly in New Orleans by serving the city's hinterland. James also entered the banking field and acquired several plantations in Mississippi and Louisiana. The two younger brothers, Charles and Henry, maintained a separate firm in New York, concentrated on the Southern trade, and made alternate annual visits to the region.[37] By the mid-1830s they were periodically at Natchez, courting Dr. James Gustine's two younger daughters. The success of their courtships made the Leverich brothers the husbands of Stephen Duncan's nieces and the brothers-in-law of William J. Minor.

In addition to these assets, the brothers were well known in New York financial circles, had long years of experience and knowledge in arranging coastal shipping charters, sugar and cotton sales, and the purchase of plantation supplies. From the late 1830s to the Civil War and after, the Leveriches performed manifold services for Duncan, Minor, Mercer, Marshall, and many other leading Natchez families. In 1848 they saved Frank Surget who had remained independent in his business connection from embarrassment at the hands of New York bankers. From that time on, the Leveriches had another important loyal client.[38] On Duncan's recommendation, the Leverich brothers obtained consignments and orders from many of the leading sugar planters in the Bayou Teche region, most notably Mrs. Mary Porter, Duncan's neighbor and heiress to the Alexander Porter estate, and William T. Palfrey.[39]

For all of these clients, the Leverich brothers performed the wide range of extra services common among factors at that time. They made advances on consignments, ordered everything for the planters from short, light hoes for younger fieldworkers to vintage wines and brandies, and looked after the sons and daughters who came north for schooling. They did even more for the Natchez nabobs. Almost every spring the Duncan and Minor families came north, visiting Philadelphia first to pay respects to close relatives there, then to New York, Saratoga, and Newport. The Leveriches often entertained them at their Long Island farm (now part of Queens), then usually joined them during August at Newport, along with Mercer, Mrs. Porter, the Surgets, and the Marshalls, for a month or more of cool breezes and association with such people as the Winthrops and Belmonts.[40] The Leveriches helped arrange many of the leases and purchases of living quarters at Newport, supplied the households with food, wine, and carriages. Duncan and Mercer com-

bined this gracious living with business, for they relied on continuous consultation with the Leveriches to guide them in making their numerous investment decisions and depended on them
to supervise their portfolios of northern railroad, municipal, and
land company securities after they returned south for the winter.[41] After the mid-fifties, the Leveriches also looked after Duncan's house on Washington Square and Levin Marshall's new
residence at Pelham Bay during the cold months.

By that time the group described here were the objects of
understandably bitter criticism from the planters still on the
make in the Natchez area. The older nabobs had ranged far
beyond their original full association with the town and its
environs and used the splendid homes they owned there primarily as winter bases from which they managed numerous,
far-flung holdings. The community received no more ostensible
benefits from the four thousand bales of cotton reportedly produced on Stephen Duncan's Issaquena County and Concordia
Parish plantations, the hundreds of hogsheads of sugar from his
and William Minor's Louisiana holdings, or the similar output
ascribed to Levin Marshall's distant properties than from the
nearby tracts run by the Hampton family of South Carolina.[42] If
the Natchez men differed from many other absentee planters in
the antebellum South it was only in the relatively modest beginnings, the steadfast loyalties, the broad range of business ability,
and the remarkable material success that such men as Duncan,
Marshall, and Mercer enjoyed. As was the case with many other
entrepreneurs before and since, family relationships were an
essential ingredient in their achievements.

Notes

1. For the early period of Natchez history, see Jack D. L. Holmes,
Gayoso: *The Life of a Spanish Governor in the Mississippi Valley,
1789-1799* (Baton Rouge, La., 1965), and William B. Hamilton, "American Beginnings in the Old Southwest: The Mississippi Phase," (Ph.D. dissertation, Duke University, 1937). For a sprightly, if not wholly accurate,

journalistic account, see Harnett T. Kane, *Natchez on the Mississippi* (New York, 1947). There are brief, but penetrating discussions in William R. Hogan and Edwin A. Davis, *William Johnson's Natchez:* The Ante-Bellum Diary of a Free Negro (Baton Rouge, La., 1951), pp. 1-64, and in Charles S. Sydnor, *A Gentleman of the Old Natchez Region, Benjamin L. C. Wailes* (Durham, N.C., 1938), passim. A more extended treatment of the postterritorial era is contained in D. Clayton James, *Ante-Bellum Natchez* (Baton Rouge, La., 1968).

2. Ulrich B. Philips, *American Negro Slavery* (Baton Rouge, La., 1966), pp. 209, 226-27; Kenneth M. Stampp, *The Peculiar Institution: Slavery in the Ante-Bellum South* (New York, 1956) passim; Charles S. Sydnor, *Slavery in Mississippi* (Baton Rouge, La., 1966) passim; Herbert Weaver, *Mississippi Farmers, 1850-1860* (Nashville, Tenn., 1945), pp. 47-53, 90, 109-110, 119-120; Paul W. Gates, *The Farmer's Age: Agriculture, 1815-1860* (New York, 1960), pp. 134-152. For a survey of writings on southern agriculture and slavery, see the useful essays by James C. Bonner and Bennett Wall, Arthur S. Link and Rembert W. Patrick, eds., *Writing Southern History* (Baton Rouge, La., 1965), pp. 147-197.

3. The suggestion that Duncan may have been the "greatest planter and slave-owner in the United States in the fifties" was made by Gates, *Farmer's Age,* p. 148; Clement Eaton, *The Growth of Southern Civilization, 1790-1860* (New York, 1961), p. 43, and John Hebron Moore, *Andrew Brown and Cypress Lumbering in the Old Southwest* (Baton Rouge, La., 1967), p. 24, contain similar statements, but there are other claimants to that title. Duncan's estimate of his wealth, by which he planned to leave each of his six children over half a million dollars each, appears in Nicholas B. Wainwright, *The Irvine Story* (Philadelphia, 1964), p. 68.

4. Samuel Postlethwaite to N. Evans, Natchez, August 26, 1804, N. Evans and Family papers, Merritt M. Shilg Memorial Collection and S. & H. Postlethwaite to Thomas Butler, November 3, 1813, Thomas Butler Papers, both at Department of Archives and Manuscripts, Louisiana State University; Kane, *Natchez,* p. 77; Katherine Duncan Smith, comp., *The Story of Thomas Duncan and His Six Sons* (New York, 1928), pp. 41-48. Stephen Duncan's father was killed in a duel over a political argument in 1793; his mother left with five children, then married the much older Ephraim Blaine and moved to Philadelphia, where her home became the center of regular family visits until her death in 1849. Duncan went to Dickinson College, which his grandfather Stephen Duncan helped found, for his B.A., and attended Pennsylvania's medical school when Benjamin Rush was lecturing there.

5. Wainwright, *Irvine Story,* pp. 34-37.

6. There is a Carlisle tradition that Stephen Duncan had married a local girl while he was still in medical school, but that she and their infant died a little more than a year later under tragic circumstances. I found no evi-

dence of this. Family connections between Margaret Ellis and other Natchez area people can be traced in Kane, *Natchez*, passim, and in Pierce Butler, *The Unhurried Years: Memories of the Old Natchez Region* (Baton Rouge, La., 1948), pp. 1-11, 24-27.

7. Stephen Duncan to Thomas Butler, April 11, 1815; S. Duncan to Mrs. Ann Butler, August 29, 1815, Butler Papers, Box 3, Folder 17, Louisiana State University; Stephen Duncan to Mrs. Katherine Minor, December 5, 1828, Minor Family Papers, Box 1, Folder 9, Department of Archives and Manuscripts, Louisiana State University.

8. For information on the Bingaman and Surget Family, see Kane, *Natchez*, pp. 144-146, Hogan and Davis, *William Johnson's Natchez*, pp. 67-68. A brief sketch of Wilkins is contained in J. F. H. Claiborne, *Mississippi, As a Province, Territory and State*, (Jackson, Miss., 1880), 1: 353. Claiborne, whose opinions were not always trustworthy, asserted that Wilkins and Duncan were the "two wealthiest men in Mississippi" before the Civil War. William B. Hamilton and Ruth K. Nuernberger, "An Appraisal of J. F. H. Claiborne, With His Annotated Memoranda," *Journal of Mississippi History*, 7 (July 1945): 131-155.

9. Wainwright, *Irvine Story*, pp. 34-37; Gustine Courson Weaver, *The Gustine Compendium* (Cincinnati, 1929), pp. 89-90.

10. James P. Shenton, *Robert John Walker: A Politician From Jackson to Lincoln* (New York, 1961).

11. Moore, *Andrew Brown*, pp. 30, 38; S. Duncan to Thomas Butler, December 15, 1827, Butler Papers, Box 5, Folder 27, Louisiana State University; S. Duncan to Josiah S. Johnston, March 28 and August 15, 1828, J. S. Johnston Papers, Historical Society of Pennsylvania.

12. Butler, *Unhurried Years*, pp. 12-64; *Jewell's Crescent City Illustrated*, (New Orleans, 1873), pp. 203-208, and Herbert J. Kellar, *Solon Robinson, Pioneer and Agriculturist* (Indianapolis, 1936) 2: 143, contain brief sketches of Mercer. Several of the generalizations here are also based on Mercer correspondence in the Butler Collection. Howard-Tilton Memorial Library, Tulane University; the W. N. Mercer Papers, Department of Archives and Manuscripts, Louisiana State University, and the Leverich Collection, New York Historical Society, New York.

13. J. Carlyle Sitterson, *Sugar Country: The Cane Sugar Industry in the South, 1793-1950* (Lexington, Ky., 1953), pp. 79-80, and his "The William J. Minor Plantations: A Study in Ante-Bellum Absentee Ownership," *Journal of Southern History*, 9 (1943): 59-74; Charles L. Wingfield, "The Sugar Plantations of William J. Minor, 1830-1860," (Master's thesis, Louisiana State University, 1950), pp. 1-29.

14. Kane, *Natchez*, pp. 191-199; *Biographical and Historical Memoirs of Mississippi*, 2 vols. (Chicago, 1890) 2: 397-398; Gates, *Farmer's Age*, p. 147. Marshall's papers are still in private hands of his descendants at "Richmond," Natchez, and there is less information about him than the

other three, but there are some revealing letters from him in the Leverich papers. Also see Theodora B. Marshall and Gladys C. Evans, *They Found it in Natchez*, (New Orleans, 1940).

15. For two interesting collections of letters spanning several generations, see Charles E. Cauthen, ed., *Family Letters of the Three Wade Hamptons 1782-1901* (Columbia, S.C., 1957) and Arney R. Childs, ed., *Planters and Business Men: The Guignard Family of South Carolina, 1795-1930* (Columbia, S.C., 1957). Family relationships are considered in a variety of ways in Clanton W. Williams, "History of Montgomery, Alabama, 1817-1846," (Ph.D. dissertation, Vanderbilt University, 1938). Both Sitterson, *Sugar Country*, and Phillips, in both *American Negro Slavery* and *Life and Labor in the Old South* (New York, 1929) have numerous examples of family ties and their importance.

16. E. Digby Baltzell, *An American Business Aristocracy*, (New York, 1962); Stephen Birmingham, *"Our Crowd:" The Great Jewish Families of New York* (New York, 1967); David S. Landes, *Bankers and Pashas: International Finance and Economic Imperialism in Egypt* (Cambridge, Mass., 1958), pp. 24-27.

17. For a further elaboration of this notion, see my article, "The Ante-Bellum South as a Dual Economy: A Tentative Hypothesis," *Agricultural History* 41 (October 1967).

18. Sydnor, *Wailes*, pp. 204-233; Jefferson College Papers, Correspondence Files, Department of Archives and History, Jackson, Mississippi.

19. Charles Stietenroth, *One Hundred Years with "Old Trinity" Church, Natchez, Mississippi* (Natchez, 1922), pp. 12, 50, 52, 67-69.

20. S. Duncan to J. S. Johnston, October 19 and December 23, 1827, Johnston Papers, Historical Society of Pennsylvania; S. Duncan to C. P. Leverich, May 21, 1857, Leverich Papers, New York Historical Society, New York.

21. Sydnor, *Slavery in Mississippi*, pp. 207-212; Hogan and Davis, *William Johnson's Natchez*, pp. 19, 226, 343; Kane, *Natchez*, pp. 204-218.

22. Wingfield, "Sugar Plantations," pp. 13-29.

23. Kane, *Natchez*, pp. 197-199.

24. The letters from these four men in the Leverich Papers in the New York Historical Society for the period from Lincoln's election to late 1861 are full and detailed revelations of their dilemma. Much the same material can be found in Mercer's diaries at Louisiana State University. Also see Wainwright, *Irvine Story*, pp. 67, 73-74, and my "Sugar and Secession: A New York Firm in Ante-Bellum Louisiana," *Explorations in Entrepreneurial History*, 2d ser., 5 (Fall 1967).

25. Butler, *Unhurried Years*, pp. 35-64; Wingfield, "Sugar Plantations," pp. 92-110; Sydnor, *Slavery in Mississippi*, pp. 45-66.

26. Wingfield, "Sugar Plantations," pp. 29-75; Theodora B. Marshall and Gladys C. Evans, eds., "Plantation Report from the Papers of Levin R.

Marshall, of 'Richmond,' Natchez, Mississippi," *Journal of Mississippi History*, 3 (January 1941): 45-55; A. McWilliams to S. Duncan, June 20, 1858, Leverich Papers, New York Historical Society; Mercer Daybooks, Mercer Papers, Louisiana State University.

27. The rate of exchange between the money from cotton sales in England and money in New York or New Orleans was almost constantly fluctuating and thus was vitally important in any planter's or merchant's reckoning. English notes usually sold at five to fifteen percent premiums, which meant a proportional discount on the planter's proceeds. Access to banking facilities or other connections that could minimize these losses were matters of vital concern.

28. Bank of the State of Mississippi, Stockholders Journal Book, Department of Archives and History, Jackson, Mississippi; Robert C. Weems, Jr., "The Bank of Mississippi" (Ph.D. dissertation, Columbia University, 1951).

29. Natchez was by no means unique in having large-scale planters dominate the local banking facilities. See William H. Brantley, *Banking in Alabama, 1815-1860*, (Birmingham, Ala., 1961) 1. The Minute Books of the New Orleans Canal & Bank Co., Howard-Tilton Memorial Library, Tulane University, show much the same pattern for at least some banks in Louisiana.

30. W. J. Minor to W. & J. Brown & Co., November 2, 1837; Minor Letterbook, 1834-38, Louisiana State University.

31. S. Duncan to A. K. Farrar, April 11, 1850 and October 7, 1858, Farrar Papers, Louisiana State University; Wingfield, "Sugar Plantations," pp. 107-110; S. Duncan to C. P. Leverich, May 2, 1861, Leverich Papers, New York Historical Society.

32. Clement Eaton, *Henry Clay and the Art of American Politics*, (Boston, 1957), pp. 74, 186; *Jewell's Crescent City*, pp. 204-205, refers to the loans from Duncan and Mercer, as did several letters from both men in the Leverich Papers, Jackson, Mississippi, dated from 1849 to 1851.

33. Washington Jackson, head of a firm with branches in New Orleans, Philadelphia, and Liverpool, visited Natchez in 1811, joined the same social club in which Duncan was a member (Butler, *Unhurried Years*, p. 26) and is listed among the first stockholders attending meetings of the Bank of Mississippi. Correspondence of various planter families in the area record visits from George Green, Peter Ogden, and other Liverpool merchants.

34. Wingfield, "Sugar Plantations," p. 19; S. Duncan, Jr., Diary of Trip to Europe, 1856, Louisiana State University; Washington Jackson & Co. to C. P. Leverich, May 6, 1844, Leverich Papers, Mississippi Department of Archives and History, Jackson, Mississippi; W. N. Mercer Memorandum Book, No. 3, 1848, Mercer Papers, Louisiana State University.

35. Butler, *Unhurried Years*, pp. 9-10; Claiborne, *Mississippi*, pp.

131-133, 163, have references to Captain Rapalje. For the New York merchant, see my "Sugar and Secession."

36. James H. Leverich to "My Dear Brother," January 29 and June 27, 1841, Leverich Papers, New York Historical Society.

37. Rothstein, "Sugar and Secession."

38. F. Surget to C. P. Leverich, April 26, 29, and July 22, 1848, Leverich Papers, Mississippi Department of Archives and History, Jackson, Mississippi.

39. For a study of the Porter plantations before 1840, see Wendell H. Stephenson, *Alexander Porter: Whig Planter of the Old South* (Baton Rouge, La., 1934). Phillips, *Life and Labor,* pp. 291-300, has a description of the Palfreys. By the 1840s, the Leveriches were also doing business with such well-known figures as Maunsel White, David Weeks, and Laurent Millauden.

40. For the association with Winthrop and Belmont, see A. Belmont to W. N. Mercer, August 16, 1862, Mercer Papers, Louisiana State University.

41. Duncan had about $500,000 invested in railroad securities alone, and was constantly buying and selling securities.

42. Cauthen, *Family Letters of Three Wade Hamptons,* shows that the family holding near Natchez was little more than an absentee plantation. The Hamptons had little to do with the town, but were friendly with Stephen Duncan and his wife until the Civil War and the discovery that Duncan was a Unionist.

THE *INDEPENDENT*:
INDISPENSABLE CONSERVATIVE IN
THE ANTISLAVERY CRUSADE

Louis Filler

I have held elsewhere that the *Independent,* even when it first began publication in 1848 as an organ of Congregationalism, with sectarian goals, and with a limited ministerial readership, exerted an influence far beyond its parochial principles.[1] This was because of the social weight of its churchmen-editors and their layman associates. In the last years before the Civil War, with a progressively growing subscription list, which reached forty-five thousand by 1860, a more readable format, and a variety of literary successes achieved by such contributors as Reverend George B. Cheever, Harriet Beecher Stowe, and especially her brother, the popular and influential Henry Ward Beecher, the *Independent* became not only a power in the national debate, but one of its most sensitive barometers.

The reason was not only its peculiar brand of liberalism, but also its peculiar brand of conservatism which probed the will and convictions of its varied northern readers and correspondents. Cheever, for example, as a young minister, had published a notorious tale, "Inquire at Amos Giles' Distillery," a dream of intemperance and retribution which dealt with a real distiller and distillery. For this libel Cheever had been publicly assaulted, successfully sued, fined a thousand dollars, and imprisoned for a month. He employed a bold, intemperate prose which gave him national identity. Henry Ward Beecher was not one of the paper's founders, and his first articles for it were tentative in style, as in "A Good Man's Departure" (November 15, 1849), composed of common pieties, and "Vicious Reform Literature" (October 11, 1849), a diatribe against periodicals like the *Police Gazette, Ned Buntline's Own,* and the *Scorpion,* which threw no light on the meaning of reform. However, Beecher developed a vibrancy of his own which charmed not only his female parishioners but their male consorts as well.

Beecher wrote with feeling about life and even about nature in ways they found stirring and evocative. There can be no doubt that he was an opportunist, and that the slavery issue caught up with him, rather than he with it. But his dramatizations of the developing crisis, his "slave auctions" conducted before thrilled and sentimental spectators, though shallow, imparted a sense of the human factor in the slavery debate which vitalized more profound arguments.

Less colorful but more consistently effective in directing and deepening the *Independent* were two others, one a layman. Many Congregationalists of the rising New York merchant class became famous for their religious and philanthropic activities; most famous were the Tappan brothers, Arthur and Lewis, whose church, education, and journalistic philanthropies served almost all moral and religion-oriented enterprises of the pre-Civil War era. They also served the mercantile community. Arthur devised the "one-price" system in over-the-counter sales. Lewis, among his many accomplishments, created what became the Dun & Bradstreet credit-rating business.[2]

However, it was Lewis Tappan's son-in-law, Henry G. Bowen, a dry-goods merchant, once one of Tappan's clerks, also from New England, who led a group of businessmen to founding the *Independent* and defending it against their conservative peers. Bowen was active in management of the paper, and helped support it until the Civil War era when, as one of the most successful and influential of northern periodicals, it was able to support him in the difficulties he encountered.

Another who dominated the *Independent* was Reverend Leonard Bacon, pastor of the First Congregational Church of New

Haven, and a true statesman of both his church and society. His reasoning was that of his times, and one measure of its mixed conservative and liberal potential. His line of thought can best be assessed by comparing it with that pursued by Abraham Lincoln. Bacon's convictions proceeded from religious tenets; the Illinois lawyer preferred legalistic ones. Both met on one issue. As early as 1823 Bacon had prepared a report for the American Colonization Society, whose general program he endorsed, condemning slavery. Other ministers of his conservative mind were unwilling to go so far. In 1846 Bacon published his *Slavery Discussed in Occasional Essays,* a volume which came into Lincoln's hands. One passage of its preface became Lincoln's anchor in his most perplexed moments: "[I] f that form of government [slavery], that system of social order is not wrong—if those laws of the Southern states, by virtue of which slavery exists there, and is what it is, are not wrong—nothing is wrong." Lincoln later echoed Bacon in a famous phrase, and acknowledged his indebtedness to Bacon.[3]

As one commentator observed, it was Bacon's ability to draw a line between the fundamental ills of slavery and the ground which had to be covered before slavery could be eradicated—it was this, rather than the mere epigram, which Lincoln learned from Bacon.[4] "Immediatism" in 1848 was no hidden cause. A generation of Garrisonians and political abolitionists had displayed every argument in its behalf. But the will of the majority, of northerners and nationists, was still to be determined. Both Lincoln and the journalist-ecclesiastics labored at tactics and strategies intended to keep them in full rapport with their constituents. The *Independent* especially, because it was constrained to cope with weekly arguments and emotions, created a tissue of language and rationalizations which was often contradictory, often self-serving, but which kept it abreast of its readers without conceding basic tenets of what were often termed "northern liberties."

The journal began with a restricted circulation. It included a letter from Boston, where it yearned to compete with Unitarianism, and from western outposts which it felt threatened by

Catholic enterprise. It faithfully reprinted long-winded sermons sometimes extending over entire pages in agate type, and reported at great length the 1849 season of annual conventions and anniversaries which drew to New York scores of religious and philanthropic organizations ranging from the American Seaman's Friend Society to the American Society for Ameliorating the Condition of the Jews, the latter an organization for converts.

The *Independent* was respectful to the New York Colonization Society sessions, even though the anticolonizationists led by the immoderate Garrison and the moderate William Jay, son of the late Chief Justice of the United States Supreme Court, had all but cleared the field of them. Their society's secretary, J. B. Finney, recently governor of Liberia, opening their convention, apologized for the absence of all the speakers who had been detained by unavoidable circumstances.

The *Independent* from time to time chided immediatist abolitionists for rude manners and deportment, but it was frequently respectful of their qualities and sincerity. As it said of Wendell Phillips, who spoke in New York at the anniversary of West India Emancipation, "We are not [of his] admirers . . . in his general course for the prosecution of the Anti-slavery cause. But his speeches often contain passages of the finest eloquence, and thoughts and arguments of great value."[5] One issue of the *Independent* reported an "Alarming Growth of Clerical Dignity!" in the tale of a young Congregationalist minister who had accepted a position in the South and promptly turned proslavery. A friend who reproved him for his conversion had received insults and abuse in return. Other issues in earlier and subsequent numbers of the *Independent* looked suspiciously at Senator Stephen A. Douglas's suggestion that California be granted statehood ("Never! until we are certain that it will not be saddled with slavery") and with cordiality the adventures of a young Negro convert in Haiti who had escaped from slavery in Brazil. A patron was solicited to help educate for missionary work in his native Africa: a work vital to the *Independent* sponsors.

Although many *Independent* causes seem today remote from liberalism, they must be viewed from contemporary lookout towers to be properly appreciated. One of the *Independent*'s formidable contributors was Reverend Horace Bushnell, who was then seen as a stormy petrel in church affairs. Arguments defending and controverting him were displayed with no sense of overdoing in the journal's pages. "The time has come," said the *Independent* in its November 15, 1849, issue, "for a sober and dispassionate examination of what Dr. Bushnell has written. We trust then that *The Evangelist, The Puritan Recorder,* and *The Christian Observer* will pursue the discussion in these more favorable circumstances. We will endeavor to do our part."

Bushnell's major tenet from modern perspectives seems innocuous enough. In his *Christian Nurture* (1846) he had argued that "the religious life of children should be fostered by and adopted into the great household of faith, the organic Christian family of the church," as his wife was to interpret it for a later generation. Although this might have appeared an obvious goal for Christians, it was less so for the pre-Civil War generation:

> So much progress has been made in this direction, i.e., in fostering the religious life of the child, that it is difficult for us to realize now the prevalence at that day of very different teachings. The Church of New England recognized no gradual growth into Christianity. None could be admitted to Christian fellowship save those who had been technically converted, passing through the prescribed stages of "conversion of sin and acceptance of salvation." Hence children had no participation in the religious life of their parents, and no rights in the Church as a home.[6]

Such standards of piety help in part to explain doctrines that might have seemed startling in much less conventional social groups. Senator William H. Seward had intended no call to anarchy when, on March 11, 1850, he denounced Henry Clay's compromise measures for settling the country, measures which included a Fugitive Slave Law. Seward had appealed to a "higher law" than the Constitution in his search for justice, but no more so than he and others had done before. To his embarrassment, the North had taken up his phrase and identified him with it in ways which were ultimately to cost him the presidency.

The *Independent* editors, and especially Bacon, played a major part in sanctifying the "higher law" as acceptable to a Christian community. As Reverend Richard Salter Storrs, one of the outstanding New York divines, a rival of Beecher in Storrs's Brooklyn Church of the Pilgrims, and an *Independent* editor put the matter: "It is the duty of each man to obey the Laws of the State except where they conflict with the Law which God has given him. . . ."[7]

It was Bacon, however, who, of the *Independent* staff, inflicted the most measurable blow to the Fugitive Slave Law in the New York area and far beyond. His Thanksgiving sermon of 1851 in support of the "higher law" brought him a letter of approval from Seward himself, mistakenly under the impression that ministerial endorsement had somehow tempered the force of his statement and given it a conservative cast. "Your sermon," Seward wrote, "clears away a mass of sophistries." Seward's subsequent defense of his "higher law" doctrine owed much to Bacon's logic and presentation,[8] though, as it proved, Seward would have been wise to have left explication to others, and avoided the unwarranted tag of radical that he acquired.

Passage of the Fugitive Slave Act inspired a group of New York merchants who longed to conciliate the South. They stood to lose much in loans and patronage if the South seceded. They therefore circulated a call for a meeting at Castle Garden in lower Manhattan to endorse Clay's compromise measures, and put pressure upon Henry C. Bowen and his business partner Thomas McNamee to join them in this project. Bowen and McNamee ensured themselves of a permanent place in antislavery lore by publishing a "card" in the New York *Herald* stating that they wished it "distinctly understood that our goods, and not our principles, are on the market."[9]

Their courage and dedication were beyond question, and their *Independent* openly proclaimed that the Fugitive Slave Law was no law for Christian men. It is significant, however, that events and public opinion in the North sustained them in their crusade. Another of their business associates, also a sponsor of the *Independent,* Simeon B. Chittenden, later a congressman, was frightened by the attendant publicity, and severed his connection with the journal. Half of its six thousand subscriptions were lost. But five thousand new ones were gained.[10] As the decade proceeded, conservative antislavery partisans could feel that popular opinion in the North comported with their own.

As North-South differences sharpened, the *Independent* reflected hardening northern views. Efforts to enforce the Fugitive Slave Law were reprobated, runaway slaves individualized, their wrongs detailed, delicacies in sectional relations given no special consideration. Stephen A. Douglas's threat to the Missouri Compromise, as reflected in his Kansas-Nebraska Bill, was met with intransigence. "Meet it now," the *Independent* advised in its February 23, 1854, issue. By then, Henry Ward Beecher was persuaded of the antislavery firmness of his congregation in Brooklyn's Plymouth Congregational Church, and elsewhere. He urged churches and parishioners to unite against passage of Douglas's bill: "Firmness will give peace; trembling will bring war."

On March 9, the *Independent* printed a column under title of "Nebraska Items": a precusor of the powerful "Kansas Bulletin" which dominated its antislavery features for several years. The column consisted simply of news briefs and comment dealing with Kansas and its future. Highlighted were such items as "Clerical Opposition," "Democracy of Old Trumbull County," "Douglas"—the latter of interest as indicating a species of discrimination which was to win the indecisive northern portion of antislavery constituents away from the Illinois senator's program for compromise, and enable them to endorse what seemed to militants the no less compromising arguments of Lincoln.[11]

Typical of the items the *Independent* printed was one published March 9, 1854, on the strength behind Douglas's bill: "The advocacy of the bill in the Northern states is confined chiefly to that portion of the press which draws its support from the patronage of the administration and to those classes of politicians interested directly or indirectly in government favor." Of interest in the process which was uniting northern opinion were the editors' views in the same issue of Horace Greeley and his New York *Tribune* with the opinions of which it had "not always [been] our fortune to agree," but which had recently been true and accurate on the Nebraska issue. The *Independent* reprinted the *Tribune's* latest article: "Read it and ponder it, ye Ministers of Christ, the country over! Shall men who have been scoffed as 'Socialists' be in advance of religious men on a theme so vast, so wide, and so momentous as this?"

Another note of comradeship, though on a different premise, was struck in "Let By-Gones Be By-Gones," published March 16. A clergyman, Dr. Taylor, had been conservative enough to have merited the praise of the *Journal of Commerce,* a paper Arthur Tappan had founded to provide the public with one free from "immoral advertisements." He had given it up because of its backsliding in this respect. But Taylor had been revolted by the Nebraska Bill. The *Independent* quoted him as believing that "it is best to be united. . . . Whig, Democrat, Abolitionist, Free-Soiler, throw it all to the wind, and go as one man for *Freedom under the Constitution of the United States."*

Independent approval of these sentiments was mixed with reservations, as it added: "If a man brings his by-gones with him, . . . if, while protesting against the Nebraska iniquity, he vociferates as loudly for the Fugitive Slave Law and its infamous concomitants, that is another question."

Taylor, the *Independent,* and Horace Greeley represented a new front rank of northern opinion which had not been there earlier and which required the *Independent* to relate. It performed this function on all levels, through religious interpretation first of all, through secular analyses of various sorts, and through its sensitivity to emotional and social nuances. Its "Editor's Table" for January 13, 1853, had noted no fewer than four novels, all directly inspired by Mrs. Stowe's *Uncle Tom's Cabin.* Of the three proslavery works, one was noticed as the best written, Robert Criswell's *Uncle Tom's Cabin: Contrasted with Buckingham Hall, the Planter's Home,* though it, with the others, was stigmatized as false. The cultural aspect of the *Independent* was given a strong life when, in 1855, Theodore Tilton was added to its staff as managing editor.

Tilton, born in 1835 and a graduate of the Free Academy (later the College of the City of New York) was much like Henry Ward Beecher whom he deeply admired: tall and imposing, emotionally religious, and personal in responsiveness. He quickly made himself noticed on Greeley's paper, then joined the Presbyterian *New York Observer,* moderate in its antislavery viewpoint. Beecher changed Tilton's opinions, he quarreled with the *Observer,* and left it to join the *Independent.* There, by reason of his enterprise, old-fashioned remnants of its journalism were swept away. Tilton brought new contributors in, and was especially active in vitalizing the *Independent*'s pages with verse; the journal "grew into a steady poetry market," and gained "a reputation for good poetry,"[12] much of it now unreadable but at the time adding a touch of grace to otherwise austere or dry pages. In time, Tilton added John Greenleaf Whittier, Elizabeth Barrett Browning, and even William Allen Butler to his contributors of verse, Butler being the author of the light-verse classic, *Nothing to Wear.* All of this lifted the journal's prose to a level which better suited a crisis that affected whole families, including their women and youth.

The editors of the *Independent* were not unmindful of the fact that events, despite their most prayerful hopes, were moving toward a climax of some sort—one which Lincoln was to define in his famous "Lost Speech," in which he held that Kansas must be free while endorsing a "reasonable" fugitive slave law; and in his equally famous prediction (which subtle northerners distinguished from Seward's more frightening perception of an "irrepressible conflict") that the Union could not endure permanently half-slave and half-free—that it must become one thing or the other. Yet such ominous clouds and foreshadowings did not perceptibly quicken the *Independent*'s tempo. There were such articles as William Allen Butler's which dealt with vacation problems. The *Independent* (February 16, 1854) "cheerfully" publicized notice of a women's rights convention prepared by Lucretia Mott, Wendell Phillips, and others, though it took occasion to assert that human life was essentially "bifold," and that woman's place was in the home. From May 1856 onward, however, it fiercely battled to help capture the presidency for antislavery.

The moral question, as James Ford Rhodes expressed it, had entered national politics.[13] The *Independent* now spoke with a new sense of authority for the antislavery enterprise. It had earlier reared in indignation at patronizing and opprobrious criticism from immediatist abolitionists, declaring that:

> [I] f there is published anywhere in these United States a paper that has done more in the last five years for the abolition of Slavery, that has done more to rally the Christian sentiment of the land against that iniquitous institution or that is more feared and hated by the abettors of Slavery at the South and at the North, we shall be happy to learn of its existence, and to do it fitting honor.[14]

It now extended its sense of mission and authority. It overcame its anti-Catholic bias in order to publicize Pope Gregory XVI's landmark Bull against slavery and the slave trade of 1837, and it sought without notable information to range poor whites of the South against their social betters.[15] It spoke with greater conviction and effect as a Republican tribune, imparting a sense of urgency to its "Kansas Bulletin," and quaintly instructing wives in methods for persuading their husbands to vote for John Charles Frémont and against James Buchanan.[16] The October 9 issue published John Greenleaf Whittier's appeal "To Pennsylvania" to vote Frémont into office. The *Independent* campaign mounted in excitement with Cheever's calls for prayer and the editors' October 30 demand for "Work! Work! Work!"

The gathering crisis continued to elicit apocalyptical prose from all the ministers as the Dred Scott decision and its implications for unleashing slavery into the North and West were made known. *Independent* prose was tempered, however, by hopes of peace and by immediate concerns which revealed as much about the public will as about the outlook of the editors and merchant-managers. Thus the financial panic of 1857 dampened abolitionist fervor. The *Independent*'s "Commercial and Financial" section was one of the more faithful northern sources of information in the area. It was conducted by Henry C. Bowen himself, as well as by his business associates. As Bowen observed in his March 12, 1857, issue:

> It is well known that The Independent is the only paper which attempts to publish, weekly, a list of all the failures, assignments, &c., which occur in every section of the country. This list is copied into all the leading journals, far and near, and except in rare instances, due credit is given to us.

Bowen solicited information from correspondents everywhere, warning against "guess-work," or rumors. Hard-headed as Bowen was in business affairs, he believed in the power of confidence, and urged reform in the credit system in the South, though warning that it could not in itself bring about "permanent commercial prosperity." What was extraordinary about his program was the fact that his firm, like many others in New York, was a heavy creditor to Southern merchants and planters who, at the commencement of civil war, would be prompt to default, temporarily ruining him.

"Trust in God," Beecher's leading article for January 21, 1858, advised, expressing the mood of prayerful waiting which the *Independent,* deflated by Fremont's defeat, felt. It shifted attention from Kansas to "Our Washington Letter," seeking to read the attitude of the new Buchanan administration. It followed the succeeding vicissitudes of the "Lecompton infamy," intended to organize Kansas on a proslavery basis, with combinations of hope and indignation. The Buchanan program for the territory became, in *Independent* pages, first a corpse, then revived. It finally passed as the Lecompton-English "swindle" in April 30, while the journal's editors sought support wherever available to delay its passage into law or implementation.

The result of its conservative approach could be seen in the bitter letter sent by Lewis Tappan to Bowen in June, expressing dismay at the *Independent*'s editorial, "Valuable and Influential Men":

> Refuting the charge of being an abolitionist! Placing stress on the fact [sic] that distinguished men, instead of God and Truth, are on the side of the paper!
>
> Such articles weaken the paper exceedingly and will, if persisted in, induce some one to establish a new paper that contends for high principles whether embraced by distinguished men or not. I feel ashamed of such an editorial. The editor should glory in the name of Abolitionist, and think it disgraceful to ... disavow the name.[17]

The apparent lags in abolitionist assertions, however, better reflected the *Independent*'s search for an effective program to combat Buchanan and his associates, than a retreat from antislavery. For the editors were constrained to deal with public apathy as well as aggressive proslavery legislative trickery. Revelations that the slave trade from abroad, barred by law, had increased to an extent that all but constituted a reopening of the traffic, and that New York harbor was its center, roused no wave of indignation, though southern and northern congressmen commented on the phenomenon from opposed viewpoints.[18] In such an atmosphere, the *Independent* could do little more than publicize so notorious an event as the landing of the yacht *Wanderer* in Georgia with over four hundred slaves who were dispersed by traders.[19] It was indicative of the *Independent*'s particular role in the antislavery crusade that its columns reflected not only "the one cause" of immediatists' concern, but other issues which its clerical board judged related to the moral myopia slavery induced. Those issues included a corrupt spoils-system in bureaucratic Washington, and even corrupt public morals, as the editors presumed to see the contemporary tragic killing for alleged adultery of Philip Barton Key by the swashbuckling Daniel E. Sickles.

On a less debatable level, the *Independent* pleaded again and again for national dignity and unity, and denied that the slavery system was popular or profitable in the South. The editors' guiding principle was a minimum program which would strengthen the North against any emergency—even for the unthinkable one of war. Until the last, the editors categorically denied its inevitability. Yet their trend of analysis by indirection prepared their readers for critical tests, as in their assessment of "The Slave Power in Missouri" (July 16, 1857), related to the Kansas struggle, and "The State of Delaware" (August 13, 1857), which utilized statistics and maps in semilogistically military fashion.[20]

The *Independent*'s steady line amid apparent waverings could be seen in its repudiation of Stephen A. Douglas, though it has been reasonably shown that he differed little in basic tenets or loyalty to the Union from his fellow Illinoisan Lincoln.[21] The New York clerics were not persuaded by such views, and brought out the one ground of difference that proved crucial to northern opinion in nuances of morality:

> Let no friend of liberty be deceived by Mr. Douglas's fiction of "popular sovereignty": nor by the like sophistries about "free labor" and free soil for *white* men. The battle of freedom in the nation must be fought on the high ground of moral principle. Better lose ten elections than abate one iota of that principle for a taking political sophism.[22]

Here was an article on which Tappan and his son-in-law Bowen could be at one. How many more there would be to join them in their stand the campaign ahead would reveal. Meanwhile, in response to the question "Who Shall Be the [Presidential] Candidate?" (September 29, 1859), the *Independent* would say only that "internal improvement, . . . the Pacific Railroad, . . . tariffs and the Homestead Bill . . . will be secondary to the one absorbing question of the future policy of the Government against slavery." It went to define a proper candidate:

> He must be ready to declare with Governor [Salmon P.] Chase, that slavery is everywhere and always a wrong; and that he is *"for intervention against wrong wherever the constitution will permit."* We do not ask that a President shall pledge himself to abolish slavery in Virginia, for he has no official right of intervention against it in that state. As a man he should hate and oppose the wrong wherever it exists; but as President he cannot intervene to put down a mob in New York, or to punish murder in Georgia;—we do not ask impossibilities;—but we do demand, the moral sense of the country demands, that the President of the United States shall pledge himself and his official power against slavery upon every inch of soil which is under Federal authority. . . .

With the October 20, 1859, issue, the *Independent* took a long step toward becoming a journal in the modern sense of the word. There was an urgent time consciousness in the article that appeared in columns one and two of the first page. Indeed, its headlines could not be missed: "THE RIOT AT HARPER'S FERRY / An Attempted Insurrection of Slaves." The article was a tangle of rumors and reports. Its editorial, however, repaid close reading:

> In another column will be found full particulars of the late exciting affair in Virginia. It seems to resolve itself into an infatuated scheme of a few men to abet the escape of slaves by a violent outbreak producing

public confusion and alarm. The instigator was a somewhat famous man, known familiarly in Kansas broils as
"Old Brown," or "Ossawatomie Brown." Exasperated
by the outrages of the Propagandists of Slavery in Kansas; having seen four of his sons butchered by the Missouri ruffians; his own life having been threatened, and
hunted for a reward; the old man was transformed from
an honest, sturdy farmer, into a lawless brigand, and
having vowed vengeance upon the authors of confusion
in Kansas, he had chosen to imitate their murderous
forays, by carrying the war into the heart of a slave-
state. As Brown was accustomed in Kansas to get up
fighting expeditions on his own account, and not as the
representative of any party in the territory, so he has
gone into this fearful venture of death, solely on his
own responsibility. Unless his movement was part of a
wide-spread scheme of insurrection, now frustrated by a
pre-mature outbreak; it was in every point of view the
height of madness; and even if it stood related to such a
scheme, it would seem to have been both foolish and
criminal.

That the slaves of the South, whenever they shall
have the intelligence to plan and the skill and strength
and courage to achieve a revolution for their own emancipation, would be justified in this, no Virginian can
deny, who respects the memory of Thomas Jefferson
and Patrick Henry, or the broad seal of his own state.
Deprived of those "inalienable rights" to "life, liberty
and the pursuit of happiness," with which all men are
endowed by their Creator, subjected to every cruelty of
oppression, would it be strange if some bold earnest
spirit among them should catch the lingering echo of
Patrick Henry's voice, crying, "Give me liberty, or give
me death," and should teach Virginia the meaning of
her own motto, *Sic Semper Tyrannis.* . . .

But feeble sporadic attempts at insurrection, when
not only the whole force of a state, but that of the

United States, backed by the public sentiment of the country, can be summoned to crush them, attempts which can issue only in the destruction of their authors, and the aggravated oppression of the colored race, are the height of madness; and any white man who lures on the ignorant and confiding blacks to such movements, is guilty of a crime against them as well as against the laws. . . .

But what a system is that which provokes such horrors, and gives such occasion for bloody insurrection! Where are now the Arcadian pictures of Southern plantations? . . . Are they not the true friends of the South who are seeking the peaceful abolition of slavery at the earliest day?

Here was a review of the insurrectionary effort, written on its heels and in the midst of ominous reports, which—barring widely bruited northern apologetics—has almost historical balance. Nothing is forgotten. Brown is disassociated from any northern parties. His alleged wrongs are recited, but his "murderous forays" are not denied. The right of slaves to revolt is asserted. The criminal nature of Brown's raid is acknowledged, but the mitigating quality of "madness"—no accidental word—is explored.

An article for the October 27 issue, "The Harper's Ferry Troubles," pointed out that "the tragic features of this affair have now given place to the judicial," and that "a mob or riot which in any well regulated town could have been quelled in a few hours assumes the gigantic proportions of servile insurrection and civil war, and for two days convulses a sovereign state and the Federal Cabinet with violent alarms."

Where, the editorial continued, were the "faithful and devoted slaves of which we have heard so much? Why does not Governor [Henry A.] Wise arm the *slaves* for the defense of that divine and beneficent institution under which it is their privilege to live?"

The November 3 issue devoted no more than half a column to Brown's trial: It was a mere report touched with sympathy for the defendant. The editorial, however, maintained the high quality of its predecessor:

> A fissure has suddenly opened at the very foundation of "the peculiar institution" of the South. . . .
>
> When Brown is executed, there will be a strong tide of sympathy for one who even dared impossibilities in the sacred cause of freedom. . . .
>
> Brown's adventures only herald a terrible train of possibilities. He has shown how easily a few resolute men can terrify the whole cowardly brood of oppressors. And if this can be done by a handful of strangers, what may not be feared when the *non-slaveholders of the South itself*—so long regarded with suspicion and contempt by the arrogant aristocracy of slaveholders—shall rise to assert their rights? . . . The voice of Dred still crieth in the Dismal Swamp, as some prophet of the Lord, "Woe to the land polluted with blood." It is idle to deny these possibilities. . . .

It was in a desperate effort to help control the national situation and keep it from falling into war and disunion that Leonard Bacon on November 14 drafted a letter to Governor Wise, a letter not so famous as that that which the erstwhile Garrisonian Lydia Maria Child sent December 17 in defense of Brown and scorn of Wise,[23] but properly capping the long *Independent* campaign for a responsible antislavery policy:

> Sir: I beg leave to communicate for your consideration one fact connected with the case of John Brown.
>
> In July 1857, I was present at a semi-centennial celebration of the settlement of Tallmadge, Summit County, Ohio. A very great concourse was assembled there from all parts of the "Western Reserve," to whom I delivered a commemorative discourse, having been invited to that service by a committee of the citizens. At the close of my discourse I was informed by some of the

gentlemen on the "speakers' stand" that John Brown was there, and that he was desirous of making an address about Kansas. I gave my opinion, of course, that any such address would be entirely inconsistent with the character of the occasion. They agreed with me on that point (though doubtless, nineteen twentieths of all in the assembly were in the heartiest sympathy with the efforts to make Kansas a free state), and I remember hearing, from some of the gentlemen around me, the remark that Brown's mind was evidently deranged on that subject. I cannot recall that I had any conversation with Brown on that occasion; but I had seen him twice at my own house in this city within the six months preceding, and my own impression was that his mind had become diseased and unbalanced in the conflicts and sorrows through which he had passed. The impression of my own was what made me remember the incident at Tallmadge and the remark that was made on the occasion.

It is not for me to argue whether this fact has any bearing on your official duty to the condemned prisoner and to the Commonwealth of Virginia. Yet I trust that I may be allowed to explain why I have ventured to make the present communication. I have thought that while you might reasonably feel yourself compelled to disregard all attempts to prove the insanity of the prisoner from nothing else than the preposterousness and desperateness of the actions for which he has been sentenced to die, you might, at the same time, be nonetheless willing to receive information of any fact tending to show that his insanity was recognized as a fact . . . more than two years ago. If you judge that an accumulation of such facts give you any light in regard to your painful duty, I doubt not that many such facts could be speedily collected. . . .[24]

Wise passed by the opportunity Bacon and the *Independent* offered. His state was unmoved by Bowen's eagerness to offer the South economic and political favors, in an article (January 26, 1860) frankly titled "How to Appease the South." Wise sent John Brown to that death which Emerson said made "the gallows shine as glorious as a cross," and the South as a whole put itself on trial, so far as northern opinion was concerned. Such *Independent* policies so closely drew northern factions together that Greeley himself became a leading contributor to its pages, though his own *Tribune* ranked first among northern papers. Greeley could now declare that the free states no longer feared that Lincoln might gain the presidency.[25] Both he and the *Independent* had practiced forms of expediency, he from a political, it from social and religious standpoints. But their brands of expediency were not to be equated with that which Hunkers and Doughfaces had employed to bury or soft-pedal the slavery issue.[26] The *Independent* more than Greeley had kept northern liberties in constant view, at least so far as chattel slavery was concerned. It had refined its differences from proslavery defenders and northerners whose apathy or intransigence was a danger to a Union policy that could hold together the border and northern states. Better than many, the *Independent* editors could state in their March 7, 1861, issue, as opinion-makers who had helped create the event: "So Abraham Lincoln is President, and the nation is glad."

Notes

1. Louis Filler, "Liberalism, Antislavery, and the Founders of the *Independent*," *New England Quarterly* 23 (September 1954): 291-306; see also Louis Filler, *Crusade against Slavery, 1830-1860* (New York, 1960), 194-197 et passim.

2. Bertram Wyatt-Brown, *Lewis Tappan and the Evangelical War against Slavery* (Cleveland, 1969), passim.

3. Theodore D. Bacon, *Leonard Bacon* (New Haven, Conn., 1931), 179ff. Bacon's church and editorial associate, Reverent Joseph P. Thompson, of New York's Broadway Tabernacle, later recalled a discussion with Lincoln on this point, in an article for the *Congregationalist*, March 30, 1866.

4. Williston, Walker, *Ten New England Leaders* (New York, 1901), p. 447.

5. *Independent*, October 11, 1849.

6. Mary Bushnell Cheney, ed. *Life and Letters of Horace Bushnell* (New York, 1903), p. 250.

7. Richard Salter Storrs, *The Obligation of Man to Obey the Civil Law; Its Ground, and Its Extent* (New York, 1850). Storrs's *Independent* associate Joseph P. Thompson took the same stand in his *The Fugitive Slave Law; Tried by the Old and New Testament* (New York, 1850).

8. Oscar Edward Maurer, *A Puritan Church* (New Haven, Conn., 1938), pp. 136-137.

9. Philip S. Foner, *Business and Slavery: the New York Merchants and the Irrepressible Conflict* (Chapel Hill, N.C., 1941), p. 44.

10. Frank Luther Mott, *A History of American Magazines* (Cambridge, Mass., 1938), 2: 367ff.

11. Lincoln in his 1858 debates with Douglas spelled out their difference in words which dovetailed with the principle that kept the *Independent* on a direct line despite numerous deviations respecting Negro-white differences as the journal's correspondents saw the, respect for Southern attitudes, and eagerness to avoid conflict. Lincoln asserted that he had no desire to bring about "social and political equality of the white and black races." He affirmed his unwillingness to make "odious distinctions" between slave states and free states. At the same time, he saw a distinction between Douglas and himself in that "the Judge is not in favor of making any difference between slavery and liberty . . . he is in favor of eradicating, of pressing out of view, the questions of preference in this country for free over slave institutions; and consequently every sentiment he utters discards the idea that there is any wrong in slavery." (Paul M. Angle, ed., *Created Equal? The Complete Lincoln-Douglas Debates of 1858* [Chicago, 1958], pp. 235, 303.)

12. Mott, *History of Magazines*, 2: 21, 175.

13. James Ford Rhodes, *History of the United States* (New York, 1892), 2: 29.

14. "Misrepresentations Abroad," *Independent*, March 8, 1855.

15. "Conscientious Catholics against Slavery," *Independent*, August 28, 1856; "The Oppression of White Men in the South," *Independent*, August 21, 1856.

16. "How Women May Vote for Col. Frémont," *Independent*, September 25, 1856.

17. *Independent*, January 10, 1908, p. 1352.

18. W. E. B. Du Bois, *The Suppression of the African Slave-Trade to the United States of America, 1638-1870* (Cambridge, Mass., 1896), 178ff.

19. "The Slave Trade Reopened," *Independent*, February 10, 1859.

20. However, not until hostilities actually were under way did the *Independent* explicitly state that "[t] he war which everybody has known to be inevitable, and which has virtually existed since the seizure of Fort Moultrie, has now become flagrant" ("The Beginning of the End," *Independent,* April 18, 1861).

21. They admired one another and considered each other friends. As Lincoln said, their differences were no more than political; when "he and I are together he would no more think of fighting me than of fighting his wife" (Gerald M. Capers, *Stephen A. Douglas, Defender of the Union* [Boston, 1959], p. 183.) Lincoln wept when he learned of Douglas's death. See Robert W. Johannsen, *Stephen A. Douglas* (New York, 1973), pp. 662ff., for an account of the Lincoln-Douglas debates of 1858, and pp. 808ff. for the responses of Lincoln and Douglas to the secession movement and the coming of war, Douglas proving somewhat more aggressive than Lincoln thought it proper to be.

22. "The Douglas Platform: Its False Issues," *Independent,* September 22, 1859.

23. Lydia Child, *Letters of Lydia Maria Child with a Biographical Introduction by John G. Whittier* . . . (Boston, 1883), pp. 107ff.

24. Bacon, *Leonard Bacon,* pp. 458-460.

25. "The Changes of Four Years," *Independent,* July 12, 1860.

26. Filler, "Dynamics of Reform: the Antislavery Crusade, and Others; with Something about the Negro," *Antioch Review,* 27 (Fall 1967): 362ff.

ANDREW JOHNSON AND THE FAILURE OF RECONSTRUCTION

Hans L. Trefousse

In no field of inquiry into American history have greater changes taken place than in the study of Reconstruction. Modern historians have completely reversed the interpretations of William A. Dunning and his successors.[1] It was a reassessment long overdue, and it is not surprising that the rewriting of post-Civil War history is continuing.

There is, however, a danger that reinterpretations not based on solid evidence will gain acceptance merely because they are challenging. When we are told that in view of Southern intransigence, any policy based on Southern cooperation was doomed to failure from the beginning,[2] we must reexamine the facts, no matter where such inquiry may lead. And while there are assuredly indications that the ex-Confederates were obstinate, it is nevertheless not at all certain that no northern policy based on Southern collaboration could have worked. Such an assumption underestimates President Johnson's actions, and, as James Ford Rhodes pointed out long ago, Johnson played a crucial role in Reconstruction.[3]

When Johnson became President, his basic views were not fully understood. Southerners feared him; Democrats considered him an apostate; and radicals hoped for executive support for their policies. "Johnson, we have faith in you," Benjamin F. Wade said to him on the day after Lincoln's death. "By

135

the gods, there will be no trouble now in running the government." "You can judge my policy by the past," replied the
President. "Everybody knows what that is. . . . Treason must be
made infamous and traitors impoverished." In subsequent conferences with his erstwhile associates on the Joint Committee
on the Conduct of the War, he expressed the hope that leading
rebels would be executed. So bloodthirsty did he seem that the
radical Ben Wade feared the President might go too far.[4]

Johnson, however, had not formulated any thoroughly matured plans. While he favored punishing insurgent leaders, fundamentally, he distrusted the radicals. He was a Southerner,
albeit a passionate Unionist. Before the war, he had even owned
a few slaves. And much as he despised the wealthy landowners,
aristocrats whom he held responsible for secession and its con-
sequent disasters, he was convinced that blacks were inferior to
whites. He fervently believed in democracy, but restricted its
application to the white race. Blacks must remain subordinate.[5]

It was a great pity that the President of the United States
entertained such ideas. The period immediately following the
surrender was decisive. If any policy was to be undertaken with
hope of success, it had to be initiated at that moment, even if it
were to be unpopular in the former Confederacy. And since the
success of Reconstruction finally came to depend on black suffrage, this was the time to introduce it.

In April of 1865, the South was prostrate. Its territory devas-
tated, its plantations ruined, and its labor forced scattered, it
was stunned. Hoping for little, it expected the worst. All that
Southern whites knew was that they had been defeated. They
had no idea what the victors would do or demand of them.

Evidence of this feeling of submission is easy to find. News-
papermen, travelers, and government agents reported it, and
testimony taken early in 1866 by the Reconstruction Committee
seemed conclusive on this point. As John Minor Botts, the famous Virginia Unionist, told the committee: "At the time of
the surrender of General Lee's army and the restoration of
peace . . . there was, not only a general, but an almost universal,
acquiescence and congratulation among the people that the war

had terminated, and a large majority of them were at least contented, if not gratified, that it had terminated by a restoration of the State to the Union. At that time, the *leaders,* too, seemed to have been entirely subdued . . . and a more humble, unpretending set of gentlemen I never saw than they were at that time."[6] Soon after Appomattox, the writer John T. Trowbridge, journeying through Virginia, heard pledges of loyalty from former insurgents, while Watkins James, the Unionist Assistant Federal Assessor at Winchester, described the people in the Shenandoah Valley early in 1865 as "quiet, peaceable, disposed to submit to almost anything."[7] Loyalists found the inhabitants of Richmond willing to welcome them back, and Jonathan Roberts, the Unionist sheriff of Fairfax County near Washington, corroborated this testimony. "As soon after the surrender of Lee as the rebels could get home," he told the committee, "they all seemed to be perfectly happy with everything."[8]

Parallel conditions prevailed in the Carolinas. In North Carolina, the editor of the Raleigh *Press* told the journalist Whitelaw Reid that he was anxious for the speediest possible restoration of civil authority and believed the people to be willing to acquiesce in whatever basis of reorganization the President might prescribe. If he had his way, he would not countenance Negro suffrage; even that humiliation, however, would be preferable to remaining unorganized and would be accepted by the people, although it would cause great dissatisfaction.[9] His statements were confirmed by one of John Covode's correspondents, who informed the radical Pennsylvania Congressman that the people of the Old North State inclined "strongly towards reunion."[10] And even in South Carolina, the cradle of secession, the defeated insurgents, hostile though they were, were not actively resisting in order to save themselves, at least according to General Quincy A. Gillmore, who had recently been in command of the Department of the South.[11]

Similar reports came from Alabama. As Mailton Safford, a local Unionist, remembered: "Immediately after the surrender of the Confederate forces, the rebel influence was very much appalled, overthrown, and destroyed there. The rebels were very much subjugated . . . and made strong professions of submission to the government." George E. Spencer, a northern officer who later represented the state in the national Senate, corroborated Safford's statement. Testifying before the Reconstruction Committee, he recalled that "immediately after the surrender of the armies of the Confederacy the people were willing to accept the condition of things as they were. They only asked to be allowed to live there."[12]

Elsewhere in the South, the situation was no different. Reid found that the population of Georgia was willing to submit, without opposition, to whatever the government might demand.[13] General Israel Vodges assured Chief Justice Salmon P. Chase that in Florida planters were willing to let bygones be bygones, provided their cotton was not confiscated, and in Louisiana, according to the Unionist Judge Rufus K. Howell, immediately after the surrender, the two parties, loyalists and their opponents, were almost evenly balanced.[14] When General George A. Custer first arrived in Texas, he found the inhabitants "as regards their sentiments towards the government, to be as satisfactory as any loyal man could wish. They made use of no expressions hostile to the government . . . or against the policy of the government. On the contrary they regarded the result of the war as final . . . and were willing to conform to any conditions the general government might see fit to impose."[15] In Memphis, old residents held a Meeting of Southern People from Western Tennessee, Mississippi, and Arkansas, which adopted resolutions pledging their active cooperation to any measures that might be thought best to effect the restoration of the government, and all the Little Rock *Arkansas State Gazette* hoped for was a mild peace. The paper reprinted a letter from the abolitionist Gerrit Smith warning against executions.[16] Even such extreme measures were not believed to be beyond the realm of possibility.

Summing up the evidence, Whitelaw Reid asserted that in May and June 1865, "the National Government could at that time have prescribed no conditions for the return of the rebel

States which they would not promptly have accepted,"[17] a conclusion in which Carl Schurz fully concurred. As he wrote in 1865 in his official report, "The public mind was so despondent [in the South] that if readmission at some future time under whatever conditions had been promised, it would then have been looked upon as a favor."[18]

Under these conditions, action was called for at once. In April 1865, Virginia federal Judge John C. Underwood, a lifelong Unionist, expressed this very clearly in a letter to the Chief Justice. "It seems to me that a *little* vigor now would be worth more than *much* hereafter," he warned, cautioning against the malignancy of returning insurgents. Carl Schurz likewise alerted his friends. "No time should be lost," he wrote to Charles Sumner on May 9. "If we only make a vigorous start in the right direction the problem will be easily solved. But if too much latitude is given to the mischievous elements in the South for the next few weeks, it will be exceedingly difficult to set matters right again. . . . "[19]

Andrew Johnson missed this opportunity. Anxious to bring back the Southern states with minimum guarantees before Congress met, he announced his lenient policy on May 29. Offering amnesty to all but high Confederate officials and those worth more than twenty thousand dollars, he called on the legal voters of the South to reorganize the government, first of North Carolina, and then of other states. Even the exempted classes had no trouble receiving special pardons. All that the new governments were asked to do was to nullify the secession ordinances, repudiate the Confederate debt, and ratify the Thirteenth Amendment, conditions upon which Johnson did not always insist. Since the legal voters were those who had been enfranchised in 1860, Negroes were not given the suffrage, and the President did not make much of an effort to extend it even to the most qualified and intelligent blacks.[20]

Johnson's actions had an immediate effect on the morale of Southern conservatives. Apparently the federal government was not only going to be lenient, it was about to return to power those who only recently had sought to overthrow it.

The result was electrifying. When Whitelaw Reid arrived in Alabama, the President's amnesty proclamation had just been published, and the journalist noticed a marked change from the atmosphere he had encountered on the Atlantic coast. "There they were just as vehement in their protestations against negro suffrage," he wrote, "but they ended in entreaties that the conquerors would spare the infliction of such disgrace. Here [in Mobile] came threats. Everywhere else it was manifest that if the restoration of civil authority depended on negro suffrage, then negro suffrage would be accepted. Here, for the first time, we were told the people would not stand it! The explanation is simple. They were just beginning to get knowledge of the North Carolina Proclamation, and to imagine that the President was willing to concede to them more power than they had dared to hope. . . . They had been offered an inch; they were soon seen to be clamoring for ells."[21]

Reid's observations were borne out by others. Trowbridge found that in New Orleans, the President had disheartened Unionists by restoring their enemies to office, and Howell insisted that "after the policy of the President began to be understood [in the city]," the old feeling of hatred returned.[22] In Texas, Custer discovered that the conservatives became "more defiant" after the promulgation of the proclamation, and in Virginia, Jonathan Roberts noticed the unfavorable effects of the President's policy.[23] Unionists in Richmond found themselves shunned as soon as Johnson's course became known; they were sued when leading Confederates received pardons.[24] The Assistant Superintendent of the Freedmen's Bureau in Culpepper County made similar observations. Johnson's policy, said W. L. Chase, "has been the cause of their [the Confederates'] demanding what they had no right to demand, and making them more bitter to government generally, especially to the people of the north."[25] As if to underline this testimony, on May 30, 1865, the Petersburg *Daily News,* commenting on the proclamation, boasted that it had been right about Johnson. He had proven that he was not "likely to stand idle, while black stars were substituted for white in the banner of the Union."[26]

Others reported similar developments. "Whatever genuine Unionist sentiment was forming and would in time have grown up," the Mississippi Republican R. W. Flournoy wrote to Thaddeus Stevens in November, "has been checked by Mr. Johnson's course. He has made a great mistake. He is now the favorite of all the disaffected elements here. . . . "[27] Even Johnson's own appointee, Governor William W. Holden of North Carolina, after suffering an electoral defeat, wrote to him in December: "In May and June last these rebellious spirits would not have dared to show their heads, even for the office of constable; but leniency has emboldened them and the copperhead now shows his fangs."[28] F. Y. Clark told the President the same thing about Georgia. "Before the pardons were granted," he reported, "political instigators were held in check. They were all endeavoring to see who could do the most for you and magnifying little acts of courtesy to Union men during the war into great deeds. Now that they all have their pardons they are on the other track. . . . "[29] In South Carolina General Quincy A. Gillmore reported the former insurgents were delighted with Johnson, and Gideon Welles heard that the subdued feeling generally prevailing in June and July had given way to one of obstinacy and bitterness, especially in the Palmetto State.[30] The Little Rock *Arkansas State Gazette* pointed to "the singular fact" that the states rather than the federal government were to decide the suffrage qualifications;[31] throughout the South, conservatives had been given renewed hope.

Southerners themselves fully realized what they owed to the President. The man who had once been excoriated throughout the Confederacy as a traitor to his section now became a hero to his conservative supporters. One railroad official, who claimed to have saved Johnson in 1861 from an infuriated mob in Lynchburg, insisted that he was happy to have performed so important a service for the country. He had been a rebel, believing in the secessionist cause. But now he and his associates considered Johnson's course to have been "just, independent, an highly satisfactory," and they prayed to God that the President might be permitted to remain at the head of the government.[32] A. O. P. Nicholson, a well-known Tennessee secessionist, also praised his fellow citizen in the White House. "My hope and that of our people has been centered on you," he wrote, "and I can safely say, that at no time of your life have you enjoyed so much of the confidence of our people since your policy as President has been developed."[33] The South Carolina constitutional convention passed resolutions of cooperation and appreciation, and the Raleigh *Daily Sentinel* suggested that the South support Johnson for the Presidency in 1868.[34]

The most varied testimonials of Southern conservatives' good will reached the White House. The rector of St. James' Church in Richmond commented upon people's great respect for the President. Even the women were becoming "harmonized," he asserted, and while they still considered the Southern cause right in itself, they thanked God that Andrew Johnson of Tennessee was in the executive chair.[35] A. G. Brown of Mississippi, who had once served with Johnson in the national House of Representatives, thought that the President's course was giving the South peace and all the prosperity it could hope for.[36] The prominent North Carolina conservative, Kenneth Rayner, assured the President that there was but one feeling prevailing with unanimity in the South, a strong and abiding faith in Johnson's ultimate triumph and success. It was all that sustained Southerners against despair. "President Johnson is our only hope," was the usual comment.[37]

The most striking tokens of appreciation came from the leaders of the defunct Confederacy. General Robert E. Lee declared that the people of the South, desiring the restoration of civil government, looked upon "the policy of the President as the one which would most clearly and most surely reestablish it."[38] It was a sentiment with which Alexander H. Stephens, the Vice-President of the insurgent regime, fully agreed. "With hopes that you may be sustained in your physical strength to bear you through your Herculean work, & that your patriotic efforts at restoration of union harmony & prosperity may be successful," he wrote, "I need not repeat . . . the assurance of my cordial and earnest cooperation with you in your exertions."[39]

Thus Johnson, by his policies, had reanimated the Southern spirit. As a former Confederate officer confessed to him, twelve months earlier he was as bitter in his feelings toward the President as it was possible to be because he regarded Johnson as the exponent of that faction in the North "who made, and still make it their religion to insult and oppress the people of the South." He did not entertain any better feelings toward that party now, he concluded, "but as for yourself, you have created an admiration and enthusiasm in my breast that really astonishes myself. I look upon you as the savior of the South."[40]

Johnson's successful interference with Republican plans for Reconstruction was a continuing effort. In 1865, he failed to take advantage of Southern submissiveness and gave the former insurgents new hope. In 1866 and early 1867, his adamant opposition to congressional proposals rendered these nugatory. The unsuccessful attempt to remove him in 1868 only encouraged the conservatives further.[41]

It is at least conceivable that in the winter of 1866-67, an adjustment might still have been made. Southern cooperation for a Reconstruction program might have been won had not the administration interfered. In June 1866, both houses recommended to the states the adoption of the Fourteenth Amendment. Because its requirements were not unduly harsh, it might have served as a basis for restoring the South with Southern cooperation. But the President said no.

The provisions of the amendment required little of the South. It was then not fully understood that the due-process clause would revolutionize the Constitution. The possible reduction of representation for states that discriminated against large classes of potential voters was not an unreasonable demand, and the nonpayment of the Confederate debt was a condition Johnson himself had recommended. The only punishment for insurgency was the disfranchisement of those leading Confederates who had previously sworn to uphold the Constitution of the United States, and even they were eligible for an amnesty. When Tennessee ratified the amendment, the state was promptly restored.

The radicals were not at all satisfied with the amendment. Charles Sumner voted for it only with reluctance.[42] The New York *Herald* considered it a repudiation of Thaddeus Stevens's ideas.[43] The *National Anti-Slavery Standard* characterized it as a surrender of the Negro, and the *Independent* scathingly critized Congress for its abandonment of principle.[44] Years later, the old radical George W. Julian still referred to it as "a proposition to the Rebels that if they would agree that the negroes should not be counted in the basis of representation, we would hand them over, unconditionally, to the tender mercies of their old masters."[45] But Congress made the offer, and there seemed to be a chance that the President and the South would accept it.

Johnson disliked the amendment from the beginning. Having expressed his objections as it was being considered in committee, he saw no reason to change his mind when it was passed.[46] He denounced it "in the most decided terms of hostility" to Secretary of the Interior Orville H. Browning. When Secretary of the Navy Gideon Welles told him there were rumors that it would serve as a basis for compromise between the administration and Congress, he interrupted to say that he was opposed to any amendment while any portion of the states were excluded from Congress.[47] He had already vetoed the Civil Rights Bill; his objections to its provisions applied with equal force to the amendment.

Nevertheless, there was widespread speculation that he might change his mind. The New York *Herald* believed the controversy between the President and Congress might be settled if the Southern states adopted the constitutional change; others agreed, and especially after the first Republican victories in the fall, there seemed to be some hope that the President might give in.[48]

But these expectations were to be disappointed. On October 24, the Secretary of the Interior published a letter condemning the proposed amendment, and his opinion was widely interpreted as an expression of the President's stance. As Eric L. McKitrick pointed out some years ago, the South was not slow to notice.[49]

When the majority Republicans decisively won the elections of 1866, a new opportunity arose to secure Southern acceptance of the amendment. Several Southern notables, among them the Governors of Virginia, Louisiana, and Arkansas, recommended such a course. But public opinion in the former Confederacy was opposed, especially to the disfranchisement provisions.[50] Without help from Washington, the amendment could not be ratified.

Instead of extending help, the President encouraged opposition. Secure in the knowledge of Johnson's stand, Southern newspapers proclaimed that they preferred his policies to those of Congress,[51] and the result was a foregone conclusion. In state after state, the amendment failed by overwhelming majorities.

The President's known opposition to the amendment might have been sufficient to defeat it, but his direct interference sealed its fate. In Alabama, Governor R. M. Patton, after first counseling resistance to the proposal, finally recognized that it might be the best solution for the South. Consequently, he informed his legislature that Congress would never offer any better terms and urged ratification. But just before the lawmakers were about to vote, Lewis E. Parsons, the former Governor then in Washington, sent a message advising rejection. Thereupon, on December 7, 1866, Alabama voted not to ratify.

Patton, however, refused to give up. Seeking to secure a reconsideration, he hoped to obtain support. But whatever chance he might have had was ruined by the arrival of still another message from Washington, this time from Johnson himself. Addressed to ex-Governor Parsons, who had sought the President's advice, it stated:

What possible good can be obtained by reconsidering the constitutional amendment? I know of none in the present state of affairs; and I do not believe the people of the whole country will sustain any set of individuals in attempts to change the whole character of our Government by enabling acts or otherwise. I believe, on the contrary, that they will eventually uphold all who have

the patriotism and courange to stand by the Constitution, and who place their confidence in the people.
There should be no faltering of those who are honest in
their determination to sustain the several coordinate
departments of the Government, in accordance with its
original design.

Needless to say, the legislature did not reconsider its vote.[52]

At the same time that Alabama politicians were wavering in
their opposition, South Carolina lawmakers were also contemplating a last-minute switch. A senate caucus selected Colonel
J. C. Weatherly to travel to Washington in order to ascertain the
attitude of the President as well as of the leading Republicans.
Did they consider the Fourteenth Amendment a final condition
for readmission? The colonel's findings would be decisive back
home.

When Weatherly arrived in the capital, he found that he could
not obtain any definite answers from congressional leaders. But
be had no trouble discovering Johnson's position. The President
was unequivocally opposed to the amendment. Thereupon the
South Carolina legislature abandoned all plans to reconsider.[53]

In Virginia, too, the prospects for ratification were not entirely unfavorable. The Governor urged acceptance, and General
John M. Schofield, the local commander, lent his influence to
secure a positive response. He even visited Washington to obtain
assurances that the amendment would be the final condition for
the restoration of the state. When he returned to Richmond,
however, "other influences, understood to come from some
source in Washington (probably President Johnson), finally prevailed." The amendment was rejected.[54] The President himself
had squelched a promising development in the South.

One final piece of evidence exists to show that Southern cooperation for Reconstruction could have been obtained. Toward the end of January 1867, when radical Reconstruction
measures were being prepared in Congress, Johnson finally began to contemplate a compromise of his own. He signified his
approval of a constitutional amendment which would state the

Union to be perpetual and contain all the provisions of the Fourteenth Amendment except disfranchisement. Senator James Dixon introduced it, and Johnson conferred with such Southern emissaries as William L. Sharkey of Mississippi, William Marvin of Florida, James L. Orr of South Carolina, and Jonathan Worth of North Carolina.[55] Such sponsorship by governors and former governors might have been successful, but it was too late. The North refused to give up the disfranchisement clauses of the Fourteenth Amendment.[56] Nevertheless, the consideration of the alternate plan demonstrates that with Johnson's help his Southern supporters might have been much more cooperative.

It is therefore evident that assertions of the utter impossibility of any Reconstruction scheme depending on Southern collaboration are incorrect. It was with considerable justice that Christopher Memminger, the former Confederate Secretary of the Treasury, concluded in 1871 in a letter to Carl Schurz:

> I think you are right in saying that if we had originally adopted a different course as to the negroes, we would have escaped present difficulties. But if you will consider a moment, you will see that it was as impossible, as for us to have emancipated them before the war. The then President held up before us the hope of a "white man's government," and this led us to set aside negro suffrage."[57]

The President did have the power to intefere; he used it, and he must bear much of the blame for the failure of Reconstruction.

Notes

1. Eric L. McKitrick, *Andrew Johnson and Reconstruction* (Chicago, 1963); W. R. Brock, *An American Crisis: Congress and Reconstruction, 1865-1867* (New York, 1963); John Hope Franklin, *Reconstruction After the Civil War* (Chicago, 1961); LaWanda Cox and John H. Cox, *Politics,*

Principles, and Prejudice, 1865-1866 (New York, 1963); Kenneth P. Stampp, *The Era of Reconstruction, 1865-1877* (New York, 1965); Hans L. Trefousse, *The Radical Republicans: Lincoln's Vanguard for Racial Justice* (New York, 1969).

2. Michael Perman, *Reunion Without Compromise: The South and Reconstruction, 1865-1868* (London, 1973), pp. 10ff. et passim.

3. James Ford Rhodes, *History of the United States from the Compromise of 1850* (New York, 1895), 6: 115ff. Professor Perman concedes that Johnson's "shortcomings aggravated the difficulty." (Perman, *Reunion Without Compromise*, p. 10.)

4. "George W. Julian's Journal, The Assassination of Lincoln," *Indiana Magazine of History*, 11 (December 1915): 335; James G. Blaine, *Twenty Years of Congress* (Norwich, Conn., 1884), 2: 14.

5. Charles Nordhoff to W. C. Bryant, February 2, 1867, Bryant-Godwin Collection, New York Public Library; William G. Moore Diary, April 9, 1868, Andrew Johnson Papers, Library of Congress, Washington, D.C.; Cox and Cox, *Politics, Principle, and Prejudice*, pp. 151ff.

6. *Report of the Joint Committee on Reconstruction*, H. R. No. 30, 39 Cong., 1 sess., 1866 (hereafter cited as *RJCR*), pt. 2: 120.

7. J. T. Trowbridge, *The South: A Tour of Its Battle Fields and Ruined Cities, A Journey Through the Desolated States and Talks with the People* (Hartford, Conn., 1866), pp. 188-189; *RJCR*, pt. 2: 42.

8. *RJCR*, pt. 2: 140, 33.

9. Whitelaw Reid, *After the War: A Tour of the Southern States, 1865-66*, ed. C. Vann Woodward (New York, 1965), p. 44.

10. John W. Gauss to Covode, April 23, 1865, John Covode Papers, Historical Society of Western Pennsylvania, Pittsburgh, Pa.

11. Q. A. Gillmore to Chase, July 27, 1865, Salmon P. Chase Papers, Historical Society of Pennsylvania, Philadelphia.

12. *RJCR*, pt. 3: 60, 9.

13. Reid, *After the War*, p. 153.

14. Israel Vodges to Chase, June 7, 1865, Salmon P. Chase Papers, Library of Congress, Washington, D.C.; *New Orleans Riots*, H. R. No. 16, 39 Cong., 2 sess., 1867, p. 50.

15. *RJCR*, pt. 4: 73.

16. Chicago *Tribune*, May 10, 1865; Little Rock *Arkansas State Gazette*, May 10, 15, 1865.

17. Reid, *After the War*, p. 295.

18. *Speeches, Correspondence and Political Papers of Carl Schurz*, ed. Frederick Bancroft (New York, 1913), 1: 282.

19. John C. Underwood to Salmon P. Chase, April 28, 1865, Chase Papers, Library of Congress; Schurz, *Speeches*, 1: 255.

20. He suggested to the Governor of Mississippi that the most intelligent and wealthy blacks be enfranchised so that the radicals would be

"foiled." Edward McPherson, ed., *The Political History of the United States of America During the Period of Reconstruction* (Washington, D.C., 1871), pp. 19-20.

21. Reid, *After the War*, pp. 219-20.

22. Trowbridge, *The South*, p. 406; *New Orleans Riot*, p. 50.

23. *RJCR*, pt. 4: 73; pt. 2: 33.

24. Ibid., pt. 2: 140, 34.

25. Ibid., pt. 2: 96.

26. Petersburg *Daily News*, May 30, 1865.

27. R. W. Flournoy to Stevens, November 20, 1865, Thaddeus Stevens Papers, Library of Congress.

28. W. W. Holden to Johnson, December 6, 1865, Johnson Papers, Library of Congress.

29. F. Y. Clark to Johnson, December 4, 1865, Johnson Papers, Library of Congress.

30. Q. A. Gillmore to Chase, July 27, 1865, Chase Papers, Historical Society of Pennsylvania, Philadelphia; Mark Howard to Welles, November 13, 1865, Gideon Welles Papers, Library of Congress, Washington, D.C.

31. Little Rock *Arkansas State Gazette*, June 7, 1865.

32. E. H. Gill to Johnson, November 22, 1865, Johnson Papers, Library of Congress.

33. A. O. P. Nicholson to Johnson, December 1, 1865, Johnson Papers, Library of Congress.

34. Sidney Andrews, *The South Since the War* (Boston, 1971), p. 384; Raleigh *Daily Sentinel*, January 4, 1866.

35. J. Peterkin to Johnson, January 16, 1866, Johnson Papers, Library of Congress.

36. A. G. Brown to Johnson, February 24, 1866, Johnson Papers, Library of Congress.

37. Kenneth Rayner to Johnson, April 10, 1866, Johnson Papers, Library of Congress.

38. *RJCR*, pt. 2: 131.

39. A. H. Stephens to Johnson, April 17, 1866, Johnson Papers, Library of Congress.

40. P. M. Cloud to Johnson, April 21, 1866, Johnson Papers, Library of Congress.

41. Hans L. Trefousse, "The Acquittal of Andrew Johnson and the Decline of the Radicals," *Civil War History*, 14 (June 1968): 148-161.

42. David Donald, *Charles Sumner and the Rights of Man* (New York, 1970), pp. 264ff.

43. New York *Herald*, June 15, 1866.

44. *National Anti-Slavery Standard*, July 16, 1866; *Independent*, August 2, 1866.

45. George W. Julian, *Political Recollections, 1840-1872* (Chicago,

1884), pp. 272-73.

46. Raleigh *Daily Sentinel,* May 3, 1866.

47. Orville Hickman Browning, *The Diary of Orville Hickman Browning,* ed. Theodore C. Pease and James G. Randall (Springfield, Ill., 1933), 2: 80; Gideon Welles, *Diary of Gideon Welles,* ed. Howard K. Beale (New York, 1960), 2: 533.

48. New York *Herald,* June 15, September 28, 1866; James Dixon to Welles, September 26, 1866, Gideon Welles Papers, Library of Congress; James S. Brisbin to Zachariah Chandler, October 5, 1866, Zachariah Chandler Papers, Library of Congress, Washington, D.C.; B. R. Cowen to Marcus Ward, October 11, 1866, Marcus Ward Papers, New Jersey Historical Society, Newark.

49. *New York Times,* October 24, 1866; Cox and Cox, *Politics, Principle, and Prejudice,* p. 229; McKitrick, *Andrew Johnson and Reconstruction,* p. 469.

50. Richmond *Whig,* December 5, 1866; Charleston, S.C. *Daily News,* January 29, 1867; Little Rock, Arkansas *Daily Gazette,* November 14, 1866. Former Confederate Postmaster John H. Reagan and the Mississippi politician James Lusk Alcorn also favored ratification. Richmond *Whig,* December 1, 1866; Raleigh *Daily Sentinel,* February 1, 1867.

51. Raleigh *Daily Sentinel,* October 11, 1866; New York *World,* October 27, 29, 31, 1866, quoting Southern papers,

52. Wager Swayne to Chase, December 10, 1866, Salmon P. Chase Papers, Library of Congress; *New York Times,* January 14, 1867; McPherson, *Reconstruction,* pp. 352-353; McKitrick, *Andrew Johnson and Reconstruction,* pp. 471-472; New York *World,* December 8, 31, 1866; January 2, 1867.

53. *Harper's Weekly,* January 19, 1867; New York *World,* January 10, 1867.

54. John M. Schofield, *Forty-Six Years in the Army* (New York, 1897), pp. 394-395; Richmond *Whig,* December 5, 1866; Rhodes, *History,* 6: 119.

55. Welles, *Diary,* 3: 31-32, 38; *Cong. Globe,* 39 Cong., 2 sess., p. 1045; *New York Times,* February 5, 1867.

56. *New York Times,* February 8, 1867.

57. Christopher Memminger to Carl Schurz, April 26, 1871, Schurz Papers, Library of Congress.

UNITED STATES FOREIGN POLICY
AND ITS DOMESTIC CRITICS, 1900-1913

Milton Cantor

Ideas do not spring, like Athene, full blown from the brow of Zeus. They are victims and possessors of the past. Understandably, foreign policy priorities so common today, and the radical critique of these policies, were nearly nonexistent before the 1890s. The United States had overwhelmingly insular concerns in these years. Few writers, reformers, social or economic critics challenged the fiercely proprietary spirit with which Americans with minor exceptions viewed their country's overseas practices. That some of their countrymen were being being radicalized in these first frenetic years of the new century is indisputable—membership rolls of the Socialist Party of America (SPA) and the Industrial Workers of the World (IWW) attest to it—but the swelling leftist criticism, when not diverted by Progressivism or absorbed into liberalism, was turned inward.

Indeed, only the anti-imperialists and a scattering of pacifists looked past national affairs. Henry Cabot Lodge, then, was right when he observed, writing in 1889, that "our relations with foreign nations today fill but a slight place in American politics, and excite generally only a languid interest." Businessmen stepped up their overseas investments, to be sure; our Latin American interests developed apace; and the the government began to think about a two-ocean navy, spurred in large part by the spacious propositions of Alfred Thayer Mahan. But Americans remained parochial in their outlook. They were busy with internal affairs, with repairing the destruction of Civil War, absorbing new ethnic groups, building an industrial empire, settling a continent. Populist and Progressive alike were considered menacingly "radical" by most voters, but both, like the majority itself, endorsed a big navy and continued commercial expansion, and only a handful of Americans resisted the missionary urge and the moralistic-pietistic strains which played an axial role in our overseas affairs.

The most articulate and familiar criticism of administration foreign policy was along traditional lines. Republicans tended to support the actions of three successive Republican Presidents after 1900; the Democrats generally opposed them. Even Progressives were indifferent to foreign affairs, which again reflected the insouciant disregard of nearly all Americans down to 1914. Fighting Bob La Follette, to be sure, did deliver vigorous expansionist speeches when campaigning for governor of Wisconsin in 1900. Aside from these speeches, however, he was markedly inattentive to overseas developments. He was "having a devil of a time," he admitted during the campaign, "reading the Congressional Record trying to find out something about the Philippines, etc., etc. . . . " His "imperialist flirtation" has even been attributed to no more than a desire to demonstrate party regularity, which was necessary for a successful gubernatorial campaign. In much the same way, William E. Borah of Idaho seemed to be an expansionist about 1900—for he had bolted to the Silver Republicans in 1896 and imperialist sentiments served as penance.[1]

THE ANTI-IMPERIALISTS

Overseas expansion reached a critical stage at the end of the nineteenth century. It coincided with the closing of the frontier and the completed settlement of the continent. It had waited upon a new technology—in the form of steamship, cable, and telegraph, which contributed to a shrinking world. The railways were now built, the home markets approached saturation, the West Coast clamored for naval protection, the urban East thought in terms of markets abroad, the industrial system came of age. Expansionism, then, was coterminous with the rise of the city, the influx of "new" immigrants from southern and eastern Europe, the maturation of a manufacturing giant, and climaxed a sudden and dramatic awakening to a sense of world power by Americans. It was paralleled by the appearance of an energetic and youthful band of expansionist spokesmen who demanded an adventurist foreign policy. Their rallying cry for a "large policy" in the Caribbean, the Pacific, and the Far East was "manifest destiny," a refurbished Jackson period slogan that would be shared by politicians, businessmen, scholars, clergy, and the general public.

The hue and cry for more land, more trade, and more power first focused on Cuba. From the days of Jefferson and the 1854 Ostend Manifesto, Cuba had been an object of special interest to the United States and regarded as legitimately within the American sphere of interest. As long as Spain owned the island, most Americans were inclined to leave things alone, but the 1868 Revolution in Cuba revived the possibility of ultimate acquisition. Indeed, considerable sentiment was generated in favor of intervention as the revolt continued. Spanish political and economic oppression provoked another rebellion in 1895, and this time events in Cuba synchronized with America's swelling economic power and a propaganda compaign.

The whole lamentable story is well known—how Spain was suddenly confronted by an American public awake and psychologically as well as economically ready for war; how the Madrid government was afflicted by a series of unfortunate developments, such as the sinking of the *Maine* on February 11, 1898; how, during the war itself, Spain went from disaster to disaster; how, having tasted empire, an overwhelming majority of Americans greeted the naval victories of the Asiatic and Atlantic squadrons as well as Theodore Roosevelt's land exploits with tumultuous acclaim and called for the annexation of Spain's overseas possessions. For many businessmen, expansion triggered visions of extracontinental commerce and markets. For navalists such as Captain Alfred Thayer Mahan, it meant the necessity of protecting our commercial interests abroad—which took the shape of a two-ocean navy and geopolitical concepts. For intellectuals like Brooks Adams and John Fiske, for clergymen like Josiah Strong, for senators like Albert Beveridge, it meant that a burgeoning role for the United States in international affairs was a fact of life.

If the conflict proved a disaster for Spain, it seemed to some Americans scarcely less so—at least in a moral and political sense—for the United States. A small group of old-fashioned reformers and liberals contended that expansion betrayed our national origins and inheritance, that it meant a drastic departure from America's traditional isolation (and they invoked Washington's Farewell Address), that it was contrary to democratic principles and a violation of our moral obligations, that it was inconsistent with our great heritage—of the Monroe Doctrine, Jefferson's and Lincoln's doctrine of consent of the governed, that it abandoned the propositions that had historically protected us from the rivalries and corruptions of the Old World.[2] Andrew Carnegie, the great iron and steel magnate, defined the issues succinctly; it was "Americanism" versus "imperialism"—with the former surrogate for the principles of freedom and the latter for domination of alien peoples. Edwin Mead, the Boston civic reformer and peace worker, added his voice, claiming that America's rule in the Philippines was a travesty of our noblest democratic ideals. Most of the anti-expansionists joined the Anti-imperialist League, which had its beginning at Faneuil Hall on June 15, 1898. Other branches were organized in such major cities as St. Louis, Chicago, and San Francisco, but Boston remained the center; and its leaders were thosy old-fashioned New Englanders, descendants of the Conscience Whigs and nonresistants, militants who took their democracy seriously. They sought to "organize the moral forces of the country."[3] They were mostly Bostonians like Gamaliel Bradford, a retired banker and publicist of reform causes, and Moorfield Storey, the outspoken lawyer who presided over the league for fifteen years. Serious, dedicated, high-minded, instilled with a sense of noblesse oblige developed over a century and more, they had a finely wrought sense of the moral righteousness of their ways; and they set forth their purposes inside the cover of every piece of literature the league distributed:

> This League is organized to aid in holding the United States true to the principles of the Declaration of Independence. It seeks the preservation of the rights of the people as guaranteed to them by the Constitution. Its members hold self-government to be fundamental and good government but incidental. It is its purpose to oppose by all proper means the extension of the sovereignty of the United States over subject peoples. It will contribute to the defeat of any candidate or party that stands for the forcible subjugation of any people.[4]

Naturally, then, many of the anti-imperialist leaders thought expansionism could best be combated by lobbying within the political and social system. That system had been good to them and they never considered working outside of it. Consequently, they supported planks in the platforms of both major parties in the 1900 elections and endorsed William Jennings Bryan, the Democratic standard-bearer. But they had misjudged their man. After an initially promising start, Bryan emphasized economic problems, the silver issue in particular, and ignored imperialism.

Despite such disappointments and successive political defeats, the anti-imperialists continued to meet, to give speeches, to disseminate literature urging reversal of administration policy. For a while their membership mushroomed, swelling to half a million by 1899. Their confidence also ballooned—to the point where it bore no relation to numbers or to reality; they would succeed, they thought, because their cause was just. And so they were to struggle vainly against American expansion for some twenty years.

These anti-imperialists cannot be labeled "radical" by any stretch of the imagination. The Boston spokesmen were typical. They were mostly Harvard alumni, distinguished lawyers, editors, bankers. Virtually renaissance types, they belonged to the best clubs and the most exclusive societies—to the University Club, the Somerset Club, the Sons of the American Revolution, the Society of the Cincinnati, the Colonial Society. At a time when only ten percent of Americans had a college education, over seventy percent of the league leadership could boast of it—and could claim old New England ancestry as well. They shared the same interests, cherished the same values, fought together for the same good causes—clean government, sound money, lower tariffs, civil service reform—and they got old fighting for them. Indeed, league officers were, by 1900, generally older than most of the pacifist and reform leadership, their average age being over sixty (while officers of peace groups averaged in the late forties and Progressivism was even more of a youth movement).[5]

These former Mugwumps found expansion a far greater and more urgent menace than municipal corruption had ever been. After all, it seemed to threaten their view of American democracy as well as the quality of American life. Hence they could not admit defeat and the Boston group carried on the anti-imperialist crusade long after the various branches had withered away. But it did so with diminished vitality after 1903, and within ten years had become an empty fortress, its guiding spirits having died off. It displayed a consistent opposition to annexation of the Philippines and to American investments there. Its members were more frequently involved in domestic issues over the next decade, but it nonetheless censured United States involvement in Mexico, Nicaragua, and Honduras.[6] These Bostonians proposed independence for the Philippines (and/or neutralization, a resolution of Carl Schurz); they denounced Theodore Roosevelt's customs house intervention in Santo Domingo; they condemned the Panama machinations of 1903—as "the natural fruit" of "the criminal blunder" in the Philippines.[7] Their attack lacked bite, however, for it was carried forward by elegant and faded patricians—by graybeards who were tired, timid, and bookish, who lacked the sharp edge of radicalism or even a principled overview that went beyond devotion to democratic ideals.

PACIFISM AND PACIFISTS: AT THE CROSSROADS

Most anti-imperialists were not greatly interested in the peace movement. The league's three most energetic officers after 1900—Erving Winslow, David Haskins, and Moorfield Storey—were, to be sure, all members of the American Peace Society (APS), but they were so deeply involved in league activities that their work for the society was negligible. Peace workers were generally younger than the anti-imperialists; their number included a more generous sprinkling of women; they were seemingly less elitist; and they prided themselves on their practicality, their awareness of the complexities of modern life, and their sense of international community.

Peace societies had long been a fixture on the national scene, going back to the colonial period. Most of them never recovered from the trauma of civil war, and those which reemerged in the Gilded Age did so in altered form. Take for example, the venerable American Peace Society, the best known and most influential of antebellum peace groups.[8] Founded in Boston in 1828, it remained provincial and impoverished throughout the nineteenth century, deriving its strength from continuity with the New England intellectual traditions. It lived in the shades of Emerson, Garrison, Horace Mann, Theodore Parker, Bronson Alcott, Dorothea Dix. Its journal, *Advocate of Peace,* carried articles that were highly moral in tone and cautiously reform-oriented. Like comparable Jackson-period organizations, it had a Quaker character and harbored a suspicion of government that verged on antistatism. Most of its members had been abolitionists, and all were Unionists. The Civil War changed it. APS members remained committed to philanthropic activities and ameliorative public service, but they became more practical in orientation as well. The old ethical absolutists lost control to newcomers who wished to accommodate the society's peace program to the national interest. The principled leadership of Quaker persuasion could be counted upon to oppose the Spanish-American War—for which they were criticized—but a surprising number of recent members approved the "splendid little war" and its results.[9] In any case, the society's superannuated membership did not seem a promising source of militancy in the peace movement in the decades ahead.

Joining the APS in the Gilded Age was the Universal Peace Union, organized in Philadelphia by the young Quaker textile manufacturer, Alfred Love. Its leaders could also boast Adin Ballou, founder of the Christian Socialist community at Hopedale, and some former members of the American Peace Society. The union, which was founded in 1866, was for years the sole organized expression of radical pacifists outside the peace sects (such as the Mennonites) and the lineal descendants of the Garrisonian nonresistants. Like most postbellum pacifist organizations, it attacked military training in the schools and championed international disarmament.[10] Like most, it was impoverished. So desperate was its condition that the union sought affiliation with the APS after 1912—and its plea was rejected.

New societies joined these nineteenth-century groups after 1900, chief among them the New York Peace Society, the Church Peace Union, the Carnegie Endowment for International Peace, and the World Peace Foundation.[11] They all had something of the character of business organizations: permanent staffs, complex fund-raising operations, research and publication departments—quite unlike their forebears. They were eager to endorse business efficiency and practicality. They were fueled by new money and had new, far more limited, goals than did the earlier "impractical" societies. Edwin Ginn, a trained lawyer and practical scientist by profession, financed a broad educational campaign directed toward teachers and schoolchildren, since with the latter "our greatest hope lies."[12] Ginn's organizational forum was the World Peace Foundation, which he envisioned as a centralized agency for the coordination of peace work, especially educational work, on a national scale. His working director, Edwin Mead of Boston, was editor of the reformist *New England Magazine*, a vice-president of the APS, and longtime peace worker who espoused Ginn's idealistic internationalism. Their foundation financed the peace movement in schools and colleges—in an effort, according to its constitution, "to promote . . . the interests of international justice and fraternity." To this end it promoted peace days, essay-writing contests, and educational materials.

Educators at Columbia—as well as lawyers, editors, and clergymen—founded the New York Peace society in 1906, and hired an Iowa farm boy, William Short, as executive secretary. Becoming one of the most important of the new peace groups, the society lobbied through its thousand-member organization for world federation, arms limitations, and an international naval force. Its ranks were dominated by businessmen, with Andrew Carnegie becoming the society's first President in 1907, though lawyers and clergymen bulked large. In effect, therefore, it became the symbol of what a number of peace societies had evolved into: an organization composed of the affluent and the influential. Short, in describing the society, stressed the role of jurists, industrial and financial leaders, and socially prominent women in the organization as well as in the peace movement at large.[13]

The prestigious Nicholas Murray Butler of Columbia University, a recent convert to pacifist ranks in antebellum years, was the moving force behind the Carnegie Endowment for International Peace, which was founded in December 1910. Together with Edwin Mead, Samuel Dutton, and Hamilton Holt of the New York Peace Society, he persuaded Carnegie to donate ten million dollars for their planned endowment. This agency, while reflecting the old Scottish warrior's longtime interest in peace work, would also confirm the growing respectability of the peace movement as well as its founders' fear of anything tinged by radicalism. For its trustees were of a wholly conservative stripe, without a really principled or idealistic pacifist among them.

The peace movement, in other words, had become respectable and institutionalized to a degree unknown before 1900. It had emerged as *the* establishment movement. As might be expected, many members of the older peace movement, before the new century, had been opposed to American overseas expansion. They had belonged to an old, familial, community-rooted elite. Principled, socially conservative, educated in a Protestant evangelism that emphasized self-discipline, moral righteousness, a finely honed sense of stewardship, and the cultural heritage of New England, they were or had been Mugwumps, supporters of good government leagues and civil service reform.

But the new pacifists, for the most part, put anti-imperialism behind them after 1900. Like the modern business corporation, to which many of them belonged, these novitiates introduced large-scale corporate practices into the new (and old, too, on occasion) societies. Most of them were financiers, industrialists, educators, corporate or international lawyers—like publisher Edwin Ginn, banker Foster Peabody, educator Nicholas Murray Butler, like Elihu Root, president of the American Society of International Lawyers, who simultaneously served as Theodore Roosevelt's Secretary of State. They had been won by arguments demonstrating the mutual dependence of American corporations and peace societies, of stable world conditions and uninterrupted trade, of political connections and technical expertise. Many of them had been drawn into peace work by the arguments of lawyers; indeed, many of them were lawyers, as noted. Inevitably, their organizations were conservative. For, as Arnold Paul has pointed out, the trend toward professionalism in the law, combined with the reemergent judicial supremacy of the Waite-Field Supreme Courts, established the judiciary "as the principal bulwark" of conservatism in America and shaped lawyers into the prime defenders of social stability as well as property rights.[14] International lawyers among them were simply products of the evolving specialization in the law itself, and they reflected both the growing professionalism and the high legal standards that emerged after the American Bar Association had been established (in 1878). That Elihu Root, the leading international lawyer in the United States, became president of the Carnegie Endowment, was natural and inevitable.

These new peace workers were internationalists, but the term, broadly conceived as it was, is elusive. Certainly it should not suggest lack of patriotism or convictions running counter to national policy. To the contrary, peace workers accepted America's virtues as unique and celebrated her humanitarian past. They held endless discussions on ways to substitute international order for anarchy, and to establish democratic government on a world scale. Implicit in their thought, it followed, was emphasis on American democratic institutions as the global model. Small wonder, then, that Presidents Taft and Wilson both found peace societies consonant with their views of the national political character and the international scene; so did Secretaries of State Root, Bryan, Bacon, Knox, and Lansing.

Peace workers, even before the Spanish-American war, supported commercial expansion—so long as it could be attained peacefully; and, though some demurred from the *method* by which our trade advanced into the western Pacific, most of them supported the war itself.[15] Hostilities abroad, of course, did disrupt the existing peace societies and paralyzed their activities. Some peace workers, like Carnegie, became resigned to hostilities and settled for a quick victory. The APS limited itself to a hapless condemnation of the yellow press, while the usually combative Universal Peace Union praised President McKinley's "calmness, moderation and wise firmness."[16] The society's anti-imperialist *Advocate of Peace* did not object to retention of Puerto Rico. Nor did its readers and editors condemn the administration's Philippine policies or exclude expansionists from membership in the APS. Anti-imperialism and imperialism were issues limited to 1898, and not widely debated thereafter. Furthermore, both sides were heartened by and attracted to the pseudoscientific racism of social Darwinists like John Fiske, sharing with them a vision of an orderly and stable world order that was a product of America's international influence and responsive to her political institutions. And once the distasteful Filipino insurrection was silenced, imperialist and anti-imperialist alike were dazzled by a nationalist vision of the "civilizing effects" of American economic and moral expansion.

With men like Carnegie, Ginn, and Butler setting the tone, such reactions should occasion little surprise. It is predictable that pacifists would display greater tolerance of expansionism than did pre-1900 peace workers, that they would contribute to a relatively conventional establishment movement, that they would find little to reform in American life or institutions, that their statements on international affairs would be bland, vague, and restrained. (By the eve of World War I, to jump ahead, Elihu Root and William Howard Taft were members of peace societies and they were also the major architects of American overseas expansion.) These new peace workers believed in free trade, and they would support that liberal internationalism which was a cornerstone of Wilson's postwar vision; they would hardly go beyond such propositions.

Understandably, therefore, these pacifists failed to ask the hard questions; they were ineffective as lobbyists, unlike the Navy League; they were unable to mount large-scale campaigns and unwilling to woo minority or labor blocs, content instead to attract a relatively small number of distinguished and prominent figures. (Hamilton Holt, John Bates Clark, and Jane Addams, fearing that the APS would become exclusively middle class, deliberately solicited the support of organized labor.) Not one peace leader publicly criticized the Taft-Knox policy of Dollar Diplomacy in the Far East or in Latin America, of which more later. Nor were peace workers even unanimous in opposing the more obvious potential dangers of this prewar decade: the international arms race, the strident big-power militarism, the competition for power and profits. For example, Boston's American School Peace League, a pacifist organization financed in part by the World Peace Foundation, had as its governing educational theme the vaguely liberal and wholly orthodox goal of inculcating schoolchildren in the ideal of "service to the nation and good will to men"—hardly goals that clashed with the morality.[17] Equally suggestive of the blandness and conservatism of the peace societies was the response of the Carnegie Endowment to the murderous Balkan Wars. It did not vigorously oppose them; it did not denounce the belligerents or even promote mediation. Rather it established an international commission to study the causes of the war.[18] Indeed, the endowment's usual efforts of these prewar years were along such lines. It established scholarly programs in economics and in international law, and it even sought to maintain "centers of influence" upon the continent.[19] Like other peace societies, the endowment reflected the views of a middle-class professional elite. True to its background, it identified with American foreign policy.

The twin passions of peace workers from the 1880s were international institutions and international arbitration. Anglo-American arbitration treaties and the Hague peace conferences, beginning in 1899, occupied them, though the latter provoked little national interest because of America's preoccupation with Cuban and Philippine military exploits. Out of this conference came the Permanent Court of Arbitration, the first international court in history. It was central to the practical program of peace workers and gave stimulus to the paired causes of arbitration and interparliamentary union.[20] These causes were further quickened, and kept before the public, by the annual conferences on international arbitration, which had been convening at the Lake Mohonk meeting resort hotel of Quaker Albert Smiley since 1895.

The four-day Mohonk meeting of the National Arbitration and Peace Congress, on the eve of the second Hague conference, brought new converts to pacifism, men who stressed the "realistic" rather than the "idealistic" content of the peace movement, men who tempered any criticism of the Spanish-American war with professions of loyalty to the nation. These same converts would remain silent while the United States, in the name of its international responsibilities, pursued an adventurist foreign policy in Latin America. Smiley himself emphasized arbitration, not pacifism, at the Mohonk conferences. He inevitably sought a genteel program, one that would not alienate those business, military, and political delegates who were in attendance. These same delegates staffed the American Peace Society, as those older societies which lingered on were staffed with "practical" members; that is, international lawyers and businessmen.

Delegates to the various national and international arbitration meetings also were prominent in education, publishing, busi-

ness, government, and the law. Speakers at Mohonk, for instance, included Justice David Brewer of the Supreme Court;
John Bassett Moore, an authority on international law; Daniel
Coit Gilman, president of John Hopkins. International lawyers,
especially after 1900, gravitated toward this attractive solution
to the problem of global instability. Legal figures like Justice
Brewer, Chief Justice Melville Weston Fuller, Joseph Choate,
and Simeon Baldwin shared more than a common conservative
outlook on domestic and world affairs; they had a common
background and training; they were held by a common vision of
international order; they endorsed the Supreme Court as a
model for an effective international organization; and they
shared Root's enthusiasm for a judicial world court, believing it
would embody the vaunted principle of judicial objectivity.
They believed that the causes of war and disputes among nations could be eliminated, as Root proposed, by administering
law in accord "with the rules of justice."[21]

"Realistic" though they were, such men often viewed both
pacifism and arbitration—and these terms are not necessarily
interchangeable—as moral and religious questions. They constantly exuded a confidence that was simply not in harmony
with the growing international tensions of prewar Europe. Reverend Frederick Lynch of the Church Peace Union predicted in
1912 that the twentieth century would be "an age of treaties
rather than an age of wars. . . ."[22] He later recalled the attitude
of most peace delegates to the Hague meeting: "We felt that
with the assembling of the Hague Conferences a new era
dawned upon the world and that the peace problem was being
brought down out of the world of idealism, where all movements are born, and was becoming a practical, political question."[23]

Nor did the course of events dispel such hopefulness. The
Hague Court, a permanent tribunal, spun out of the second
conference, which seemed to indicate progress. Successive Presidents, Roosevelt and Taft, endorsed the cause of international
arbitration, not finding in it anything inherently hostile to national sovereignty. Such men could be counted upon to reject

anything that smacked of anarchy or even disrespect for law and order. War itself, to these genteel pacifists, was consonant with the "lower passions of men"—and, understandably, "Lower passions" were identified with "lower men," with the lawless and disorderly, here and abroad.

Between 1908-1909, some twenty-five arbitration treaties were negotiated. Arbitration, by this time, had become the cowbird of the peace movement, crowding all other possibilities and issues out of the nest. Protests against the increasing militarism at home and abroad, against the payment of taxes to a government preparing for war, and against the rising expenditures on armaments, filtered into the columns of the peace journals, but the cause of international arbitration captured the headlines.

The prominence of arbitration was further indication that the peace movement had markedly changed, grown respectable, completed an earlier stage. The older peace societies changed with it or died. Witness, for instance, the Universal Peace Union, which declined in numbers and in energy as the older members died off, and the new and young recruits to pacifism chose new and younger societies. Garrisonian nonresistance seemed curiously old-fashioned and idealistic, out of touch with contemporary life. New money, funneled into peace societies, both old and new, by reputable and wealthy converts, guaranteed moderation, gentility, and vacillation in times of international crisis. Delegates to the 1907 National Arbitration and Peace Conference included William Jennings Bryan, two cabinet officers, four Supreme Court judges, one governor, ten mayors, twenty-seven millionaires, thirty labor leaders, forty bishops, sixty editors—and such men could be counted upon to do nothing and say nothing remotely critical of government policies.

SOCIALISTS: THE PREWAR YEARS

Among critics of American foreign policy before World War I, the Socialist Party (SPA) and the Industrial Workers of the World (IWW) regarded themselves as the only authentic radical voices. Both groups were relatively new to the national scene. The organized life of the IWW did not begin until 1904; the Socialists appeared in 1901, twelve years after the Second International had been formed as a loose overseas federation of socialist and radical labor parties.

American socialism, at the turn of the century, had been the property of rival factions. There was the Socialist Labor Party (SLP) of Daniel DeLeon and the Social Democratic Party (SDP), which evolved out of the Social Democracy of America, founded by Eugene V. Debs and Victor Lewis Berger in 1897. The SDP barely lasted out 1898, the year of its founding (and it became the SPA in 1901), and would be identified with Debs.

A Curacao-born Marxist, DeLeon rejected chimerical gains like shorter hours and higher wages for America's workers; that is, he disavowed "reformist" parties and labor unions. A theoretical Marxist, DeLeon attempted to keep the faith untainted by the bourgeois nationalism and monopoly capitalism that stained the bright ideals of expansionists. He scored the corrupting nature of middle-class values, urged industrial unionism, held tenaciously to such Marxist canons as the increasing pauperization of labor and the radical overthrow of existing capitalist institutions. Preoccupied with internecine warfare, his party from the outset exhibited those qualities of conflict and fragmentation which would characterize radicalism in the twentieth century. For example, as early as 1898 one SLP splinter group broke away from the parent body and joined the Debs-Berger Social Democracy.

DeLeon mistrusted the motives of Cuba's revolutionaries. He wished the Cubans freed of Spanish oppression, but not at the cost of another capitalist war which would only deliver Cubans into the hands of American capitalism. He hammered home, in the weekly *People* (it became a daily in July 1900), the SLP official organ, the notion that imperialism was evil, a view shared by Debs. Both socialist leaders agreed that the worker would pay all the costs of empire and the capitalists would reap all the profits; both perceived that war over Cuba would serve only to advance the cause of monopoly capitalism.

DeLeon, in the *People*'s columns, attempted to alert his readers to the dangers of imperialism and to the primacy of the class
struggle. His arguments, then, were very different from those of
the Anti-Imperialist League and the patricians who supported it.
War, he taught, was an opportunity for capitalist powers to
break union organizations by appealing to nationalist sentiments while using the proletariat as cannon fodder. The 266
sailors killed on the *Maine*, he told SLP'ers, were insignificant
when compared to the thousands who died annually from over-
work in sweatshops or from the bullets of police employed by
the bosses. One editorial in the *People* revealed that both the
American Sugar Trust and the Tobacco Trust were actively supporting the Cuban revolutionary junta, a disclosure which con-
verted some readers to DeLeon's position that the rebellion
would only transfer ownership of Cuba from Spain to American
capitalism. Later, when reports of slavery and forced concubin-
age in the Sulu archipelago reached his desk, DeLeon explained:

> . . . while at one end of the islands the American flag is
> to be forced upon the untractable Aguinaldo and his
> Tagals by means of bayonets and Winchesters as an em-
> blem of civilization, the same emblem is, by cash pay-
> ment, sought to be raised by our general in command
> over polygamy and chattel slavery. The American
> flag . . . is, in the hands of the labor-fleecing capitalist
> class, in danger of being the swindle rag of the mock
> auctioneer.[24]

The radical anti-expansionist protest was more disorganized
and less effective than that of the conservative Anti-Imperalist
League. It was also less consistent. The 1900 campaigns of both
socialist parties hardly touched on the annexation issue. To be
sure, DeLeon himself was unrelenting. He insisted that "the
question of territorial expansion has become an issue that vitally effects the wage workers";[25] and he ceaselessly criticized
United States intervention in Cuba. But he failed to swing his
SLP into an unequivocal antiwar position.

Debs, too, scored war and imperialism, but did not carry all his followers into the anti-expansionist camp. W. J. Ghent, a leading socialist, endorsed McKinley's actions; so did the Yiddish-language *Daily Forward,* the leading organ of Jewish socialists in the United States. In accepting the presidential nomination of the SDP, Debs declared that imperialists and anti-imperialists alike were capitalists who enforced wage slavery, a position to which he repeatedly returned during the campaign that followed.[26] His sentiments were understandable. Coming out of union ranks, Debs himself was part of the central experience of American labor, as well as the hero and symbol of socialism in the United States. He would have no traffic with the major political parties; he opposed capitalism because it was "inherently unjust, inhuman, unintelligent"; he rejected socialist participation in the AFL. But Debs represented a doctrinal mix that was scorned by ideological purists such as DeLeon. Indeed, he embodied the unity of Populist, Marxist, militant trade union, and Judeo-Christian traditions that fused to form the Socialist Party in 1901. His Social Democratic Party, at its 1898 convention, adopted a platform that included the fashionable Progressive measures as well as more advanced proposals that came to fruition during the New Deal: "cooperative production and distribution"; accident, unemployment, and old-age insurance; "a system of public works and improvements for the employment . . . of unemployed"; the "reduction of the hours of labor in proportion to the increasing facilities of production"; "equal civil and political rights for men and women"; and "the adoption of the initiative and the referendum." The Social Democratic Party, therefore, and the Socialist Party as well—since it took over the SDP platform virtually intact—pressed for "immediate demands," which DeLeon contemptuously called "palliatives" and which could only maintain and deepen the bitter feud that was rife in American radicalism.

It would be oversimplification to find that the SPA, which was born in a "bloomin', buzzin', confusion" in 1901, was an amalgam of Debsian and dissident DeLeonite socialists. Populists, for instance, were an important source of party member-

ship; so, too, were Christian socialists, who came to SPA
through a belief that life on earth could approach the kingdom
of God. Then there were other strains in the party: the boyish
romanticism of Jack London, the messianic piety of George
Herron, the syndicalist bravura of Big Bill Haywood and the
IWW bloc, the do-good settlement worker constituency, the mil-
lionaire socialists like J. G. Phelps Stokes, the upper-class converts like William English Walling and Robert Rives La Monte,
and the culture radicals—the bohemian writers and artists—who
fought for birth control, women's suffrage, and uninhibited so-
cial-sexual norms.

Given the unstable political chemistry of these elements, it is
surprising that all reacted with studied indifference to peace
workers and peace societies as well as to foreign policy matters.
Neither the "parlor socialists," as the party intellectuals were
sometimes called, nor the older socialist writers, expressed any
marked interest in events outside the United States. The *International Socialist Review,* the *Christian Socialist,* the reform-
minded *American Fabian,* DeLeon's *People*—all of them generally ignored both America's overseas policies and her peace societies. Regarding the latter, whenever socialist periodicals did
take notice of pacifists, it was only to dismiss them summarily
as "bourgeois." Vincent St. John, an important IWW official,
even attacked the peace societies. They were, he wrote, "nothing more or less than schemes whereby certain parasites of the
present [capitalist] system amuse themselves or gain a liveli-
hood. There is no record that they ever accomplished anything
except create a demand for printer's ink, paper, and furnish an
avenue by which some individuals can exploit their ego."[27]

The socialist attitude toward pacifists is understandable—and
it was reciprocated. Peace workers were markedly hostile to the
socialist interpretation of war and imperialism; they eschewed
doctrinal discussion of the roots of conflict and they shunned
radicals as pariahs. Neither the World Peace Foundation nor the
American Peace Society, to cite two instances, ever commented
upon the economic and social causes of conflict. It was a rare
prewar event, such as the landing of American troops at Vera-

cruz, that resulted in socialist-pacifist cooperation and, on this occasion, in a twin-pronged drive against Wilsonian actions.[28]

Socialist indifference to pacifism, it should be understood, had not taken the high ground of principle at this time. The socialist just-war view, the belief that conditions sometimes required revolutionary turbulence and civil war, was not an issue. Party leadership simply was not interested in the pacifist or, for that matter, the anti-imperialist, program; and the peace movement left it cold. Socialist convention resolutions and campaign literature did denounce military training in the schools and the use of the army as strikebreakers; they did (at the June 1898 convention of the Social Democratic Party of America) demand the "abolition of war as far as the United States are concerned and the introduction of international arbitration instead."[29]

More characteristic, however, were the thirty-three planks of the 1912 Socialist Party platform, not one of which mentioned foreign affairs.[30] The major theoretical journals of socialism almost never alluded to overseas policies. Algie Simons filled the pages of the *International Socialist Review* with comments on rural institutions or problems in American history; and Ernest Untermann, a German immigrant and Marxist, contributed pieces on abstract doctrinal matters; Robert Rives La Monte, an important socialist writer, confined himself to conditions under capitalism and to Marxist exegeses; Charles Kerr, the notable socialist entrepreneur and publisher, also restricted his analyses to the domestic scene (both before and after 1908, when he took over the editorship of the *Review*); Louis Boudin, a critic of Untermann and a leading socialist intellectual, also rarely touched upon foreign affairs; and William English Walling, another prominent theoretician, was almost wholly preoccupied with corruption and politics in those articles which he wrote for socialist and muckraking non-socialist journals. He did, to be sure, organize the Friends of Russia, and rallied liberals and radicals to the aid of the 1905 Russian Revolution, but such overseas efforts and interests were sputtering and sporadic at best.

ON THE WORLD STATE

Both Theodore Roosevelt and William Howard Taft maintained aggressive overseas policies. Taft, for instance, intruded in China—in an ongoing big-power dispute over financing and control of China's railways. But State Department initiatives, specifically in Manchuria, evoked no criticism from the peace societies. Nor were pacifists alone in ignoring these maneuvers. They were joined by socialists and even by anti-imperialists, who at best registered feeble protests. In sum, none of the groups that might be expected to object to the policies of Taft and his Secretary of State Philander Knox voiced anything resembling tough and forthright criticism; and there was no organizational protest to fill the vacuum.

Silence also greeted Taft's Latin American measures. Indeed, those who should have been most concerned seemed almost wholly unaware of the activities of successive Republican administrations in the Caribbean. Only Carl Schurz and a scattering of other anti-imperialists came down hard on Roosevelt's 1904 corollary to the Monroe Doctrine.[31] Only the Anti-Imperialist League went on record against Roosevelt's meddling in the internal affairs of the bankrupt and violence-torn Dominican Republic. Pacifists, belonging to an uncontroversial establishment reform movement, could not be expected to protest; and socialists focused on America's working class and on domestic affairs. They also failed to criticize State Department-National City Bank intervention in Haiti. Nor did they dissent when the United States provided moral and physical support to Nicaraguan revolutionaries who toppled José Zelaya, the country's ironhanded dictator.

Taft dealt with Caribbean trouble spots much as Roosevelt had done. He also intervened to establish a protectorate over Nicaragua and finally, when trouble broke out there in 1912 and President Adolfo Diaz requested United States assitance, Taft obliged with a contingent of marines who remained in that fractious land until 1925.

Peace workers, unlike socialists and anti-imperialists, even approved presidential efforts to protect American investors and to stabilize "backward" Caribbean nations.[32] Such reactions were predictable. The peace societies were managed by political and social moderates. Mildly reformatory in outlook, they were often social and economic conservatives. Elihu Root, President of the Carnegie Endowment, received the 1913 Nobel Peace Prize, but General Leonard Wood, a big-army advocate, considered him a friend of the military and was delighted "to see this award given to one who has been so strong an advocate of preparation as being the best means of preserving peace."[33] Nor did John Hays Hammond, a founder of the American Society for the Judicial Settlement of International Disputes and a participant in the 1911 National Peace Congress, perceive any conflict between peace and militarism. He even sponsored a contest "for accuracy in bomb dropping" at the Harvard-Boston Flying Meet of 1910.[34] Jacob M. Dickinson, the president of the second National Peace Congress, which met in Chicago in 1909, was also Secretary of War in Taft's administration. He authored a sensational report to Congress, during the 1910-1911 debate over military appropriations, which declared our coastlines defenseless against invasion and that the army was lamentably inadequate.[35] No less than eleven leaders of various peace societies, one scholar points out, were simultaneously officers of the Navy League. One of them, Lyman Abbott, was a vice-president of the American Peace Society. He saw nothing contradictory about signing a Navy League petition urging more battleships in 1913 or, in the following year, addressing a dinner of the Navy League. Charles W. Wliot, observing developments in the Far East during 1911-1912, recommended that the Carnegie Endowment "recognize frankly the present necessity of maintaining in all countries armed forces for protective duty against aggression from without or disintegration from within."[36] Usually the confirmed militarist was denied admission into pacifist ranks, but even this unwritten rule was violated. General Horace Porter served as an officer in the New York Peace Society to complement his activities as president of the Navy League. In so doing he stretched the already wide provision—for the NYPS was on record as ready to include "both those who deny all place to armaments, and those who fear, in the present state of civilization, to abolish large armies and navies."[37] The society readily approved Carnegie's assertion that "this Society does not oppose such armament as may be necessary for adequate national protection."[38] Equally suggestive of the close cooperation between the military and peace leaders were proceedings at the 1913 American [National] Peace Congress. Those who led it allowed big-navy propagandists, such as officials of the Navy League, to address its meeting. Arthur Dadmun, league secretary, told delegates to the disarmament panel that it was difficult to distinguish pacifist from militarist. He quoted a tribute to the navy from Joseph Choate, a prominent peace official, and noted how Root, when senator, "as a lover of peace had voted for three new battleships."[39]

There were peace workers who did campaign against increasing armaments. Edwin Ginn, the publisher, denounced arms spending as contrary to professions of peace. Oswald Garrison Villard, in the *Nation* and in the New York *Evening Post* arraigned those who called the United States defenseless or urged naval increases. But there were many like Eliot and Albert Smiley of Mohonk who thought it "impractical" to expect any arms reductions while no international tribunal existed. Moreover, a 1911 referendum of the New York Peace Society on the addition of two battleships to the U.S. Navy produced twenty percent in favor of the proposal. Even more, almost one-third, favored fortification of the Canal Zone, rather than neutralization.[40] Even Edwin Mead, surely an opponent of a large navy, cooperated with big-navy organizations like the American Peace and Arbitration League: "We have got to look at these things fairly. Where we can work together, let's work together."[41]

None of the peace societies, being so compromised, ever criticized congressional naval expenditures; they confined themselves to promoting arbitration treaties, establishing friendship organizations, and financing educational exchange programs. Such examples of cooperation with government agencies, by men of goodwill and democratic scruples, and such instances of indifference in the face of an adverturist foreign policy deprived pacifism of whatever bite and energy it might have had. Indeed, these examples of cooperation smacked of collusion, but no one seemed to notice or to care—except for an occasional socialist, and the SPA record in such matters was hardly better.

WILSONIAN POLICIES

Wilson assumed office at a time when the world was at peace; but the peace was deceptive and these crepuscular years were rife with potentially malevolent events. Japanese maneuvers in Manchuria threatened the "Open Door Policy"; Colombia was still angry over Roosevelt's machinations in regard to the Panama Canal; England was alienated owing to our discrimination in favor of United States coastwise shipping through the Canal; American marines bivouacked on Nicaraguan soil; and Mexico was gripped by revolutionary turbulence which threatened our economic interests south of the border. Wilson at first ignored overseas events, possibly in the hope that they would disappear. His inaugural address had not mentioned foreign policy, nor had he discussed it in his campaign; yet his first administration was largely concerned with international affairs and his second was overwhelmed by them.

The pacifists' response to Wilsonian measures was predicable. They strongly identified with the incoming President—with his program of domestic reform, with his internationalism and his lofty purposes, and his faith in moral law and progress. Such visionary qualities, after all, corresponded to their own, and they reacted intuitively and positively to Wilson's conviction that a new era had arrived, believing as they did that the day of permanent peace was at hand. It was all part of their faith in progress, of their intense pride in America's extraordinary history, of their conviction that evolution toward a time of social harmony was inevitable. The peace workers, we have seen, were internationalists. They were confident that global progress could be measured to the degree that it resembled the United

States. They would arouse their countrymen to their world responsibilities; and, in so doing, peace workers were merely calling upon a hallowed doctrine of stewardship; only now it took the form of helping backward peoples along the path to righteousness and civilization.

Such views bulked large among government leaders as well as peace workers, and there was an understandable identity of men and ideas shared between them. The cherished view of a virtuous and chosen nation in a sea of corrupt and uncivilized societies remained a highly attractive proposition, convincing Americans—as it always had—that their country was uniquely equipped to exercise world leadership. Peace workers untiringly recalled to their country the time-honored view that America acted for unselfish reasons, that it had no military hungering for glory, no world empire to protect, no desire for territory and conquest. The only altruistic nation on earth, the United States had a mission to set right the wrongs of the great powers of the Old World.

Such views were central to Woodrow Wilson's approach to foreign affairs. The peace workers, it followed, were preparing the way for his leadership in overseas matters, including the war to end wars. Small wonder, then, that Edwin Mead—one of the more militant peace workers!—believed the President would actively promote the cause of world peace. Wilson seemed surrogate for all their hopes—with faith in arbitration, his sense of mission, his belief in America as a virtuous nation in a nonvirtuous world, and his desire to incorporate rules of morality into foreign affairs.[42] Wilson favored the rule of law, and Frederick Lynch of the Church Peace Union naively predicted, like other peace workers, that the twentieth century would be "an age of treaties rather than an age of wars. . . . " David Starr Jordan, President of Stanford University and a prominent pacifist, urged Wilson to end American support for the six-power railway consortium in China and to adopt a policy of nonintervention in Mexican affairs.

Bryan's appointment as Secretary of State confirmed their roseate view of the incoming chief executive and buoyed their spirits. "The great commoner" seemed one of them. He was not an absolute pacifist, of couse, and he had warmly supported the war with Spain. But the turn of events had greatly sobered him by 1900; and the fact that a just war to end Spanish tyranny could be transformed into an imperialist war appalled him. Besides, Bryan applied Christ's teachings to international relations; he urged that *Machtpolitik* be replaced by Christian morality as the guide to foreign policy; he proposed conciliation treaties that included clauses for "cooling off" periods; and he generally advocated conciliation and mediation. Bryan, then, shared a touching faith in international arbitration with pacifists, and concluded thirty agreements which submitted all disputes to arbitration and which provided for a one-year "cooling off" period before resort to arms. In sum, both Bryan and Wilson seemed to confirm the early hopeful expectations of the peace workers.

Nor were these expectations immediately dashed. Wilson did reverse some of his predecessors' foreign policies. He withdrew support from the proposed bankers' loan to China as incompatible with Chinese sovereignty; he committed the United States to withdrawal from the Philippines under the 1916 Jones Act and inaugurated far-reaching political and administrative reforms; and, finally, he officially repudiated Dollar Diplomacy.

Of the potential critics of Wilson's meddling in the Caribbean, and of the administration's failure to act in the Philippines before 1916, only the Anti-Imperialist League took public exception. Moorfield Storey, then the league's president, told Charles Francis Adams (in a letter of May 16, 1913) of his great disappointment that "Wilson takes no position on the Philippine question."[43] The league, commenting on administration actions in Santo Domingo, Nicaragua, and Honduras, claimed that "the imperialistic spirit still prevails in less aggressive form." In 1916, referring to events in the Western Hemisphere, a league memorandum declared: "No spheres of influence, protectorates, or trusteeships should be undertaken here by the United States."[44] Other than the league, there was organizational bankruptcy when it came to critics of America's overseas policies. Very few groups or individuals publicly, or even privately, proclaimed that the conventional interventionist policies of Roosevelt and Taft were still in effect. Yet Wilson's administration carried out more armed intervention than did his predecessors in the White House. And once again Latin America provided the *mise-en-scène* of executive action.

Riotous conditions on Haiti prompted fears of foreign-power interference and a threat to America's lifeline, the Panama Canal. It also produced anxieties about financial investments on the island, and, in December 1914, an American military presence, as marines landed at Port au Prince, seized half a million dollars from Haitian bank vaults, and transported these funds to the National City Bank. Marines arrived in force in August 1915 and pacified the island, after fighting which cost two thousand Haitian lives. They also went ashore in the Dominican Republic in May 1916. But neither intervention disenchanted pacifists and reformers. Nor were they noticeably critical of the 1914 treaty that Bryan negotiated with Nicaragua, which seriously infringed on her sovereignty, or of the meddling of General Enoch Crowder, Wilson's personal emissary, in Cuban politics.

Finally, there was the Mexican dilemma, another legacy of earlier days inherited by the Democrats; and it, too, troubled Wilson from the moment that he assumed office in March 1913. Thirteen months later, he ordered armed intervention—in the form of ten naval vessels and a marine regiment which waded ashore at Veracruz. But Mexican troubles did not then subside. Rather they flared up more violently than ever when Pancho Villa, the able lieutenant of Venustiano Carranza (who had replaced Victoriano Huerta in office), massacred eighteen United States citizens at Santa Isabel in January 1916 and then, two months later, sacked Columbus, New Mexico, leaving seventeen more Americans dead. To chastise Villa and end these border incursions, Wilson ordered General John Pershing and several thousand cavalry into Mexico in futile pursuit of Villa.

Some peace workers were disappointed by Wilsonian policies vis-à-vis Mexico, for his actions seemed no different from Roosevelt's or Taft's. Edwin Mead, David Starr Jordan, and former Congressman Joseph Slyden were especially unhappy.

The Monroe Doctrine, they charged, furnished quasi-legal pre-
text for interference in Latin-American affairs, and they wanted
to amend or eliminate it.[45] Most of their colleagues, however,
reacted mildly or indifferently to Mexican developments. They
acquiesced when Wilson failed to recognize Huerta's regime.
They praised the chief executive's policy of "watchful waiting."
They mildly objected to Pershing's expedition; but they were
slow to dissent, and their criticism, when it came, was drowned
out by an approving symphony of interventionist sentiment in
and out of Congress.

Democrats by temperament and tradition, and instinctive
allies of the President, peace workers were hostile to Huerta's
unconstitutional vault into power and to his repressive regime.
Understandably, then, they never protested Wilson's diplomatic
drive to isolate Huerta from the international community and
to bring him down. Even Andrew Carnegie, on record as opposing United States intervention in Mexico, was ready to give
presidential policy a chance to work.[46] Like most Americans,
finally, peace workers supported the chief executive's actions
after Tampico and condemned Mexico's authorities for failure
to offer an immediate and unconditional apology.

But, for the first time, many peace workers became restive.
Not to be completely identified with patriots, they were
troubled by the military intervention. When successive Mexican-American crises culminated in Veracruz, some of them
even joined Wobblies and Socialists in open opposition to
United States actions.[47] The response of the New York Peace
Society was typical. Its members, at the Society's April 24,
1914, meeting, rejected any administration action that might
lead to war with Mexico. The Commission on Peace and Arbitration, of the Federal Council of Churches of Christ, sent a
resolution to the President as well as to each cabinet officer and
member of Congress warning against "mischief-makers and . . .
certain vested interests whose aggrandizement is furthered by
war."[48]

At this acute crisis, Wilson gladly accepted the proposal from
Argentina, Brazil, and Chile for a joint mediation; and his ac-

ceptance cheered peace workers. Some of them praised the chief executive. Hamilton Holt, for example, hailed Wilson and Secretary of State Bryan: They "have shown a political genius equalled only by their humanity." Carnegie's praise was even more fulsome: "This is the happiest moment of my life," he exclaimed. "War has been averted. . . . There will be no more hostilities. . . . The United States should expect Mexico and all other Latin American republics to take care of their own affairs, and should not meddle in them."[49]

SOCIALISTS AND MEXICO

Socialists made impressive electoral gains from 1910 to 1912, but the rank and file as well as most of the leadership limited their activities to the American scene. Witness, for example, the SPA 1912 convention, where the most fierce antagonisms swirled around the antisabotage plank; or the writings of Walling and La Monte, both of whom failed to consider American expansion abroad; or the articles of Austin Lewis and Anton Pannekoek, the Dutch-born left-socialist, which appeared in the columns of the *International Socialist Review* and which were given over to attacks on the ruling class and the condition of the proletariat; or the contributions of Ernst Untermann, one of the most learned of socialist intellectuals, actually favoring Pershing's foray across the border. In this sentiment he was joined by Jack London, the most famous of American socialists, one who still signed his letters, "Yours for the Revolution." But a real revolution, in Mexico, had already disenchanted London. He had alienated former party comrades by writing in *Collier's* that American troops should have occupied Tampico as well as Veracruz, that Mexican oil should be owned and exploited by foreign interests, and that the main trouble with American intervention was that it was not sufficiently forceful. The Mexican revolutionaries, he stated, were only bandits who were fighting for loot and for the pleasures of pillage; and their country would be "mismanaged and ill treated" until the United States "took over the whole country" as the "big brother of the countries of the new world."[50]

Socialists were understandably unhappy with London's surrender to all his worst instincts of Nordic supremacy and looked for another hero. They found him in John Reed, the poet-journalist, and their newest and most brash *Wunderkind*. Reed covered the Mexican scene for *Metropolitan*, the New York *World*, and the *Masses*, which, naturally enough, considered revolutionary events south of the border of great importance. He identified with the peons, admired Villa because he was a fighter, marched with this "Friend of the Poor, the Mexican Robin Hood" on Torreon and—brave, generous-hearted, and romantic—became a legend in his lifetime. Reed was anti-Huerta, but believed that intervention would get out of control, that the interventionists would seize the opportunity to conquer all of Mexico, and he sought to counteract agitation for all-out invasion. He persuaded aging publisher Joseph Pulitzer to take an unambiguous position against it, arguing that land for the peons, not oil for English and American exploiters, was the real issue, and a *World* editorial, arguing that land for the peons, not oil for English and American exploiters, was the real issue, reflected Reed's influence. In the *Metropolitan* of June 1914, Reed warned that "the first American soldier across the Rio Grande means the end of the Mexican revolution. . . . We went to debauch the Mexican people," he continued, "and turn them into little brown copies of American businessmen and laborers, as we are doing to the Cubans and Filipinos." Writing even more uninhibitedly in the *Masses*, he declared that nothing more catastrophic could happen to Mexico than the imposition of "our grand democratic institutions—trust government, unemployment and wage slavery."[51] Reed was not alone. Lincoln Steffens also traveled down to Mexico, and, deeply influenced by this first major Latin American social revolution, he reported, much like Reed, that the peons supported Villa because "he was at least a bandit," while Carranza, the Mexican President, was middle class. The official Socialist publication, *Party Builder*, flatly condemned United States intervention "in the name of humanity and civilization." The party's National Executive

Committee belatedly, in June 1916, demanded that Wilson re-call the troops and "capture the Americans who have inspired the Mexican raids across the borders." Louis Fraina, a major Socialist Party official, also attacked the United States role in Mexico. More than any other party member, he seemed aware of the implications of the Monroe Doctrine in the American "imperialist" scheme, and more aware of administration activities in Latin America. Like the Socialists, the anarcho-syndicalists blamed the entire affair upon America's "financial interests." Anarchist Emma Goldman, warning against the possibility of intervention below the border even before it took place, from an early date, relentlessly flailed away at administration policy toward Mexico. But it was the reports of Reed, the twenty-seven-year-old golden-haired boy out of Greenwich Village, that caught the public eye and that crystallized whatever there was in the way of popular opposition to Wilson's measures.[52]

Certainly the old anti-imperialist bloc, now confined to the best clubs and drawing rooms of proper Bostonians, was ineffectual in rallying public sentiment against American actions vis-à-vis Mexico. The most articulate and indefatigible spokesmen—Carl Schurz, Ernest Crosby, Leonard W. Bacon, et al.—were dead, and the bloc's argument against overseas possessions and interventionist practices eclipsed by the darkening clouds of European war.

Nor were the Socialists any more effective. They continued to limit their efforts to "boring from within" and capturing trade unions, restricting their energies and speculations to the arraignment of capitalism at home. Victor Berger even affirmed the need for military preparedness, and his moderate bloc followers were sharply divided from the party's antiwar majority. In sum, America's socialists, having no consistent or vigorous antiwar record up to 1914, maintained their customary silence on international affairs. Only with the outbreak of hostilities on the continent did they become aware of the need to take a stand—a realization that would crystallize bitterly antagonistic leadership positions and a deep rift in SPA ranks.

The peace movement, which had few uncompromising pacifists, also ignored Mexican-American affairs, being ineluctably drawn to Wilson—out of the desire of its members to advance their own special reform projects or their indentification with the Administration's progressive program. Pacifist ranks, like those of the socialists, would be shattered by overseas conflict from 1914 to 1917—with many peace workers idealistically supporting the "moral" conflict; or finding their continued efforts in the cause of pacifism in conflict with their patriotism, or equating both; or concluding that further support of pacifism was a menace to their reputation or to their work in behalf of one or another civil reform, which had always been their primary objective. Then, too, continued loyalty to the peace cause might jeopardize their influence in the circles òf power—something they valued highly. The old peace workers, after all, comprised a national elite of clergymen, educators, laywers, journalists, and philanthropists—successful and confident men who greatly esteemed social stability and authority. Too great a devotion to the peace issue became an increasing liability for these silver-haired veterans of the older international arbitration campaigns. And their ongoing commitment to the great cause was made untenable by the rush of events overseas and by dramatic shifts in the personnel and objectives of the peace movement itself. By late 1914, new peace societies—such as the Women's Peace Party and the American Union Against Militarism—had rejected many of the initial assumptions and reform objectives of prewar pacifism. Unlike their predecessors, who were always apprehensive about radical challenge to the social order, these younger men and women were not ecstatic about American diplomacy, did not find national political institutions paradigmatic, would not join in the campaign for military preparedness or in the war effort. Rather they found fault with both American institutions and foreign policy, and the overseas conflict would prompt them to reexamine social priorities and to develop a social ethic unknown to the earlier peace societies.

The First World War, then, had a mixed impact on the putative critics of our foreign policies. Although the Anti-Imperialist League, despite its being withered, did not officially expire until

1920, the overseas conflict hastened its end by demonstrating its ineffectiveness. The war produced disarray and schism in both socialist and pacifist ranks. For the socialist Party, the major radical organization in the United States, it catalyzed factionalism and—immeasurably helped by public opinion and repressive government actions—splintered and enfeebled the party's infrastructure. The war exposed the old peace societies for what they were, eliminating them from consideration as a bloc of critical observers and activists. But it also shaped a radicalized pacifism—with a constituency sharply critical of American society, with a social ethic unknown to the former peace groups, one that seamlessly wedded Christian idealism to social and industrial justice, and that would be of growing influence and importance over the next half century.

Notes

1. Padraic C. Kennedy, "La Follette's Imperialist Flirtation," *Pacific Historical Review*, 29 (May 1960): 131-144; Marian McKenna, *Borah* (Ann Arbor, Mich., 1961), pp. 37-38.

2. E. Berkeley Tompkins, *Anti-Imperialism in the United States: The Great Debate, 1890-1920* (Philadelphia, 1970), is a well-researched and useful study, and I have drawn upon it.

3. [Anti-Imperialist] Scrapbook, Widener Library, Harvard University, Cambridge, Mass.

4. On the antiimperialist appeal to the faith of the fathers, see, for instance, George G. Mercer's speech at the "Eastern Conference of Anti-Imperialists," reported in the New York *Evening Post*, "Special Anti-Imperialist Supplement," February 24, 1900. See also, Joseph Tulchin, "The Reformer Who Would Not Succeed: The Aberrent Behavior of Edward Atkinson and the Anti-Imperialist League," *Essex Institute Historical Collections* (April 1969), pp. 76-79; Charles Francis Adams, "Imperialism and the Tracks of Our Forefathers," *Anti-Imperialist Broadside*, no. 2, (December 20, 1898) Widener Library, Harvard University, Cambridge, Mass.; Senator George F. Hoar, in *Congressional Record*, 55th Cong., 3d sess., p. 544; George Boutwell, "In the Name of Liberty," Boutwell Papers, Massachusetts Historical Society.

5. Tompkins, *Anti-Imperialism*, pp. 236, 269-70. To be sure, several of the most eloquent pamphleteers were men in their early thirties; e.g., Rev.

Adolph A. Berle (see his essay in *Free America, Free Cuba, Free Philippines: Addresses at a Meeting in Faneuil Hall*. . . . [Boston, 1901], pp. 50-56) and Charles Warren (see his *The Development of a Policy, and the Contradictions Which May Arise Therefrom*. . . . [Boston, 1900]).

6. *Report of the Seventeenth Annual Meeting of the Anti-Imperialist League* (Boston, 1916), p. 14.

7. *Report of the Fifth Annual Meeting of the New England Anti-Imperialist League* (Boston, 1903), p. 17.

8. For the definitive study of the peace sects, from the outset of settlement into the twentieth century, see Peter Brock's massive *Pacifism in the United States* (Princeton, N.J., 1968). See also C. Roland Marchand, *The American Peace Movement and Social Reform, 1898-1918*, pp. 5-11, a work I am indebted to.

9. Sondra Herman, *Eleven Against War* (Stanford, 1969), p. 16.

10. Ibid., pp. 4, 6, 7.

11. Marchand, *American Peace Movement*, pp. 5-11. Most helpful is David Patterson, "The Travail of the American Peace Movement, 1887-1914" (Ph.D. dissertation, University of California, Berkeley, 1968).

12. *Report of the Lake Mohonk Conference* (1901), pp. 20-21. See also, *Universal Peace Congress, Report* (1904), p. 218; *National Arbitration and Peace Congress, Proceedings, 1907*, pp. 154-155.

13. Frederick Lynch, *The Peace Problem: The Task of the Twentieth Century* (New York, 1911), pp. 81-82. See also, *Proceedings of the Second National Peace Congress* (Chicago, 1909), p. 365.

14. Arnold Paul, *Conservative Crisis and the Rule of Law: Attitudes of the Bar and Bench, 1887-1895* (Ithaca, N.Y., 1960), pp. 2, 64, 81.

15. Walter LaFeber, *The New Empire* (Ithaca, N.Y., 1963), p. 416. See also Thomas J. McCormick, commentary, in *Studies on the Left* (1962), 3: 31-32.

16. *Peacemaker*, 16 (March 1898); 165-169, 170-172; (April 1898); 190, 191-192, 193. Gathered under peace banners within a few years would be men like Theodore Marburg, who urged war against Spain; Nicholas Murray Butler of Columbia University, and Reverend Lyman Abbott, both of whom advocated Philippine annexation; Elihu Root who, as Secretary of War, had diligently pressed the campaign against Filipino guerillas. See, on link between pacifism and expansionism, Michael Lutzker, "The 'Practical' Peace Advocates: An Interpretation of the American Peace Movement, 1898-1917" (Ph.D. dissertation, Rutgers University, 1969).

17. *Third Annual Report of the American School Peace League* (Boston, 1911), pp. 44-45. For a précis of this program, see Fannie Fern Andrews, "A Course of Study in Good Will," *Religious Education* 6 (January 1912): 570-573.

18. Marchand, *American Peace Movement*, pp. 128, 142.

19. This phrase, used by Nicholas Murray Butler, was used to indicate the distinction between the practical peace societies and their work—supported by the Carnegie Endowment—and the "peace propaganda . . . primarily rhetorical and fleeting in character" (Carnegie Endowment for International Peace, *Year Book for 1913-1914*, p. 57).

20. Herman, *Eleven Against War*, p. 18.

21. *Proceedings of the Third Annual Meeting of the American Society of International Meeting of the American Society of International Law* (Washington, D.C., 1909), p. 19.

22. Herman, *Eleven Against War*, p. 3.

23. Frederick Lynch, *Personal Recollections of Andrew Carnegie* (New York, 1920), p. 24.

24. *People,* August 20, 1899, p. 2.

25. Ibid., October 3, 1900, p. 3. DeLeon attacked Bryan's endorsement of the treaty as hypocritical; Bryan simply needed a good campaign issue: "Any lie, any subterfuge to get votes, is the rule of the capitalist politician" (ibid., October 13, 1900, p. 1).

26. Eugene Debs, *Debs: His Life, His Writings and His Speeches* (Chicago, 1908), p. 358.

27. Vincent St. John, "The Working Class and War," *International Socialist Review* 15 (August 1914): 117.

28. On joint or separate Socialist and pacifist meetings, see *Advocate of Peace* 76 (May 1914): 112. On Socialist willingness to join pacifists in an anti-interventionist campaign, see resolution, April 25, 1914, in *Socialist Congressional Campaign Book, 1914,* pp. 279-280. See also, *The Party Builder,* April 24, 1914, pp. 1-14.

29. *Social Democracy Red Book,* pp. 121, 122. See also Daniel Bell, "Marxian Socialism in the United States," in Donald Egbert & Stow Persons, eds., *Socialism in American Life* (Princeton, N.J., 1952), 2: 266; Howard H. Quint, *The Forging of American Socialism* (Columbia, S.C., 1953), passim.

30. *Proceedings of the National Congress of the Socialist Party, 1912.* Socialists did indeed criticize American "imperialism"—much as Debs attacked war as the product of the "master class"—in general and abstract terms. There were few specific charges leveled until the early 1920s. For a representative criticism, see John Spargo's attack on the Monroe Doctrine and on America's Latin American policies, in "The Monroe Doctrine, Its Democratization," *The Intercollegiate Socialist* (1917), pp. 8-9; Lilian D. Wald, *The House on Henry Street* (New York, 1915), pp. 230-233; Alice Stone Blackwell, *The Little Grandmother of the Russian Revolution: Reminiscences and Letters of Catherine Breshkovsky* (Boston, 1917), pp. 111-125, 332-333; Jane Addams, *Twenty Years at Hull House* (New York, 1926), chap. 17.

31. Tompkins, *Anti-Imperialism,* p. 265.

32. A fairly typical endorsement of Dollar Diplomacy, in an editorial endorsing a Chinese loan and United States financial intervention in Latin America, may be found in *Advocate of Peace* 74 (November 1912): 231.

33. Leonard Wood to Elihu J. Root, December 27, 1913, Root Papers, Library of Congress, Washington, D.C.

34. Adams D. Claflin to John Hays Hammond, November 9, 1910; Hammond to Claflin, copy, November 11, 1910, Box 5, Hammond Papers, Yale University.

35. New York *Tribune,* December 16, 1910. See also *Proceedings of the Second National Peace Congress* (Chicago, 1909), pp. 9, 22-24.

36. Charles W. Eliot, *The Road Toward Peace* (Boston, 1915), pp. 55-56.

37. New York Peace Society, *Annual Reports, Constitution . . . for the Year 1906-1907,* p. 5.

38. "New York Peace Society Minutes," January 7, 1913, New York Peace Society Papers, Box 1, Swarthmore College Peace Collection.

39. *The Navy,* 7 (June 1913): 250-256; *Advocate of Peace,* 75 (June 1913): 124-126.

40. William H. Short to Hamilton Holt, copy, March 3, 1911, Box 4, New York Peace Society Papers, Swarthmore College Peace Collection.

41. *Proceedings of the American Peace Congress,* (1913), p. 148.

42. Members of the Anti-Imperialist League shared the same convictions. They simply assumed that Wilson would implement the Democratic Party's plank on the Philippines and issue "an immediate declaration of the nation's purpose to recognize the independence" of the islands. *Report of the Fifteenth Annual Meeting of the Anti-Imperialist League* (Boston, 1913), pp. 17-18.

43. Quoted in Mark A. DeWolfe Howe, *Moorfield Story: Portrait of an Independent* (Boston, 1932), p. 305. Storey was so disappointed with Woodrow Wilson's performance that he voted for Charles Evans Hughes in the 1916 presidential election.

44. *Report of the Seventeenth Annual Meeting of the Anti-Imperialist League* (Boston, 1916), p. 10.

45. Arthur Link, *Wilson: The New Freedom* (Princeton, N.J., 1956), p. 324. See also David Starr Jordan, *America's Conquest of Europe* (Boston, 1913), pp. 35-37.

46. *New York Times,* November 26, 1913.

47. *Advocate of Peace,* 76 (May 1914): 112.

48. *Annual Report of the Federal Council of the Churches of Christ in America, 1914* (New York, 1915), pp. 31-32.

49. Andrew Carnegie, Letter to the *New York Times,* April 26, 1914.

50. Richard O'Connor and Dale Walker, *The Lost Revolutionary* (New York, 1967), p. 128.

51. Quoted in Granville Hicks, *John Reed* (New York, 1936), p. 139.

52. In an exception to the rule of radical disregard of overseas affairs, Emma Goldman had earlier urged liberty for the Cuban and Filipino people, though she was aware that America's delusive mission was to "civilize" them—which, she recognized, would bring slavery (*Mother Earth*, September 1906). For further examples of Socialist opposition to intervention in Mexico, see "Imperialism Rampant," *The New Review*, 1 (March 1, 1913): 257-259; "Democratic Imperialism," ibid., 2 (January 1914): 5-10; "Villa or Wilson—Which is the Bandit?", *The Blast* (March 15, 1916). An earlier expression of opposition to United States policies below the border may also be found in *Mother Earth*, for Emma Goldman warned of "the sinister design to invade Mexico" in "Observations and Comments," ibid. (May 1911).

TOM MANN AND WILLIAM D. HAYWOOD:
CULTURE, PERSONALITY,
AND COMPARATIVE HISTORY

Melvyn Dubofsky

In a 1966 essay analyzing the origins of working-class radicalism in the American West, I concluded that "today we need
fewer vague generalizations about the uniqueness or significance
of the frontier.... We ... need comparative studies placing
American labor history in the broader context of world-
wide ... history where all workers, regardless of nationality,
tasted the fruits, both bitter and sweet, of the capitalist order."[1]
Frankly, since then, I have barely explored the treacherous ter-
rain of comparative history. Like most historians, I have a fond-
ness for the unique and the particular, a suspicion of the abstract; and, thus far, most comparative historical studies have
been based either on sweeping abstractions or on loose generalizations. Nevertheless it can be argued that a firm historical
basis exists for comparing the experience of Britain and the
United States, especially for the years from roughly 1880 to
1919.

In this essay similarities and differences in Anglo-American
history will be explored through an analysis of the lives,
thoughts, and beliefs of Tom Mann and William D. Haywood,
among the most eminent and active labor radicals in their respective societies. In the course of their lives and careers both
men followed a trajectory that carried them from working-class
obscurity to radical notoriety. Mann, the son of an English Mid-
lands miner, and Haywood, a child of the American West, both

189

participated prominently in the most significant trade union
and radical political developments of the era 1890-1920. They
rose to prominence initially within traditional trade unions,
later became advocates of working-class politics and socialism,
grew more radical and revolutionary with time, and ultimately
linked themselves to the Bolshevik Revolution and Soviet communism. No two labor leaders in pre- and post-World War I
Britain and the United States were more indelibly associated in
the popular mind with working-class radicalism, massive industrial conflicts, and labor violence. An examination of their lives
thus promises to shed new light on the role of radicals in British
and American society.

Before analyzing the careers of Mann and Haywood in greater
detail, however, one might fairly ask: Are the English and the
American experiences at all comparable? A quick and easy
answer would be, NO! For those scholars who have most often
compared English and American history, such men as Seymour
Martin Lipset, Louis Hartz, and Daniel Boorstin, assure us that
the American experience has been exceptional, if not at all
points, certainly at those most vital in the shaping of national
character and consciousness.[2]

What precisely are the attributes or conditions of American
exceptionalism? First there is the inescapable fact that the United States came into being without a distinct feudal tradition in
the European sense and without a hereditary, conservative social class. Lacking an *ancien regime* America produced no radicals committed to overthrowing it and no reactionaries dedicated to restoring a lost golden age of aristocratic virtues. Instead, as Louis Hartz sees it, all American citizens functioned
within an agreed Lockean postfeudal consensus. Indeed, Lipset
has asserted that from its birth America has been a nondeferen-
tial, nonascriptive society, which produced the second basic attribute of American exceptionalism: the extent of social mobility and the fluidity of class lines.[3]

Talk about the "promise of American life"—men who rose
from log cabins to the White House and from steerage passage
to business imperium—has been among the commonplaces of

the national mythology. In a society in which men rose and fell solely on the basis of their abilities and in which there was always room at the top, no place existed for radical theories of social change or for radical economic and political organizations to effect such changes. There was simply no point in challenging Hartz's Lockean consensus, for as Werner Sombart once commented: American socialism was shipwrecked on reefs of roast beef and shoals of apple pie.[4]

Which brings us to the third attribute of American exceptionalism: the lack of a substantial socialist tradition. For the reasons cited above and others too numerous to mention here, such historians as David Shannon have concluded that the rhetoric, the mystique, the symbols of American labor politics are different, that "it is natural to expect the Chicago workingman of, say, 1900, to have political ideals and loyalities different from those of his counterpart in Lyon, the Baltimore truck driver to think differently politically from the Newcastle shipyard worker. . . . "[5] And these different traditions of class and thought doomed socialism in America.

Finally all these exceptional characteristics combined to produce the unique national value structure that Lipset has analyzed with immense subtlety. Americans are dominated by what he labels an achievement-egalitarian syndrome. The American devotion to equality is tempered by a similar commitment to individual achievement, and the resultant tension, or dialectic, between equality and individualism has caused the lower-class American "to drive *himself* to get ahead," unlike the working-class European, who tends to emphasize "collective modification of the class structure."[6] Hence, once again, peculiar American values preclude the possibility of a radical or socialist tradition.

Still, I would hazard to argue that during the lifetimes of Tom Mann and William D. Haywood, such differences between English and American society were more apparent than real, and to them, at least, insubstantial. Let me explain.

To begin with we have the question of whether history is to be written, or indeed viewed, from the top down or the bottom up. For industrialists, the implications of a feudal tradition are clear enough: Societies with aristocratic traditions preserve rul-ing-class values that are not necessarily gratifying to capitalists; aristocratic values are not those of economic man, particularly his scientific-technological variant. Moreover, industrialists must struggle to establish their values as preferable and often them-selves can rise to the top of society only by assimilating aristo-cratic traditions.[7] But workers in either case are still ruled by factory masters, who set the terms of work and the rewards for labor. Mann and Haywood, perceiving society from the bottom up, viewed their respective "masters" in much the same way.

Social mobility also looks quite different, whether viewed from the bottom or the top of society. Asa Briggs's successful mid- and late- Victorian men and women for example sound remarkably like Lipset's Eisenhower-era Americans. Briggs's middle-class Victorians saw a society in which a marked degree of individual mobility existed; where the dividing line between classes was extremely difficult to draw; and in which divisions within class lines were often more significant than conflicts between classes. And Beautrice Webb in her autobiography re-members values inculcated during her childhood that are nota-bly congruent with Lipset's American ideal-type values.

> It was the bounden duty of every citizen to better his social status; to ignore those beneath him, and to aim steadily at the top rung of the ladder. Only by this persistent pursuit by each individual of his own and his family's interest would the highest general level of civili-zation be attained.[8]

But down at the bottom of society in both England and the United States what Haywood and Mann saw was mass insecuri-ty, squalor, and poverty; the fortunate few might indeed rise, but only at the expense of the vast majority doomed to remain in the class of their birth.

Furthermore, during the lifetimes of Mann and Haywood la-bor politics in England and America perhaps did not appear as different as later historians have perceived it. In both nations socialism and radicalism touched a relatively small minority, yet the ruling classes dreaded social turmoil and even revolution. If England had a Labour party before World War I, America had a Socialist party that seemed equally a potential threat to the political hegemony of the two established parties. That English labor would rise as American socialism declined, neither Mann nor Haywood could foresee before 1918, by which date they had formed their fundamental notions about labor, radicalism, and politics.

Let me now turn away from abstraction and examine more closely the lives and thoughts of Mann and Haywood. In both cases, however, a dearth of historical sources complicates the task of comparison and analysis.[9] The lack of sources notwithstanding, we can piece enough together about the lives of Mann and Haywood to reveal a similar developmental pattern.[10] Both men lost one parent at an early age,[11] lacked formal education, and turned to wage-earning early—Mann started work in a coal mine at age nine and remained in the pit for four years; Haywood, scrambling for the various jobs available to an uneducated, working-class youth, spent his preadolescent days around Salt Lake City and several Utah mining camps. When Mann's father moved the family to Birmingham, Tom, at age fifteen, was apprenticed to a toolmaking firm where he learned the engineering craft. Haywood at fifteen also discovered his primary occupation: Together with his stepfather he went down into the silver mines of Nevada, and a hard-rock miner he would stay until 1900. Mann, the skilled engineer, and Haywood, the skilled nonferrous miner, seldom remained long enough in one place to establish roots. After completing his Birmingham apprenticeship in 1877, Mann spent the next five years working in various capacities in London, and Brooklyn, U.S.A., and visiting Paris. Haywood during the initial years of his working life drifted about the widely scattered mining camps of Utah, Colorado, Nevada, and Idaho, until he finally settled down for a time in Silver City, Idaho.

Both men encountered the labor movement at various stages

in their early working lives but at first committed themselves to it less than enthusiastically. Indeed, Mann would not become a truly active member of the Amalgamated Society of Engineers until socialism touched his heart and mind. In Haywood's case we have no substantial evidence of interest in trade unionism before 1896. But in that year the president of the Western Federation of Miners (WFM) visited Silver City to charter a local which Haywood joined. Over the succeeding decade he was to rise within the union hierarchy and to serve as a conscientious official, until socialism became his new passion.

Mann and Haywood turned to socialism for similar reasons. Their experiences with "bread and butter" forms of unionism convinced them of its inability to solve the essential "social problem;" equally important, non-working-class socialists transformed both men into prominent public personalities. Mann and Haywood would also find at roughly the same time socialism less than a complete solution to industrial society's ills, and, disillusioned with the prospects of socialist revolutions, they became syndicalists.

Syndicalism in turn propelled Mann and Haywood into the communist movement. Mann, a charter member of the British Communist party, remained loyal to it until his death in 1941. For Hayward communism led to political exile in the Soviet Union, where he died in 1928, having failed to promote radicalism in the land of his birth or to build his version of the new society in the land of his exile.

There are several other striking similarities in the lives of Mann and Haywood. Though they had families, evidence indicates that they were not family men. Indeed, Mann scarcely mentions wife and children in his memoirs and there is the distinct possibility that he in fact maintained two separate and distinct families. Haywood, a physically attractive man, wed to a frail and increasingly superstitious woman, took to satisfying his sexual needs outside the home.[12]

Also notably congruent in the careers of Mann and Haywood was their commitment to internationalism in theory and practice. Mann, for example, twice visited the United States and

South Africa; spent a decade in Australasia; traveled in the Soviet Union; and devoted considerable effort to establishing European trade-union federations. Haywood in 1910 and again in 1913 toured the continent and Great Britain, where he addressed various trade-union and socialist audiences. And, of course, he spent the last eight years of his life in the Soviet Union.

It is indeed noteworthy how, despite their dissimilar immediate environments, their quite different crafts, and the divergent character of the trade unions to which they belonged, Mann's and Haywood's careers and values followed parallel paths. Birmingham and London were obviously worlds apart from Salt Lake City and Silver City. Practically the same can be said of the Amalgamated Society of Engineers and the Western Federation of Miners. The ASE, which Mann joined in the 1870s, was a proven success. Despite enormous changes in the social and economic environment of England, the society maintained its traditional posture of craft exclusiveness and union moderation. Representing the aristocrats of the British labor movement, it functioned within the limits set by Victorian working-class respectability and lower middle-class morality.[13] The Western Federation was another matter. The union, which Haywood joined in 1896, had barely survived the first three years of its life and had a future that looked anything but healthy. But Haywood's recruitment coincided with an upturn in the union's prospects, an improvement that proceeded hand-in-glove with radicalism. Committed to militant notions of class struggle, the union practiced as well as preached solidarity. Its practices and beliefs cut against the grain of the American labor movement, most of whose affiliated unions were cut out of the same cloth as the English Amalgamated Society of Engineers.[14] In other words, Mann became a radical despite his union affiliation, while Haywood learned his radicalism in union service.

Nothing in the early union careers of Mann and Haywood hinted at the distance that they would travel in their radicalism. Before leaving Birmingham for London, Mann had devoted himself to temperance and viewed life from an orthodox Christian

perspective. Even after his conversion to socialism early in the
1880s, he essentially remained moderate. During the famous
London dock strike of 1889, which made him a national per-
sonality, Mann served more as the conscientious union official
than the militant agitator. His moderation won him appointment to the Royal Commission on Labour, a position he held
for three years. During that time he spoke regularly to middle-
class reform and church groups, and indeed seemed so close to
clergymen that rumors arose that Mann was about to take
church orders. It was such behavior that caused Friedrich Engels
to write: "Of their leaders, Tom Mann is upright but boundless-
ly weak, and he has been made half-crazy by his appointment as
a member of the Royal Commission on Labour."[15]

Similarly, Haywood, the Silver City, Idaho, trade unionist,
concentrating upon job security, higher wages, shorter hours,
and union-sponsored protection against illness, injury, and
death, cautiously led his fellow workers along the accepted
route of American trade unionism from 1896 to 1900. No wonder the chief engineer of the mine at which Haywood worked
considered Big Bill a model citizen![16]   After 1900, when he left
Silver City to become secretary-treasurer of the WFM, Haywood, by then a socialist, still acted moderately and cautiously.
Confining his radicalism mostly to editorials in the union journal, Haywood, on the eve of the most brutal conflict in his
union's history, remarked: "We are not opposed to employers . . . it is our purpose and aim to work harmoniously and
jointly with employers as best we can under this system, and we
intend to change the system if we get sufficiently organized and
well enough educated to do so."[17] Mann, at a comparable stage
in his own career, had observed that the work of trade unionists
was "so to organize ourselves and to get workers generally so
effectively organized, that we can insist on the necessary
changes taking place."[18]

Yet even during the moderate phase of their socialism, the
factors that would later transform two conscientious union officials into radical gadflies to their respective societies were in
gestation. This is much clearer in Mann's case and has been

documented both in his memoirs and in Dona Torr's biography. Haywood's public arrival as an agitator was much more sudden, if equally understandable. After toiling as a worker and union official for some ten years in what Englishmen would refer to as the provinces, Haywood was suddenly catapulted into the national spotlight. Arrested for his part in the alleged conspiracy to assassinate ex-Governor Frank Steunenberg of Idaho and brought to trial for murder, he became a martyr to the cause of labor and radicalism. From his Boise prison cell, he stood in 1906 as the Socialist candidate for governor of Colorado. Thereafter he seldom drifted far from the radical limelight. Four years before his arrest, however, Haywood had had premonitions of what his future role would be. Writing in the union journal, Haywood extolled the contributions of the agitator to civilization and asserted that the agitator "is the advance agent of social improvement and fully realizes that reforms are not achieved by conservative methods."[19] A decade earlier Mann, in more Biblical terms, had written similarly of his own function: "Cry aloud, spare not, lift up thy voice like a trumpet, and show My people their transgressions. Upon the agitators rests the stupendous task of awakening the nation . . . to yearnings for a worthier life. For all effective agitators . . . we have cause to be devoutly thankful. . . ."[20]

These two self-proclaimed prophets of radicalism carried the same message to their respective societies. Fastening their gazes, as all good prophets are wont to do, upon society's disinherited, those unable to adjust to industrialism or destroyed by it, they warned in the words of Haywood at the founding convention of the IWW: ". . . society can be no better than its most miserable."[21] But the Anglo-American labor movement, as perceived by Mann and Haywood, neglected the disinherited. They observed nations in which capital was concentrating into immense industrial combines whose technology obliterated traditional skills, while trade unions remained devoted to crafts that had lost social and economic significance. As early as 1886 Mann had bemoaned the typical trade unionist of his time, whom he characterized as "a man with a fossillized intellect, either hopelessly apathetic or supporting a policy that plays directly into the hands of the capitalist exploiter."[22] Four years later he and Ben Tillet ridiculed the deadly stupor of such tight craft unions as the Amalgamated Society and pleaded that "clannishness in trade matters must be superseded by a cosmopolitan spirit, brotherhood must not only be talked of but practiced. . . . "[23] Haywood proved equally severe in his condemnation of American trade unions which represented a small minority of workers inculcated with the spirit of craft selfishness, who tried to monopolize union benefits for the favored few. And Haywood, like Mann, asserted that the true friend of labor should see that: "The diversity of labor is incapable of craft distinction. . . . The machine is the apprentice of yesterday, the journeyman of today. But the industrial union is the evolution of the labor movement confronting and competing with the strides of the machine in industrial progress . . . it is also the open door of organized labor."[24]

Separated by three thousand miles of water and another twenty-five hundred of land, never having met personally (at least at this point in their lives), Mann and Haywood nevertheless shared thoughts about the labor movement, expressed those thoughts in comparable ways, and consistently sought to practice their theories of industrial unionism and labor solidarity.

Their transcendent faith in the value of workers' organizations also made both men uncertain socialists. Socialists largely by instinct, their politics were more of the heart than the mind. As socialist agitators they stirred the emotions of workingmen with glowing pictures of a new and better world-to-be, not with learned exegeses of Marxian economics or politics. And their roles as agitators playing upon crowd emotions made them uncomfortable with socialists primarily concerned with the finer points of theory or the gathering of an additional vote or two. As self-taught working-class intellectuals, Mann and Haywood sometimes had strained relations with university-educated radicals.

From the first Mann never believed that socialist politics was as important as working-class economic organizations. During his active years in the Social Democratic Federation (SDF), roughly 1884 to 1890, Mann was uneasy about Hyndman's hostility toward trade unions. Irked by the SDF's neglect of the labor movement, Mann quietly ceased his work for the federation. His subsequent relationship with the Independent Labour Party (ILP) also troubled him. Though Mann served as secretary of the ILP from 1894 to 1896, collaborated amicably with Keir Hardie, and stood as a party candidate in several elections, he was never secure in a party that veiled its socialist paternity and that seemed to him to be a vote-grabbing machine. In the period between his break with the SDF and his activity within the ILP, Mann expressed his fundamental attitude toward politics in these words: "The real worker for the people is the man who is changing their habits and thought, and he must work amongst the rank and file. Always remember that Parliament will not change the people, but as the people are changed, they will very soon change the Parliament."[25] And nine years of almost continuous agitation for socialism in Australasia, where he observed labor governments in action, reinforced Mann's suspicions about politics. "It was plain to me," he wrote just before leaving Australia in 1909, "that economic organization was indispensable for the achievement of economic freedom. The policy of the various Labour Parties gave no promise in this direction, nor did the superadding of political activities to the extant type of trade-union organization seem any more hopeful."[26] Taking note of syndicalism in France and Italy, as well as the IWW in the United States, he observed: "Whether parliamentary action was to be dropped or not, increasing importance would evidently attach to industrial organization."[27]

Haywood's relationship to socialism proved more strained than Mann's, and for comparable reasons. In a party eager to appear respectable, Haywood publicly gloried in his disdain for the capitalist law. The implications of the dynamiting of the Los Angeles *Times'* building in 1911, which frightened many socialists, led Haywood to plead for more direct action and sabotage. To a party, many of whose leaders were professional men and women, Haywood challenged: "To understand the

class struggle you must go into the factory and you must ride
on top of the boxcars or underneath ... you must go down
with me into the bowels of the earth ... there by the rays of a
tallow candle you will understand something about the class
struggle."[28] Worse yet, Haywood derided parliamentary reforms
and declared instead that: "I want to to say ... it is decidedly
better ... to be able to elect the superintendent in some branch
of industry than to elect a congressman."[29] As a result of such
declarations and his public actions, Haywood was recalled from
the Socialist party's National Executive Committee in 1913;
thereafter he devoted himself to the IWW and to syndicalism.

For both Mann and Haywood the transformation from socialist to syndicalist entailed no violent rupture with their earlier
beliefs. Indeed, continuities in their patterns of thought were
more apparent than discontinuities. Throughout the 1880s and
1890s, as he agitated for socialism, Mann constantly asserted
that organization of the working class remained the single most
important radical objective. So, too, in Haywood's case. At the
moment he became an active socialist, Haywood noted: "The
essential thing for the producing class is to control and supervise
the means of production and distribution. ... This can only be
accomplished by workers themselves organizing an industrial
government."[30]

In such comments lay the seeds of syndicalism: faith that the
workers by organizing themselves fully and engaging in direct
action at the point of production, without the mediation of
political parties or parliaments, could seize industry and operate
it in the best interests of society. Again, it should be stressed
that neither Mann nor Haywood presented blueprints detailing
how workers would attain total organization, oust the capitalists from economic and political power, and run their new society. Theory and analysis were not their strong points—agitation
was, and the style and content of their agitation for syndicalism
was indeed similar.

Both men advised workers to ignore politics, because it only
served to confuse and divide labor, fomenting sectarianism
where solidarity was required. Traditional trade unionism was

equally to be disdained. In place of politics and business unionism would arise the revolutionary union, which in Mann's
words, would make possible concerted action whereby the
workers may be enabled to decide the conditions under which
production shall be carried on."[31] The essence of the revolutionary union was its unremitting adherence to the class struggle—in Haywood's words: "We deny that any identity of interest can exist between the exploiter and the exploited."[32] Or as
Mann noted: "The object of the unions is to wage the Class War
and take every opportunity of scoring against the enemy."[33]
Mann and Haywood thus opposed binding agreements with employers, which could only serve to paralyze the will of the labor
movement and vitiate labor solidarity. Workers and their unions
had to remain free at all times to act as fighting organizations,
willing and ready to use any means of direct action necessary to
achieve the social revolution.

Although Mann and Haywood never explained precisely how
direct action would usher in the revolutionary commonwealth,
their scenarios for revolution were basically similar. Mann simply advised workers to "cease to function as workers and this
would force the employers to make the required concessions,
including the complete capitulation."[34] Haywood concurred: "If
labor was organized and self-disciplined it could stop every
wheel in the United States tonight—every one—and sweep off
your capitalists and State legislatures and politicians into the
sea."[35] One could only wonder why if employers and governments were superfluous they had dominated society so long?
And if instead they were powerful and essential, why they
would meekly surrender their powers and privileges to an organized working class?

Vaguer still were Mann's and Haywood's notions concerning
the administrations of a syndicalist society. Of one thing we can
be sure: Parliamentary politics had no place in their utopia.
Industrial government would replace parliamentary institutions,
trade unions would substitute for political parties, and union
officials would take over from civil-service bureaucrats. Trade
unions, as the primary social institutions, would in the words of

Mann, "assume the responsibilities of provisioning, clothing, and housing the people."[36]

Paradoxically, for syndicalists who asserted the primacy of industrial democracy and rank-and-file participation in all matters, Mann and Haywood shared a singular penchant for the type of scientific efficiency approaches then so popular among English Fabians and American Progressives.[37] References to the efficient, scientific organization of society form a recurrent theme in the writing and remarks of both men. As early as the 1889 London dock strike, Mann's solution to the problems of waterside labor was the scientific reorganization of the London docks under municipal control. Six years later in an ILP pamphlet, he asserted: "What is now imperatively demanded is a national scientific supervision of the Nation's Work . . . scientifically adjusting our own energy so as to harmoniously balance the nation."[38] Indeed, the struggle for his syndicalist utopia was to be waged scientifically by scientifically organized industrial unions.[39] Haywood's allusions to scientific efficiency scarcely differ; again and again he reverted to the theme that workers would not be emancipated until their unions were established upon a scientific basis and that his syndicalist state would be organized along lines more scientific and more efficient than those of anarchistic capitalism.

Not surprisingly, Mann and Haywood never resolved the contradictions inherent in their images of a revolutionary rank-and-file working-class movement that would achieve power scientifically, or of a syndicalist society that would be founded on absolute democracy and individual participation in decision-making and yet would be totally scientific and efficient. Such beliefs placed them closer to middle-class technocrats and bureaucrats than to less militant social democrats or ordinary rank-and-file workers. Perhaps this explains part of their inability to form mass movements among English and American workers and also their final turn to communism.

One can only hypothesize that in Lenin and the Bolshevik Revolution Mann and Haywood saw a revolution actually achieved by nonparliamentary means, by what indeed could be considered direct action; and that Lenin personified the efficient, scientific revolutionary who coolly displaced the capitalists and their bureaucratic henchmen. The "dictatorship of the proletariat," it could be argued, was simply a preliminary stage in which the revolution was defended against counterrevolutionary terror while the scientific basis was laid for a future society of free men and women.

Mann had no apparent difficulty in reconciling communism and syndicalism. Of the Bolsheviks, he could simply say: "They hold that parliament is outworn, and that the growing economic power of the workers must fashion new forces of political expression." Of himself: "We should not rigidly adhere to past policies for the sake of consistency when these no longer make for perfect solidarity." The experience of world war and revolution had altered Mann's beliefs, leading him now to conclude that "the Communist International is the unifying force that must bring together and organize all the militant workers in their right relationship, so that each can play his part in the common struggle."[40] To that conception Mann remained true until his death in 1941.

Haywood's switch to communism had a less rationalized base. Whether he went into exile because of his attraction to communism or simply out of a desire to avoid imprisonment is unclear. Most likely his flight resulted from a combination of the two. Whatever the reasons for his flight to Russia, his exile was not a happy one. Out of his depth in the new society being created by such men as Lenin and Trotsky, not really a Bolshevik, and in fact seriously ill, Haywood saw his dream of building a Wobbly utopia in Russia quickly sour. By 1923 he was in semi-, if not permanent, retirement in Moscow, a desperately lonely man, who remained something of a character in the world of American exiles in Russia. Ailing and frequently hospitalized, he finally died on May 28, 1928.[41]

What conclusions, then, can one draw about the comparability of the English and the American experience in the industrial era from such a brief glance at the lives of Mann and Haywood? Obviously one cannot and should not make too much of simi-

larities in transnational experience derived solely from a comparison of two individuals, exceptional as they both may have
been. Still, there are so many obvious similarities in their careers, their perceptions of society, and their patterns of thought
that one must question David Shannon's assertion that "it is
natural to expect the Baltimore truck driver to think differently
from the Newcastle shipyard worker" (one might also observe
that it would be just as natural to expect the Yorkshire coal
miner to think differently from the Cornish tin miner). For here
we have a Birmingham engineer and a western American hard-
rock miner who shared a common rhetoric and value system.
Until we examine in more detail the rhetoric and value systems
of other Anglo-American leaders and trade unions, and choose
leaders, individual unions, and federations of unions that are at
least comparable, we are in no position to assume ipso facto
that American working-class values differed fundamentally from
English ones. The same caution holds for Lipset's assertions
about the uniqueness of the general American value structure:
his achievement-egalitarian syndrome. To Mann the tension between equality and individualism was as intense among organized sectors of the English working class as among their American counterparts, and caused workers on both sides of the
Atlantic to drive themselves ahead rather than joining together
collectively with all other workers to modify the class structure.
Indeed, the history of Anglo-American labor movements is rife
with examples of the tension between individualism and equality, selfishness and self-sacrifice, as even a cursory reading of the
sources must indicate. Again, until we examine individuals and
institutions on both sides of the Atlantic in comparable social
situations, we are in no position to draw firm conclusions
about fundamental differences or similarities.

The lives of Mann and Haywood do, however, reveal one
clear similarity in the Anglo-American experience and one sharp
difference. Their careers certainly dislcose how marginal a place
the principled and militant working-class radical has held in
Anglo-American society. The more radical both Mann and Haywood became, the more they led or spoke for organizations out

of touch with the mass of workers, except in times of unusual crisis. But English society has always maintained that extra measure of tolerance for deviancy that America has lacked, that English tolerance for eccentricity that Kenneth McNaught in his suggestive essay on the failure of American socialism[42] has posited as the cause for the tenacity of English radicalism in contrast to the evanescence of American radicalism. Tom Mann, the English radical and communist, could end his life in his native land, after receiving birthday tributes from Emmanuel Shinwell and Clement Attlee. Haywood died a miserable exile, having to be satisifed that American communists distorted and romanticized his contributions to the American labor movement and to radicalism.

Notes

1. Melvyn Dubofsky, "The Origins of Western Working Class Radicalism, 1890-1905," *Labor History*, 7 (Spring 1966): 154.

2. Seymour M. Lipset, *The First New Nation: The United States in Historical and Comparative Perspective* (New York, 1963); Louis Hartz, *The Liberal Tradition in America* (New York, 1955); *The Founding of New Societies* (New York, 1964), pp. 69-122; Daniel Boorstin, *The Genius of American Politics* (Chicago, 1953); *The Americans,* (New York, 1958, 1965), vols. 1, 2.

3. Hartz, *Liberal Tradition;* Lipset, *First New Nation.*

4. Cited in Daniel Bell, *Marxian Socialism in the United States* (Princeton, N.J., 1967), p. 4.

5. David Shannon, "Socialism and Labor," in C. Vann Woodward, *The Comparative Approach to American History* (New York, 1968), p. 249; Carl Degler cites Shannon's essay as ". . . one of the most incisive and fresh explanations for American exceptionalism in print. . . ." (*Journal of Southern History*, 34 [August 1968]: 429.) Cf. John Laslett, *Labor and The Left* (New York, 1970), p. 304; and Kent and Gretchen Kreuter, *An American Dissenter: The Life of Algie Martin Simons, 1870-1950,* (Lexington, Ky., 1969), p. 220, for the following remark: "Socialism was a fragment torn from the culture of another continent, and to live successfully in a new environment it had to unite itself with indigenous forms of life that were already thriving. . . . Yet he [Simons] underestimated the vigor of the life to which he sought to attach this foreign graft. It was socialism that was choked out."

6. Lipset, *First New Nation,* p. 175.

7. For the problems of businessmen-capitalists in an aristocratic society, see David Landes, "French Entrepreneurship and Industrial Growth in the Nineteenth Century," *Journal of Economic History,* 9 (1949): 49-61; "French Business and the Businessman: A Social and Cultural Analysis," in E. M. Earle, ed., *Modern France: Problems of the Third and Fouth Republics* (Princeton, N.J., 1951), pp. 334-353.

8. Asa Briggs, "The Language of 'Class' in Early Nineteenth-Century England," in Asa Briggs and John Saville, *Essays in Labour History* (London, 1967), pp. 43-73, especially pp. 70-71.

9. In Mann's case we are more fortunate than Haywood's. Although there is no substantial collection of Mann's private papers and documents, we do have his own understated and quite believable autobiography, (*Memoirs* [London, 1923]), as well as Dona Torr's *Tom Mann and His Times,* vol. 1, 1856-1890 (London, 1956); Edward Thompson's, "Tom Mann and His Times, 1890-1892," *Our History* (Pamphlet No. 26-27, Summer-Autumn 1962); and Dona Torr's *Tom Mann* (London, 1936).

For Haywood we are less fortunate. His autobiography, about which there is still some dispute as to authorship, is exaggerated and at places clearly not in accord with the facts of his life. See *Bill Haywood's Book: The Autobiography of William D. Haywood* (New York, 1929). A biography that scarcely transcends the insights of the autobiography and can be equally misleading (though it contains some new information, particularly on Haywood's Russian exile) is Joseph R. Conlin, *Big Bill Haywood and the Radical Union Movement* (Syracuse, N.Y., 1969). For a somewhat different version of Haywood's life and career see my own, "The Radicalism of the Dispossessed: William Haywood and the IWW," in Alfred F. Young, ed., *Dissent: Explorations in The History of American Radicalism* (DeKalb, Ill., 1968), pp. 177-213.

10. Unless otherwise cited, the material for the biographical sketches comes from Mann's *Memoirs,* Dona Torr's biography, Haywood's autobiography, and my essay on Haywood.

11. Mann lost his mother when he was only two and a half; Haywood's father died when Bill was three.

12. Confidential information on Mann from English sources; for Haywood's extramarital activities see, "Relating to the Western Federation of Miners, 1906-1907"; Pinkerton Reports, Idaho State Historical Society (microfilm); and Mabel Dodge Luhan, *Intimate Memories,* vol. 3, *Movers and Shakers* (New York, 1936), pp. 89, 186-187.

13. J. B. Jeffereys, *The Story of the Engineers* (London, 1946).

14. Melvyn Dubofsky, "The Origins of Western Working Class Radicalism"; Vernon Jensen, *Heritage of Conflict* (Ithaca, N.Y., 1950).

15. Engels to F. Sorge, August 9-11, 1891, in Karl Marx and Friedrich Engels, *Letters to Americans, 1848-1895* (New York, 1953), p. 235.

16. The State of Idaho v. William D. Haywood, et al., microfilm copy, Idaho State Historical Society, (1891) vol. 3.

17. Stenographic Report of the Advisory Board Appointed by Governor James H. Peabody to Investigate and Report upon Labor Difficulties in the State of Colorado and More Particularly at Colorado City, pp. 80, 81, 84, 109, 118, in James H. Hawley Papers, Idaho State Historical Society.

18. Mann, *Memoirs*, p. 106.

19. *Miner's Magazine*, 3 (February 1902): 6.

20. Mann, *The Programme of the I.L.P. and the Unemployed* (London, 1895), pp. 1-2.

21. *Proceedings of the First Annual Convention of the Industrial Workers of the World* (New York, 1905), p. 18.

22. Torr, *Tom Mann and His Times*, p. 218.

23. Tom Mann and Ben Tillett, *The "New" Trade-Unionism: A Reply to Mr. George Shipton* (London, 1890).

24. *Miner's Magazine*, 6 (May 11, 1905): 6; cf., *Miner's Magazine*, 7 (November 30, 1905): 10.

25. *Yorkshire Factory Times*, August 28, 1891, cited in Thompson, "Tom Mann," p. 32.

26. Mann, *Memoirs*, p. 239.

27. Ibid., p. 243.

28. William D. Haywood, "Socialism the Hope of the Working Class," *International Socialist Review*, 12 (February 1912): 464.

29. Ibid., p. 462.

30. Haywood to Officers and Delegates at the 1906 WFM Convention, May 24, 1906, in WFM, *Official Proceedings of the 1906 Convention* (Denver, 1906), pp. 17-22.

31. Mann, "Forging the Weapon," *The Industrial Syndicalist*, 1 (September 1910); foreword to Emile Pataud and Emile Pouget, *Syndicalism and the Co-operative Commonwealth* (Oxford, 1913).

32. Haywood letter to 1906 WFM convention.

33. Mann, "Forging the Weapon," p. 7.

34. Mann in *The Industrial Syndicalist* (April 1911), cited in Torr, *Mann*, pp. 36-37.

35. *U.S. Commission on Industrial Relations, Final Report and Testimony* (Washington, D.C., 1915), 11: 10, 578.

36. Mann's foreword to *Syndicalism and the Co-operative Commonwealth*.

37. E. J. Hobsbawm, "The Fabians Reconsidered," in *Labouring Men* (London, 1964), pp. 250-271; Robert Wiebe, *The Searth for Order, 1877-1920* (New York, 1967), pp. 145-163.

38. Mann, *Memoirs*, p. 127; *The Programme of the ILP and the Unemployed*, p. 3; "Forging the Weapon," p. 4; "The Transport Workers' Strike

in England," *International Socialist Review*, 12 (December 1911): 355.

39. Ibid.

40. Tom Mann, *Russia in 1921* (London, n.d.), especially pp. 15, 24, 38, 43; *Memoirs*, pp. 323-324; Torr, *Mann*, pp. 45-48.

41. J. R. Conlin, *Haywood*, pp. 194-209.

42. Kenneth McNaught, "American Progressives and the Great Society," *Journal of American History*, 53 (December 1966): 504-520.

THE FOREIGN POLICY
OF PROGRESSIVE IRRECONCILABLES*

Fred Greenbaum

While the progressive irreconcilables have often been considered to be isolationists, an examination of their foreign policy statements renders this label inapplicable for the most part. They were generally opposed to imperialism, although not always consistently so. Their nationalism resulted in a strong sense of the sovereignty of all countries; they were usually non-interventionist and insisted upon the same treatment for weak nations as for powerful states. At the same time they believed in international cooperation in an effort to achieve a lasting peace. But, just as they differed in their perception of solutions to domestic affairs, they had divergent views on foreign policy matters.

The objections to the Treaty of Versailles voiced by the progressive irreconcilables were of such marked similarity that it has tended to obscure significant differences of opinion before their consideration of the treaty, during the debates, and in their subsequent careers. Over all, they protested that, like the Congress of Vienna, the treaty created a league of victors, determined to punish and suppress the vanquished, and to preserve imperial systems.

Robert M. La Follette of Wisconsin described the treaty as

*Part of the research for this essay was made possible by grants from the Research Foundation of the State University of New York.

"enough to chill the heart of the world." We had broken relations with Germany to preserve freedom of the seas and Wilson
had surrendered the principle to Britain at the conference table.
He had proclaimed self-determination in place of the secret
pledges—only to embody the clandestine agreements in the
treaty. He had made sacrifices for a League covenant but it
enforced this immoral settlement and betrayed American independence to European powers. Under Article 10, La Follette
charged, we agreed to preserve the political independence and
territorial integrity of all members, placing American wealth
and lives at the disposal of remote governments through en-
tangling alliances. Nationalist rebels who, like the American patriots, received outside help, would be considered disturbers of
the peace. Article 11, he insisted, extended our obligation to
preserve the internal status quo from revolution. The two would
keep the United States in a constant state of war, resulting in a
large standing army and suppression of criticism, similar to that
of the conflict that had just concluded. It did not create a real
league of nations, for many countries had been excluded. It did
not create a real league of peace, for its boundary settlements in
central Europe would create turmoil; and its unjust economic
provisions regarding Germany would bring resumption of hostilities. The treaty was unfair to an ally: It conveyed to Japan
German rights in Shantung that should properly have reverted
to China. The treaty's greatest beneficiary was England; it obtained German territories in a series of mandates and protectorates in Africa, the Near East, and Asia; the negotiators had
denied a hearing to Egypt, India, and Ireland; with the League
supervising the arms traffic the British Empire would be more
secure. Not even the International Labor Organization was satisfactory, for its labor standards would be too low to benefit
American workers. The treaty confirmed La Follette's belief
that the war had been fought for territory, trade routes, commercial advantage, and the right to exploit weaker nations.[1]

The analysis of William E. Borah of Idaho was similar to that
of La Follette. He opposed a Carthaginan peace and wanted a
settlement based on justice and equality of nations, a goal im-

possible to achieve through secret negotiations; after the final text was agreed upon it would be too late to make changes. Versailles, he found, was based on the strategic needs of the victors, and the rights of the weak, even allies, were ignored. He was disturbed that Wilson had rejected an equality-of-races provision. As a result of the treaty, Korea, Egypt, India, Ireland, Germany, Austria, Hungary, and China were left with grievances. He was most distressed by the League; the history of arbitration treaties had shown that nations ignored unsuitable decisions, and the League would have to employ force, committing the United States to unnecessary European adventures and permitting Europe to intervene in Latin America (for the Monroe Doctrine contained a dual commitment). That would require conscription, with all its drawbacks, largely to prevent revolutions like our own. Peace could not be established by force. Despite its proponents' statements, he commented, there was no requirement for disarmament in the League convenant and England was already planning her largest peacetime army. International bankers wanted the League so that the United States would underwrite their investments. The League would increase the power of the executive at the expense of Congress, for if it were endoresed, and the President dispatched troops to enforce its orders, who could say he had not been authorized? This possibility violated his strong sense of constitutional balance. The League was an undemocratic, uncontrolled, superstate which would eliminate nationalism.[2]

Unlike most opponents of the League, George Norris of Nebraska was not concerned with its limitations of American sovereignty or its infringement on the Monroe Doctrine, because he was willing to sacrifice some sovereignty for peace and disarmament and understood that the nation could not avoid European problems. Arbitration, backed by economic sanctions, was a viable tool for an honest league, he insisted. But the effect of Article 10 on the aspirations of subject nations and the League's marriage to the infamous Versailles Treaty, which embodied the secret treaties, made it a wholly unacceptable package.[3]

Of all the progressive irreconcilables, Hiram Johnson of California probably came closest to the popular notion of an isolationist. Yet even he expressed willingness to make sacrifices for some sort of properly constituted league, although he never seemed prepared to go any further than the enlargement of the Hague tribunal and the extension of arbitration to treaties. While he said that Wilson could not dry up the two oceans which provided America with a God-given geographical isolation, he did not consider the country to be isolated financially, socially, or otherwise. Article 10, he charged, dedicated America's sons to the preservation of the British and Japanese empires; he pointed to the Allied invasion of Russia and the use of Rumanian troops to restore the Hungarian Habsburgs as examples of its potential counterrevolutionary operation. A racist, and especially anti-Japanese, Johnson emphasized the Shantung provision and protested against any treaty that submitted domestic race problems to the jurisdiction of the League. He was particularly incensed at the six votes granted England and her dominion partners in the League Assembly and insisted that the Assembly was more than a debating society; at the very least it chose four of the nine members of the Council. He rejected reservations, for they would be forgotten soon after American entrance. Granting that we could not change the Versailles Treaty, he spurned arguments that we should join the League to temper its terms; the fact that you cannot prevent a burglary is no reason to join the burglars, he quipped.[4]

Although the progressive Democrat from Colorado, Charles S. Thomas, agreed with the objections of his Republican counterparts in many particulars, there were a number of differences in his analysis. He felt that the President drafted treaties under the Constitution, and the Senate could offer amendments, accept, or reject the document; but it need not be consulted in advance; when Senators were included in a peace commission they acted as executive representatives. The League attracted him as a moral force as long as no one depended upon it as a controlling influence in international affairs; it would break in a crisis just like the Hague conventions. He preferred the continuation of a league of victorious nations until other countries were reformed enough to be admitted, and particularly favored an Anglo-American entente. He rejected a resolution for the independence of Ireland as political; there was no equivalent resolution for the independence of Korea because there were few Korean votes to be garnered. Thomas was unimpressed with Johnson's request for a reservation that would have given the United States as many votes in the Assembly as the British Empire; after all, the dominions were independent, and, on many questions, Australia and Canada were as likely to vote with the United States as with Great Britain, and we would more readily depend on the Latin American bloc. It was not the Assembly, but the Council, where decisions were to be made, and there we had a veto; in fact, the requirement for unanimity would prevent Council action on most major questions. As for Article 10, he was willing to accept a five-year obligation to preserve the territorial integrity and political independence of those countries we had helped to bring into existence. His major objection to the League was to Article 13, which established the International Labor Organization. He agreed with La Follette that the twenty-four votes cast by the British Empire could be significant in this body, for a two-thirds vote was required on major questions. While La Follette objected that the international standards would not be high enough, Thomas protested that the entire conception was undemocratic, for it singled out only one class, and it created a supernational framework of organized units of labor, a minority of the workers of the world, and clothed it with executive, legislative, and judicial powers. While he felt that Germany merited any punishment visited upon her, she had not surrendered unconditionally, but on the terms of the memorandum of November 5, 1918. The Treaty of Versailles violated this understanding, imposed broad, undefined reparations, and destroyed the economic structure of Germany and central Europe.[5]

The reaction of the progressive irreconcilables to the treaty and the League was generally motivated by an anti-imperialist impulse. Yet in the harmony campaign of 1900 La Follette defended the party plank on the Philippines, asserting that the President's sole purpose was to maintain a stable government in a multilingual, multitribal area, threatened by a tyranical minority of insurgents led by Emilio Aguinaldo; as Jeffersonian expansionists, Americans desired only to spread enlightened liberty. Embarrassed, progressive Republicans generally justified this occupation as an apprenticeship in self-government which would eventuate shortly in independence. William E. Borah firmly supported Philippine independence and opposed a tariff on Philippine goods. He did not expect the islanders to be ready for Anglo-Saxon government for centuries and thought it was in their interest to remain a dependency. But this solution was not in the American interest, because the nation was not suited for imperialist governing of subjects. Norris favored independence with no strings attached—no protectorate, coaling stations, or naval bases—but while the archipelago remained a dependency he favored a tariff to protect domestic agricultural products. Johnson supported independence, but opposed the admission of duty-free coconut oil. After a fifteen-year period of independence, he wanted Fillipinos excluded from immigration like other Asiatics. As a Democrat Thomas felt free to mock the unfulfilled promise to grant independence. He argued that the acquisition of the islands was the "evil hour" when the United States first ignored Washington's admonition to keep aloof from the old world and violated the Monroe Doctrine.[6]

The progressive irreconcilables had a more limited perception of the Monroe Doctrine than most of their contemporaries. The United States should prevent European interference in Latin America; it should set an example to be followed; it should not follow Theodore Roosevelt and impose its will on weaker nations while respecting powerful, industrial, westernized countries. Otherwise, Borah warned, the Monroe Doctrine would be considered a dagger rather than a shield. These men did not approve of Wilson's interference in Mexican affairs. Borah thought Huerta was correct to refuse to accept an unaccredited emissary who came to demand his resignation. While Norris agreed with Wilson's moralistic refusal to recognize Huerta, he vigorously opposed the occupation of Veracruz; Admiral Mayo should have hidden the flag rather than allow the old butcher to disgrace it with a salute. Thomas thought the whole revolution was a struggle between agents of conflicting oil interests. While he anticipated that disturbances would force American intervention, he feared that military involvement would lead to permanent occupation and the problem of seventeen million unassimilable aliens. La Follette agreed that capitalists could gamble with their money in foreign investments, but then they had to take the gambler's risk. Neither La Follette nor Johnson wanted the executive to supply arms to Obregon to put down an insurrection; La Follette approved of the Mexican government while Johnson disapproved. Borah had an extremely important role in the final peaceful resolution of the Mexican problem during the Coolidge administration. While he joined Norris and La Follette in opposition to the occupation of Nicaragua, Haiti, and Santo Domingo by American marines, for lives and property were not actually threatened, he believed that marines could be landed if the danger were real; but congressional action would be necessary, he added, in the event of conflict with foreign troops or in an effort to control the affairs of another nation. Johnson was disturbed by the ineffectiveness of this policy of sustaining tottering governments; either enough soldiers should be sent in to do the job or we should get out; he had "no sympathy for the Borah-La Follette view that at the first time of trouble we should run." The Republican progressives opposed the payment to Colombia of $25 million to atone for Panama; Norris referred to it as conscience money, Johnson as blackmail, and both considered it a move to permit penetration by American oil interests. But Thomas thought it was worse to prevent an unoffending nation from putting down a rebellion than to invade it, and he supported reparations to Colombia; he satirized the Republicans' position—next they would call Belgium's demands for reparations from Germany blackmail. Yet he was displeased that the Virgin Islands had not been acquired because they would have safeguarded the canal. The progressive irreconcilables divided on the question of exempting American coastwise ships from Panama tolls; La Follette, Johnson, and Borah favored the plan; Thomas and Norris opposed it. La Follette and Norris were early advocates of hemispheric cooperation: La Follette commented favorably on William G. McAdoo's call for a Pan-American Conference; Norris insisted that any supervision of elections should be done in conjunction with other American nations. But Johnson was to attack the Roosevelt Good Neighbor Policy.[7]

While the termination of hostilities in Europe affected them in the same way, its commencement brought different reactions from these five progressives. Borah distrusted European motives and supported a strong navy consistent with the tradition of separation from European involvement. Fearing a large professional army as dangerous and considering militia to be inefficient and subject to political generals, he toyed with universal military training only to conclude it was the basis of militarism and decided we could meet our manpower needs with a voluntary army. He favored a policy of neutrality that insisted on the right to carry noncontraband goods to all belligerent powers and permitted Americans to travel in a war zone even if it meant arming merchant ships. He resisted the hysteria following the sinking of the *Lusitania,* comparing it to incidents in Mexico, and initially suspected the Zimmerman note to be a forgery. As late as January 1917, he favored noninterference in European affairs and only endorsed a diplomatic break to enforce neutral rights. But he voted for a war for national rights and honor; he did not think we were fighting for democracy. He wanted German capitulation, not an armistice, but demanded a peace based on justice. Like Borah, Johnson favored a strong navy (on two oceans), was reluctant about a draft, and preferred a voluntary army. Though a Roosevelt progressive, he was not carried away by the cry for preparedness; instead, he emphasized the role of social justice in creating contented citizens and good soldiers. He believed in a strict neutrality and refused to comment on the *Lusitania* affair lest it embarrass Wilson. Though impressed by La Follette's antiwar arguments, he felt he could not join him; when the administration had practically declared war he could consider no alternative; and it was necessary to protect American citizens and ideals. He justified temporary abandonment of a tradition of splendid isolation because democracy could not be continued here if destroyed abroad. La Follette, Thomas, and Norris all resisted increased naval expenditures and insisted that the demand would be deflated without a profit motive if naval vessels were to be constructed by the government. Thomas and Norris satirized the possibility of invasion: Norris described a postwar attack by European cripples, widows, and orphans transported by rafts and rowboats. Thomas did think that threats of increased numbers of airplanes and submarines might have validity, but the United States had not even manned the battleships it possessed. All three felt that nations, armed excessively, were more likely to go to war. Norris and La Follette argued that arming merchantmen was an act of war and filibustered to prevent passage of enabling legislation. Thomas insisted on the right to arm merchantmen and declared that we could not permit Germany to change any laws of neutrality by acquiescing in the sinking of armed freighters. Thomas supported the break in diplomatic relations with Germany; La Follette and Norris opposed it. La Follette and Norris felt that neutrality had not been equally applied and voted against the war resolution. Thomas joined Borah and Johnson in voting for it. All three voted against the draft. Norris and La Follette hopefully pursued all peace feelers; Thomas mocked them as German propaganda following each military disaster. And Thomas agreed with Borah and Johnson that Germany had to be thoroughly defeated.[8]

As the war drew to a conclusion the question of the spreading Bolshevik revolution had to be faced. Respect for the sovereignty of all nations and conviction that each country had to work out its own problems led Borah, Norris, Johnson, and La Follette to reject Amercian intervention in Russia and to oppose the persistent refusal to recognize its de facto Bolshevik government. While Johnson was as worried about the spread of Bolshevism as conservatives and called Lenin and Trotsky disgusting, he could not accept intervention against a revolutionary government, for this alleged shortcoming was one of his most vigorous criticisms of the League. The purpose of the expeditionary force, he said, was to secure the loans of international bankers. But the policy was self-defeating; in 1919 he declared that the Bolsheviks would have fallen if not for Allied intrusion. These Republican progressives all felt that the best defense against red revolution was to improve the economic conditions in the country, to practice democratic ideals, and to improve American democracy; they were confident of victory in open debate. They rejected the logic of nonrecognition. Norris found no evidence that Russia was trying to overthrow the United States government; statements by domestic radicals no more bound the Soviet Union than one Republican murderer made all Republicans murderers; as for the imperial debt, it was likelier to be resolved after recognition. Borah said the Bolshevik regime, while unacceptable, was less inimical to our theory of government than that of the czars. During the depression he held out the hope of increased trade. C. S. Thomas, on the other hand, insisted that Bolshevism "must be stamped out as a nest of vipers" before it enveloped the world, and justified intervention to protect American supplies at Archangel, to free the Czech troops, to combat an agent of the Kaiser, Lenin, and to secure the debt.[9]

In rejecting intervention in Russia, the treaty, and the League, the progressive irreconcilables were not rejecting all international involvement. Even Hiram Johnson maintained that he really preferred to support the League, because it appealed to his humanitarian instincts, asserted he would have endorsed one that did not relinquish our sovereignty and which really prevented war. Of course he would not permit himself to be pinned down as to how an acceptable league could be created and persistently opposed any moves that resembled entanglement; in 1935 he was credited with preventing American entrance into the World Court as affiliation with the League through the back door. On the other had, he supported the Hague Court of Arbitration, for it could not have recourse to sanctions; the World Court was backed by the sanctions of the

League, he insisted. Court reservations that prevented the tribunal from dealing with meaningful questions without approval made it meaningless, he commented. Norris was equally attracted to arbitration and felt that pursuit of the Bryan treaties rather than alliances could have prevented the shattering of peace in 1914. Reluctant about entrance into the court, he was willing to endorse American adherence to the protocol only if the Senate were consulted before questions concerning the United States were submitted. La Follette thought the force of world opinion would effectuate arbitration decisions, but it could be bolstered by cutting off intercourse with an offending nation. He hoped to resolve the problem of neutrality through a federation of neutral nations which would issue maritime regulations and define commercial rights. Borah favored arbitration as well. He suggested that Mexico arbitrate the oil dispute, though he would have hesitated to endorse American submission of a problem of similar magnitude; he did state that Mexican sovereignty would have to be waived first. While he was disturbed when he felt that his country ignored arbitration treaties and findings and resorted to force in Latin America, he opposed Norris's resolution to submit the Panama tolls to arbitration as an embarassing precedent. Borah liked the idea of the World Court, if it could be divorced from the hated League, but he wanted it to be an actual court of justice with compulsory jurisdiction, permanent judges, including an American jurist, which administered a codified international law, including a provision for outlawing war, and providing it was enforced by world opinion. Government, he argued, was not supported by force, but by loyalty and respect for the law. The federal judiciary maintained peace between the states largely through the power of public opinion, and war could be outlawed internationally on a similar basis. Norris endorsed the resultant Kellogg-Briand Treaty; Johnson, stating that it would neither help nor harm the situation, voted for the proposal.[10]

Borah's foreign policy initiatives during the 1920s were not limited to the outlawing of war and the settlement of the Mexican dispute. Determined that an armaments race should not lead to a new war, he introduced resolutions in 1921 and 1929 for meetings to limit armaments, initiatives which resulted in the Washington and London conferences. He was not satisfied with the results of the Washington Conference. Limitations of battleships were economical, but the weapons of the next naval war—submarines and airplane carriers—had not been included. And the companion document, the Four-Power Treaty, was a Versailles-like alliance to maintain the status quo. La Follette and Johnson agreed with Borah on the Four-Power Treaty; La Follette insisted that it tied us to Japan's atrocities in Korea, China, and Russia, and to British imperialism. In addition, it might inspire a countervailing alliance of China, India, Russia, and Germany. The Wisconsin Senator felt that the conference had only created a naval holiday, restored each nation to the 1914 level of preparedness, and in itself was "poor insurance against another war." Thomas approved of arms reduction either by example or negotiations, for military might increased military spirit and the possibility of war. Norris, on the other hand, voted for the entire Washington product. By 1929 Borah had hoped that a conference would do more than just restrict naval armaments. He wanted a clarification of maritime law in which the rights of neutrals would be enhanced and the definition of contraband limited to munitions. Norris was satisfied with the results of the London Conference, adding only that no agreement absent from the published text could be binding. Johnson opposed the treaty because he felt it denied to the United States the parity established at Washington and the ability to defend itself in the Pacific: "Great Britain builds as she prefers; the United States builds as Great Britain permits." It was the worst outrage since the League, he concluded.[11]

Another of Borah's initiatives was a call in 1922 for a conference to solve the question of reparations and international debts. These progressives considered reparations to be excessive, since they were not limited to direct damages, and they made strong statements against the excessive authority of the reparations commission. Johnson opposed Borah's call for an economic conference, for the nation would become entangled in European affairs; if the United States agreed to a solution it would have to help carry it out, he argued. He was disturbed that Italy claimed it could only pay a portion of the agreed interest rate while it trumpeted its solvency in negotiating a seven percent loan from J. P. Morgan. By the thirties he indicated willingness to pass up debts from nations unable to pay but insisted upon payment from those who were able to do so; nevertheless, he sponsored a bill to prohibit private loans to nations in default of their war debts. Norris and La Follette were disturbed that any reduction in the debt or interest would have to be absorbed by the American taxpayer, who was already excessively burdened. Norris pointed out that Britain was charging Persia and Australia higher interest rates than the scaled-down return she agreed to pay to the United States. La Follette was almost willing to cancel the debt to be free of entanglement, but such an arrangement would finance larger military forces with which European imperialists could enslave the world. Norris was agreeable to funding the debt and awaiting repayment, but was unwilling to cancel any part of it as long as the debtors were maintaining large armies. Norris, La Follette, and Johnson insisted that the debts and reparations were separate problems. While Borah agreed with them, he felt that Europe could not repay the debts until the reparations question was settled. He greeted the Lausanne agreement to scale down debts and reparations, but warned that without increased trade, reduced tariffs, and significant disarmament it would not be sufficient to ensure the peace. He was willing to trade debts for disarmament.[12]

The progressives' international interests were not limited to Europe. They were very sympathetic to Chinese national aspirations and opposed the transfer of Shantung to Japan. With the rise of Chinese nationalism during the 1920s, Borah commented on the Chinese predicament: Foreigners controlled her cities, resources, and tariff rates; foreign ships patrolled her coast and rivers; foreigners were exempt from her laws. In 1927, he applauded China's efforts to terminate foreign concessions. While he condemned the Japanese invasion of China, insisted that great nations should be governed by the same treaties and international law that they enforced upon weaker states, and taunted England for refusing to join the United States in refusing to recognize the crime, he still believed the United States should limit its activities to protecting its citizens and interests. Johnson chided Secretary of State Stimson for taking a strong stand on the invasion of Manchuria when he had no intention of following through.[13]

These progressive Republicans did not have a uniform reaction to Axis expansionism, though their reaction to fascism was consistently negative and they were equally sympathetic to China and the Western democracies.

By the time of the New Deal, Johnson had conceived of the country as a protected enclave, guarded by a large navy, with its producers safe behind a high tariff wall (Norris, La Follette, and Borah endorsed a tariff that reflected the difference in the cost of production between American manufacturers and international competitors). He had thought Franklin D. Roosevelt joined him in his suspicion of foreign entanglement, but he grew wary after the World Court fight. The Good Neighbor Policy was a hodgepodge that permitted Mexican appropriation of property and might lead to a greater Panamanian voice in the Canal Zone. Opposed to involvement in Ethiopia, he questioned the neutrality of an arms embargo when only one side could manufacture munitions. Roosevelt's desire for executive flexibility was a veiled seizure of the war-making power. "Cash and carry" did not take the profit out of war, only the risk, and favored the nation with the strongest navy: England in the Atlantic and the hated Japanese against China. Jolted by Roosevelt's "quarantine the aggressors" speech he rejected the private boycott it precipitated as warlike. Although he did not think the Japanese apology for sinking the Panay was adequate, he would not suggest any action. When Roosevelt requested a larger navy in response to Japanese repudiation of the Washington Conference, Johnson was torn. Though he favored naval power, he believed rumors that the program entwining us with England secretly complemented the British fleet. As war engulfed Europe he rejected an enlarged army and considered repeal of neutrality in favor of a return to international law. When Roosevelt spoke of restricting aggressors by measures short of war, Johnson assumed he meant economic sanctions and admitted he preferred a warrior grandson to starving children. And he fought against repeal of the embargo as equivalent to intervening on the Allied side. Lend-lease, he declared, deprived the United States of protection. Russia might turn the borrowed weapons on this nation. The "Four Freedoms" and the Atlantic Charter committed the country to combat and to a postwar alliance. The convoy system abandoned freedom of the seas. And when the administration requested the repeal of the neutrality laws in late 1941 he insisted that the republic was being carried into the war by deceit and subterfuge. As the hostilities drew to a close, Johnson, barely able to read and speak, but consistent to the end, opposed the United Nations charter.[14]

Borah joined Johnson in applying the lessons of World War I to the very different situation of the thirties. He persisted in promoting unfettered American independence in foreign affairs as more important than peace, but at the same time, as the only road to peace. While he was repelled by fascism and communism and protested that the fascists had behaved as butchers in Spain and Ethiopia, he felt that Nazism had not caused the war, which had resulted from a desire for power and territory. Austria's merger with Germany was inevitable and would have occurred before Hitler if not for the World Court. England had approached the United States for a joint effort to protect Ethiopia only because of the proximity of its own territories. He supported the extension of neutrality laws to the Spanish Civil War but wanted Germany and Italy included as belligerents. While Munich raised treaty violation to a tenet of diplomacy, it was a European affair. In the Far East he sympathized with China but followed neutrality, opposed the boycott of Japanese goods as dangerous and useless, and suggested the renewal of a commercial treaty with Japan, without selling munitions. Though shocked by Russia's invasion of Finland, he wanted to continue normal relations. With a general conflagration Borah argued that England and France had not acted to save the early

fascist victims and were now only fighting for their own imperialist ends. The United States must remain a model, not a belligerent. While at first he preferred freedom of the seas to the
neutrality laws, he feared a repetition of our earlier experience,
and modified his stand. Now he wanted to prohibit travel of
Americans on ships of belligerents, to forbid loans not only to
belligerents but to those who were preparing to fight, to embargo arms so that legitimate trade could continue, to forbid
loans to defaulting nations, and to prevent the arming of merchant ships. He opposed "cash and carry": It favored naval
powers; it would lead to credit; and it was equivalent to intervention because it changed laws during a war in a manner that
unequally affected the belligerents. By his death, he was spared
the sight of another American overseas conflict.[15]

Unlike Johnson and Borah, both of whom had voted to enter
World War I, Norris found a distinction between the events
preceding these holocausts. Fearful of the military and cautious
about its costs during an economic crisis, he resisted military
expansion in 1938 and the draft in 1940 (though he reversed his
position later), and persisted in removing the profit incentive
for war; he suggested a yardstick airplane factory. He tried to
avoid the mistakes that led to the Great War. Yet, frightened of
an aggressive Axis threat to Western civilization, he acquiesced
in American measures to aid the Allies. In 1936 he supported
the loyalist cause but opposed presidential discretion in the
embargo. With the fall of France he endorsed its government's
request that American shippers transport to Mexico surviving
German and Italian volunteers for loyalist Spain. By 1938 he
favored a private boycott against Japanese goods and sought to
prevent Japanese purchase of scrap metal; at the same time, he
considered an antifascist military alliance with Russia, Britain,
and France. In 1939 he advocated "cash and carry", for the
embargo aided Germany. This policy avoided some of Wilson's
errors, he explained: American vessels would not carry passen-
gers and freight to belligerents; no sales would be made on
credit; Americans would not purchase foreign bonds; and merchant ships would not be armed. The Axis, he insisted, could

not be appeased. But he evaded his earlier commitment to a referendum on war. As the battle drew to a conclusion, he advocated hard, but nonimperialist, terms to ensure a lasting peace: unconditional surrender; destruction of armament factories; permanent disarmament enforced, if necessary, by fifty years of occupation; punishment of war criminals, with militarists eliminated as a class; the cost of the war to be borne by the vanquished, with payments to be adjusted annually according to ability to pay. But the losers must not be humiliated. They must eventually be included in a league, based on the equality of nations and races. And the United States should aid the hungry among allies and enemies in the postwar world.[16]

The progressive irreconcilables reflected similarities in their frames of reference, although they differed in many specifics. Throughout long careers Senators La Follette, Thomas, Borah, Johnson, and Norris reacted individually to foreign policy issues, as they arose, with a mixture of national concern and a sense of international responsibility. While their responses varied, at no point did they ignore world problems or the place of the United States in the community of nations. During the 1930s, when international issues polarized into interventionism and noninterventionism, Borah and Johnson were noninterventionists and were castigated as isolationists. Norris, with only a slightly different perception of the relationship between nations, became an interventionist, and was heralded as an internationalist. Therefore it is time to revise the old stereotypes.

Notes

1. Robert M. La Follette, Sr. (RML) to family, March 30, April 21, 1919; RML to Belle C. La Follette (BCL) and Robert M. La Follette, Jr. (RML, Jr.), May 4, 1919; RML to RML, Jr., May 10, 1919, Robert M. La Follette Papers, Library of Congress, Washington, D.C.; U.S., *Congressional Record*, 66 Cong., 1 sess., 58 (1919): 7011-12, 7669-77, 8428-33, 8728-29; 67 Cong., 1 sess., 61 (1921): 637-51; *La Follette's*, 11 (1919): 33-35, 86, 93, 101-102; 12 (1920): 54-55; 13 (1921): 77-78.

2. William E. Borah, "The Perils of Secret Treaty Making," *Forum*, 60

(1918): 657-68; "Militarism in a League of Nations," *Forum*, 61 (1919): 297-306; U.S., *Congressional Record*, 66 Cong., 1 sess., 58 (1919): 690-95, 1737-49, 2063-68, 2075-80, 3934-38, 4349-55, 6078-79, 7320-25, 7942-50; 66 Cong., 2 sess., 59 (1920): 3934-38; 67 Cong., 1 sess., 61 (1921): 5776-81; 67 Cong., 2 sess., 62 (1922): 4000-01; *New York Times*, February 1, 1918; August 20, 1919; October 19, 1921; William E. Borah (WEB) to W. J. Bryan, December 18, 1916; WEB to E. Dewey, January 8, 1917; WEB to M. G. Rebeling, February 5, 1917; WEB to V. A. Dithmar, March 6, 1917; WEB to C. A. Varnum, December 21, 1918; WEB to Maurice Leon, September 29, 1921; WEB to W. D. Humiston, March 2, 1922, William E. Borah Collection, Library of Congress, Washington, D.C.

3. U.S., *Congressional Record*, 65 Cong., 3 sess., 57 (1918): 77, 3749-51; 66 Cong., 1 sess., 58 (1919): 2592-2600, 3564-76, 3634-35, 4361-63; 5158, 6788-6826, 7364-65, 7687-89; George Norris (GN) to my dear friend, June 1, 1919, George W. Norris Collection, Library of Congress, Washington, D.C.

4. Speech by Hiram Johnson, *Transactions of the Commonwealth Club of California*, 14 (1919): 414-32; U.S., *Congressional Record*, 65 Cong., 3 sess., 57 (1919): 71, 130, 1585, 1797-99, 1907, 2261-62; 66 Cong., 1 sess., 58 (1919): 157, 501-509; 5971, 7002, 7355-60, 8752-54; 66 Cong., 2 sess., 59 (1920): 5233-35; 67 Cong., 1 sess., 61 (1921): 4811-14, 6408-10; *New York Times*, December 3, 1918; January 18, April 25, September 12, 14, 17, 1919; June 8, 1920; Hiram Johnson (HJ) to C. K. McClatchy, January 8, 1918; April 7, 12, 1919; HJ to Hiram Johnson, Jr., (HJ, Jr.), December 7, 1918; February 24, May 8, 22, 31, August 1, 1919; HJ to HJ, Jr., and Archibald Johnson (AJ), June 22, August 23, 1919; HJ to AJ, August 7, 1919; HJ to Mayer Lissner, March 14, 1919; HJ to Albert Beveridge, July 21, 1918; HJ to Chester Rowell, July 31, 1919; Notes for an article for Sunset Magazine, 1919, Hiram Johnson Collection, University of Berkeley Library, Berkeley, Cal.

5. Sewell Thomas, *Silhouettes of Charles S. Thomas* (Caldwell, Ida., 1959), pp. 192-209; U.S., *Congressional Record*, 65 Cong., 3 sess., 57 (1919): 994-99, 1372-79, 1726-30, 6326-31, 7797-7805, 8422-23; 66 Cong., 2 sess., 59 (1920): 2991-3004.

6. Padraic Kennedy, "La Follette's Imperialist Flirtation," *Pacific Historical Review*, 29 (1960): 131-44; U.S., *Congressional Record*, 64 Cong., 1 sess., 53 (1916): 2438-47, 1792-95; 65 Cong., 3 sess., 57 (1919): 994; 66 Cong., 2 sess., 59 (1920): 3000; 70 Cong., 2 sess., 70 (1929): 3837; 72 Cong., 2 sess., 76 (1933): 372-77; 73 Cong., 1 sess., 78 (1934): 6324, 6380; WEB to J. H. Gibson, February 24, 1916; WEB to E. J. Moldenheuer, May 7, 1932, William E. Borah Collection, Library of Congress; GN to J. O. Hane, September 10, 1900; GN to W. F. Buck, January 26, 1906; GN to F. G. Arnold, May 4, 1934, George W. Norris Collection, Library of Congress.

7. U.S., *Congressional Record,* 63 Cong., 2 sess., 51 (1914): 6357-71, 6996-7000, 7532-38, 8501-06, 16520-21; 63 Cong., 3 sess., 52 (1915): 4268, 4694, 5237-38; 64 Cong., 1 sess., 53 (1916): 946-48, 1792-95, 3886-90, 4003; 64 Cong., 2 sess., 54 (1917): 4769; 65 Cong. 3 sess., 57 (1919): 996; 66 Cong., 3 sess., 60 (1921): 166, 243-248, 305-10, 465-69; 67 Cong., 2 sess., 62 (1922): 8941-45; 69 Cong., 1 sess., 57 (1926): 4753-54; 70 Cong., 1 sess., 69 (1928): 7195; *New York Times,* July 22, August 19, October 30, 1913; April 2, 10, 15, 1914; January 13, May 9, 1916; May 2, 1922; January 4, 1924; November 25, December 28, 1926; February 21, March 21, 1927; April 20, 26, 1928; January 9, 1930; January 6, April 19, 20, 1931; April 11, 1938; July 25, 1939; *La Follette's,* 4 (May 11, 1912): 1; 5 (March 1, 1913): 3; 5 (August 16, 1913): 1, 3; 6 (May 2, 1914): 1; 6 (June 27, 1914): 1; 7 (June 1915): 1, 2; 8 (January 1916): 1; 8 (August, 1916), 2; 9 (March, 1917), 1-4; William E. Borah, "Fetish of Force," *Forum,* 74 (August 1925): 240-5; "Neighbors and Friends," *Nation,* 124 (1927): 393-394; "Leadership is Needed Most," *International Digest,* 1 (April 1931): 36-38; GN to J. O. Hane, September 10, 1900; GN to M. Danielson, March 23, 1911; GN to Frank Roth, April 24, 1928; GN to John Parker, May 11, 1928; GN to R. E. Wright, September 4, 1935, George W. Norris Collection, Library of Congress; WEB to Lewiston Commerce Club, February 17, 1914; WEB to H. P. Cumrock, April 3, 1914; WEB to C. M. Kiggins, June 3, 1915; WEB to E. A. Hutto, December 12, 1916; WEB to Charles Welch, May 9, 1922; WEB to August Peterson, June 28, 1922; WEB to N. W. Murphy, November 29, 1926, William E. Borah Collection, Library of Congress; RML to BCL, April 24, 1914; RML to Fred Mackenzie, June 22, 1914; BCL to RML, March 10, 1917, Robert M. La Follette Papers, Library of Congress, HJ to C.K. McClatchy, January 14, December 31, 1927; HJ to Harold Ickes, May 2, 1931; HJ to John Bassett Moore, June 26, 1937; HJ to Redwood Export Company, August 6, 1938, Hiram Johnson Collection, University of California, Berkeley Library.

8. U.S., *Congressional Record,* 62 Cong., 3 sess., 49 (1913): 4318-21; 63 Cong., 2 sess., 51 (1914): 4267-70, 9370-72, 9640-41; 63 Cong., 3 sess., 52 (1915): 4267-70, 4694, 5237-38; 64 Cong., 1 sess., 53 (1916): 2767-68, 3485-87, 3886-97, 5201-15, 5277-84, 5408-14, 8123-24, 11480-81; 64 Cong., 2 sess., 54 (1917): 3737-38, 5004-09; 65 Cong., 2 sess., 56 (1918): 4010, 9181, 9462-66; 69 Cong., 2 sess., 68 (1927): 990-97; *New York Times,* May 9, 1915; January 6, December 13, 1916; January 12, 13, 26, February 8, April 1, 4, 1917; September 17, November 12, 1918; *La Follette's,* 4 (March 2, 1912): 4-5; 8 (October 1916): 1; 9 (April 1917): 1-3; 9 (May 1917): 2-5; WEB to Frank Plaisted, November 16, 1915; WEB to M. C. Turner, December 6, 1915; WEB to P. M. Beers, March 16, 1916; WEB to E. F. Caton, April 15, 1917; WEB to H. C. Griggs, August 8, 1917; WEB to A. C. Boyd, March 9, 1920, William E.

Borah Collection, Library of Congress; HJ to C. K. McClatchy, January 25,
1916; April 7, 1917; Speeches by Hiram Johnson, San Francisco, July 8,
1916; St. Louis, June 3, 1917, Hiram Johnson Collection, University of
California, Berkeley Library.

9. U.S., *Congressional Record,* 65 Cong., 2 sess., 56 (1918): 9053-55;
65 Cong., 3 sess., 57 (1918): 342-347, 932, 998, 1101-04; 1388-95,
2261-66, 3258; 66 Cong., 1 sess., 58 (1919): 4896-4902; 66 Cong., 3 sess.,
60 (1921): 1867-68; 71 Cong., 3 sess., 74 (1931): 4219-23; *New York
Times,* January 4, 1921; April 24, 1932; June 15, 1933; HJ to William
Allen White, April 11, 1918; HJ to AJ, Christmas 1918, Hiram Johnson
Collection, University of California, Berkeley Library; RML to family, December 27, 1918; January 19, 1919, Robert M. La Follette Papers, Library of Congress; GN to C. E. Hopping, December 30, 1920; GN to WEB,
December 21, 1923; GN to E. B. Hardemann, May 1, 1933; *La Follette's,*
11 (1919): 60, 102ff; 15 (1923): 161; 16 (1924): 4-6, 26-28, 41, 45; William E. Borah, "Senator Borah in Russia," *NEA Journal,* 20 (1931): 285.

10. U.S., *Congressional Record,* 63 Cong., 2 sess., 51 (1914): 13977; 63
Cong., 3 sess., 52 (1915): 3631-33; 65 Cong., 3 sess., 57 (1919): 2262; 67
Cong., 1 sess., 61 (1921): 6164-67; 67 Cong., 2 sess., 62 (1922): 8941-45;
69 Cong., 1 sess., 67 (1926): 2349-55; 70 Cong., 2 sess., 70 (1929): 1066,
1069, 1717, 1728, 2294, 2618-20; 74 Cong., 1 sess., 79 (1935): 695-700,
964-968; HJ to Meyer Lissner, March 14, 1919; HJ to F. P. Doherty,
October 21, 1921; HJ to HJ, Jr., April 19, 1935, Hiram Johnson Collection, University of California, Berkeley Library; GN to F. M. Willis, April
20, 1910; GN to C. C. Catt, March 7, 1932, George W. Norris Collection,
Library of Congress; WEB to C. J. Welch, May 9, 1922; WEB to August
Peterson, June 28, 1922; WEB to Lewiston Commerce Club, February 17,
1914; WEB to H. P. Cumrock, April 7, 1914; WEB to E. D. Peckham,
November 7, 1931, William E. Borah Collection, Library of Congress; *New
York Times,* January 5, July 22, 1913; May 2, 1922; December 18, 19,
1925; January 10, November 25, December 28, 1926; February 21, 1927;
William E. Borah, "Neighbors and Friends," *Nation,* 124 (1927): 392-94;
"The Fetish of Force," "How the World Court can be Perfected," *Ladies
Home Journal,* 40 (October 1923): 9, 111-112; "Civic Righteousness,"
Century, 114 (1924): 642-644; "Public Opinion Outlaws War," *Indepen-
dent,* 113 (1924): 147-149; "How to End War," *Nation,* 119 (1924):
738-779.

11. U.S., *Congressional Record,* 66 Cong., 3 sess., 60 (1921): 1189-90,
3316-17, 4043-48, 4142-46, 4168-70; 67 Cong., 1 sess., 61 (1921):
229-230, 1731-55; 67 Cong., 2 sess., 62 (1922): 231-236, 2638, 3607,
3775-84, 3792, 4497, 4621, 4227-35; 70 Cong., 2 sess., 70 (1929): 1717,
2180-89, 2294, 2618-20; 71 Cong., spec. sess., 73 (1930): 25-32, 109,
248-260, 362, 378; *New York Times,* January 5, 1922; April 26, 1927;
July 25, 1929; June 9, 27, July 12, 1930; *La Follette's,* 13 (1921): 17-18,

113-114, 161, 177-178; 15 (1923): 1-2; William E. Borah, "The Ghost of Versailles at the Conference," *Nation*, 113 (1921): 525-526; "Will Humanity be Heard at Washington," *Sunset*, 47 (December 1921): 3; "Why the Conference Must Act," *Sunset* 48 (January 1922): 18-19, 73; "The Freedom of the Seas," *Current History*, 29 (1929): 922-927; WEB to D. Scudder, April 21, 1922; WEB to H. B. Louke, May 5, 1938, William E. Borah Collection, Library of Congress; GN to E. W. Youell, November 30, 1928, George W. Norris Collection, Library of Congress; HJ to C. K. McClatchy, May 3, 1930, Hiram Johnson Collection, University of California, Berkeley Library.

12. U.S., *Congressional Record*, 66 Cong., 2 sess., 59 (1920): 2991-3004; 67 Cong., 1 sess., 61 (1921): 3528-34, 4251-54; 67 Cong., 2 sess., 62 (1922): 1674-81, 1955-57, 1966; 67 Cong., 4 sess., 64 (1923): 1046-49, 1223, 1471, 3548-53, 3741-47, 3783-84; 68 Cong., 2 sess., 66 (1925): 2984-93; 73 Cong., 1 sess., 77 (1933): 2547; 73 Cong., 2 sess., 78 (1934): 3374; 74 Cong., 2 sess., 80 (1936): 4478-79; *La Follette's*, 13 (1921): 113-114; 15 (1923): 17-20; *New York Times*, December 23, 25, 1922; January 10, 1923; July 21, 1926; July 19, 1931; January 24, 1932; January 14, 1934; June 25, 1939; Thomas, *Thomas*, pp. 194-209; HJ to C. K. McClatchy, October 5, 1921, Hiram Jackson Collection, University of California, Berkeley Library; WEB to C. E. S. Wood, July 6, 1931; WEB to R. O. Burnsley, November 20, 1931, William E. Borah Collection, Library of Congress; H. A. Wallace to GN, December 18, 1931; GN to H. A. Wallace, January 21, 1932; GN to C. G. Wilcox, July 19, 1932, George W. Norris Collection, Library of Congress.

13. U.S., *Congressional Record*, 76 Cong., 2 sess., 85 (1939): 70-75; *New York Times*, January 28, 1927; January 6, April 19, 20, September 25, 1931; August 31, 1937; March 7, 1938; November 24, 1939; *China Weekly Review*, 39 (January 1927): 120-122; *Congressional Digest*, 6 (1927): 160, 178; News Release, December 23, 1937; WEB to W. B. Langsdorf, January 8, 1940, William E. Borah Collection, Library of Congress; HJ to Elizabeth Moore, October 7, 1937, Hiram Johnson Collection, University of California, Berkeley Library.

14. Fred Greenbaum, "Hiram Johnson and the New Deal," *Pacific Historian*, 18 (Fall 1974): 20-35.

15. *Christian Century*, 48 (1931): 1242; *New Republic*, 86 (1936): 97-98; William E. Borah, "Our Imperative Task: To Mind Our Own Business," Lew Sarett and William T. Foster, *Modern Speeches on Basic Issues* (Boston, 1939), pp. 279-85; *New York Times*, January 28, 1927; February 6, September 17, December 12, 1935; December 30, 1936; June 1, August 31, 1937; March 7, September 20, October 30, 1938; November 24, December 2, 1939; William E. Borah, "Retain the Arms Embargo," "What Our Position Should Be," *Vital Speeches*, 5 (1939): 397-399; U.S., *Congressional Record*, 74 Cong., 1 sess., 79 (1935): 7977-78, 13,955; 74

Cong., 2 sess., 85 (1939): 70-75; WEB to David Stern, November 26, 1935; WEB to H. B. Quist, January 13, 1936; WEB to R. L. Buell, January 16, 1936; WEB to W. B. Langsdorf, January 8, 1940, William E. Borah Collection, Library of Congress.

16. U.S., *Congressional Record*, 65 Cong., 2 sess., 56 (1918): 3319-21, 4069-70; 66 Cong., 1 sess., 58 (1919): 5384-87; 67 Cong., 1 sess., 61 (1921): 1412-14, 1502-06; 74 Cong., 1 sess., 79 (1935): 3104-05; 74 Cong., 2 sess., 80 (1936): 3912, 3919-22, 3932, 6805; 75 Cong., 3 sess., 83 (1938): 5687; 76 Cong., 1 sess., 84 (1939): 2216, 2371; 76 Cong., 2 sess., 85 (1939): 367, 994-996; 76 Cong., 3 sess., 86 (1940): 8065-69; 9855-56, 10, 113-19; 77 Cong., 1 sess., 87 (1941): 9978; *New York Times*, March 28, April 20, July 12, 1938; March 7, April 30, 1939; May 13, 18, June 7, July 26, October 4, 1940; January 23, February 27, May 12, 25, 26, September 24, October 19, 1941; July 26, December 7, 1942; November 8, 1943; George W. Norris, "American Neutrality," *Vital Speeches*, 6 (November 1, 1939): 62-64; GN to W. A. White, April 21, 1942, *New Republic*, 107 (1942): 119-120; GN Letter to the Editor, *New Republic*, 110 (1944): 84-86; George Norris, "Germany After Defeat," *New Republic*, 110 (1944): 703-705; GN to Glenn Scott, April 12, 1911; GN to G. W. Timm, January 14, 1919; GN to Newton Baker, January 23, 1920; Baker to GN, February 2, 1920; J. P. Robertson to A. H. Fetters, July 16, 1935; J. P. Robertson to Ray Turner, January 20, 1938; GN to H. G. Harris, February 17, 1939; GN to H. J. Johnson, March 20, 1939, George W. Norris Collection, Library of Congress.